What People Are Saying About *Get Reel*

Wow! Double wow! This is the first book that consciously dives into the power of media without blaming anyone. It's an innovative and heart-stretching inquiry that will shatter your illusions of media. Using compelling research and laugh-out-loud storytelling, Dr. Mramor shifts your unconscious viewing habits to conscious, fresh insights that will never let you see the media the same way again. Hold on. It's a captivating ride!

Shawne Duperon, six-time Emmy winner

Mandatory modern medicine for your mind at every age! I love the fresh concepts Dr. Nancy presents in this eye-opening manual for surviving and thriving in our fast-paced constant bombardment of mass media. "Your TV viewing habits are metaphors for how you live your life." Dr. Nancy brilliantly bridges the connection between how our inner peace, happiness, and satisfaction with life is a real reflection of how, when, and what we watch in the media. Think about your thoughts, free your mind, and set your soul free. Read this book!

Deb Scott
Top 1 percent Kred Social Media Influence,
award-winning bestselling author

Nancy presents a groundbreaking analysis of how we unwittingly allow the media in general and TV in particular to program our beliefs as well as our viewing schedules. She shines a light into how we are unconsciously influenced by what we watch and takes us on a journey to retake control of our lives by being much more aware of how media messages either bring us closer to our true selves or take us further away. It's all in how you view ... a very important subject.

David Fraser PhD, speaker, consultant, coach, and author
of *Relationship Mastery: A Business Professional's Guide and
Leadership: Presence and Practice*, Glasgow, Scotland

Dr. Nancy Mramor has produced a winner with *Get Reel: Produce Your Own Life*. This book entertains while expertly guiding the reader to view "reel life" and the illusion marketing media presents with new eyes—to make more informed choices. Using our favorite movies and TV shows as a roadmap, Dr. Nancy takes us on a humorous journey of media and self-discovery. *Get*

Reel painlessly teaches how to de-program and re-program ourselves from the hypnosis of mass media.

This book is as entertaining as any of your favorite shows, and the best part is your IQ won't drop!

Debra Oakland, *Living in Courage*

We are all familiar with the phrase "You are what you eat" ... in other words, garbage in, garbage out. Dr. Nancy Mramor delivers the parallel yet deeper message ... you are what you watch.

In her book *Get Reel, Produce Your Own Life* ... Dr. Mramor takes us from couch potato to cocreator. She shows us that mindless TV watching can turn into a productive process of recognizing archetypes that we mirror in a positive way, and how to avoid the pitfalls of network "brainwashing."

"You are what you watch" can now mean a very good thing!

Carol Lee Espy, producer, radio and TV host

This book delivers the conscious key to produce your life as the star you are meant to be as opposed to falling short of the misguided standards of pop culture.

Mary Lee Gannon, award-winning reinvention expert, *Starting Over*

Get Reel opens and closes the discussion of whether you can watch TV and movies, read books and surf the web, and absorb the information in such a way that it supports your authentic self, and ultimately your happiness. With Dr. Mramor in the director's chair, you have the power to produce and be the star of an Oscar-worthy life!

Debbie Mancini, Dear Mama Deb, bestselling author and parenting coach

Dr. Nancy Mramor's breakthrough, master guide shows us how to tune in to what we really need and start "consciously viewing" and get reel!

Elizabeth Hamilton-Guarino, Hay House author of *Percolate—Let Your Best Self Filter Through*

Get Reel
Produce Your Own Life

Nancy Mramor Kajuth, Ph.D.

BALBOA.
PRESS
A DIVISION OF HAY HOUSE

Author Credits:
Award Winning Author of Spiritual Fitness, Media Psychologist, Coach and Speaker

Balboa Press books may be ordered through booksellers or by contacting:

Balboa Press
A Division of Hay House
1663 Liberty Drive
Bloomington, IN 47403
www.balboapress.com
1 (877) 407-4847

Print information available on the last page.

ISBN: 978-1-5043-3566-9 (sc)
ISBN: 978-1-5043-3567-6 (hc)
ISBN: 978-1-5043-3568-3 (e)

Library of Congress Control Number: 2015911243

Balboa Press rev. date: 07/28/2015

CONTENTS

Foreword vii

Get Reel xi

Why Get Reel? xv

Chapter 1   Watch Two Shows and Call Me in the Morning 1

Chapter 2   Politics and the News: The Facts, Ma'am, Just the Facts.. 16

Chapter 3   TV Guide to Love and Sex 37

Chapter 4   All in the Family 62

Chapter 5   Let's Make a Deal 77

Chapter 6   Reality TV Unplugged 103

Chapter 7   CSI: Crazy, Scary, Intense 126

Chapter 8   Do You Believe in Magic? 154

Chapter 9   The New Adventures of the Old You 186

References 211

FOREWORD

Dr. Nancy Mramor defines the world that joins modern media with the field of health. Since her early days as a psychologist, she has been practicing, researching, and appearing as a media expert in every type of media—print, radio, TV, and even the Internet. On the air, Dr. Nancy speaks easily and expertly about psychology, personal fulfillment, and self-awareness. All you have to do is ask her, and the events of everyday life become crystal clear. Whether there is misbehavior in the NFL, a new pope is elected, or David Letterman has an affair at the office, Nancy breaks it down for you. And when it comes to understanding yourself, look out! Because she is such a natural at taking psychology and turning it into understandable, everyday terms, she is the perfect person to write *Get Reel*.

When I met Dr. Nancy, I was producing a talk show for WQED-TV, PBS. Our host was the amazing Eleanor Schano, one of the first female newscasters in America. Eleanor, Nancy, and I bonded early in our work together because of our mutual goal: to present the truth in quality programming that would bring more knowledge and purpose to viewers' lives. As a producer in television and radio for many years, my work has taken me from serious issues in talk programming to children's shows and sports programming, documentaries and field production on both local and national levels. Every aspect of my experience has proven what an impact the media has on people's lives, positively as well as negatively.

Television and movie productions can create the illusion of what is considered perfect. While doing so, imperfect people and things are designed to look much better than they really are, making the average viewer feel less adequate comparatively. Although many viewers recognize that such illusions are fantasy, for others it is hard to differentiate reality from fiction. Even when you are watching a well-researched documentary, the creators' "take" on the event can determine what information is left out and what is given center stage.

Get Reel was prompted by Dr. Nancy's practice and research that led her to understand why people who come to her office aren't happy. Some of the main reasons are: unrealistic expectations about their goals, how quickly they should achieve them, their looks, their income, their social circles, and the skills necessary for a happy life. As she began to explore where these self-defeating beliefs came from, she discovered that it was primarily from family, peers, and media. Most often, the expectations about life, others, and themselves were so unrealistic that they could be traced back to some life event, parental expectation, trauma, or disappointment that was inconsistent with what they were seeing in the movies and on TV. Her work revolved around reconstructing these beliefs, the hurts they had caused, and ways to move away from them into a better place. Sometimes it meant limiting time with certain family members, reviewing expectations about how much support to expect from friends, or changing the TV channel from drama to comedy.

Get Reel gives you sound advice about how to enjoy watching and listening to media while also offering a cautionary tale of how to avoid the pitfalls. While the media's messages about love, relationships, politics, families, and religion are not necessarily intended to represent reality, it is nearly impossible not to take them in and view them as goals or beliefs that you live by unconsciously. After all, television and media are some of your most influential teachers. But what if the messages aren't entertainment? What if they are running your life?

Get Reel will take you on an entertaining journey through your favorite movies and TV shows while awakening you to the reality of the ideas presented through media. On this journey, be prepared to learn how personal fulfillment, success, and happiness can be increased or decreased by your media intake. But once you wake up, there is no turning back. After beginning to consciously view media, you will also have the skills to view everything in your life more consciously.

If you want to learn more about yourself than you ever dreamed possible and let go of the media illusions so skillfully crafted to direct your life, entertain you, and make you spend money, then laugh your way through *Get Reel*. You may walk away happier because you will be a much more self-accepting person. So hold on for the ride! Let's go from Getting *Reel* to Getting *Real* and become the producer of your own life!

Debbi Casini Klein
Multi-Emmy-award–winning producer, television and radio

GET REEL

DISCLAIMER/ATTITUDE ADJUSTMENT/ EXPLANATION/GOOD REASON

Any aunt/friend/colleague/neighbor/sister-in-law's daughter, dog, colleague's dog, or other individual mentioned in *Get Reel* could be a composite of a real or imagined person/pet/neighbor's pet/comedian/thief/ conscious reader/drama viewer/other.

If your favorite/least favorite/grandma's favorite/electrician's favorite/ boss's least favorite/mayor's favorite television program was not mentioned in *Get Reel,* please rest assured that the omission was unintentional. Any reality show/news show/comedy/dramedy/sci-fi thriller/car race/horse race/ flea race, or other program that is not included was not ignored; the experts just told me to keep it to around two hundred pages. Enjoy reading/reading the parts that interest you/reading and discussing/reading for fun/reading for transformation/reading and lending the book *Get Reel*

Seriously though, *Get Reel* should not be considered psychotherapy. (1) This disclaimer governs the use of this book. By using this book, you accept this disclaimer in full.

(2) Credit

This disclaimer was created using an SEQ Legal template.

(3) *Get Reel* is not a substitute for professional therapy or medical advice.

The book contains information about hypnotherapy. You must not rely on the information in the book as an alternative to medical or psychological advice from an appropriately qualified professional. If you have any specific questions about any medical or psychological matter, you should consult an appropriately qualified professional.

If you think you may be suffering from any medical condition, you should seek immediate medical attention. You should never delay seeking medical advice, disregard medical advice, or discontinue medical treatment because of information in this book.

(4) No representations or warranties

To the maximum extent permitted by applicable law and subject to section 6 below, we exclude all representations, warranties, undertakings, and guarantees relating to the book.

Without prejudice to the generality of the foregoing paragraph, we do not represent, warrant, undertake, or guarantee that the use of the guidance in the book will lead to any particular outcome or result.

(5) Limitations and exclusions of liability

The limitations and exclusions of liability set out in this section and elsewhere in this disclaimer govern all liabilities arising under the disclaimer or in relation to the book, including liabilities arising in contract, in tort (including negligence) and for breach of statutory duty.

Nancy Mramor and Transformedia LLC will not be liable to you in respect of any losses arising out of any event or events beyond reasonable control.

Nancy Mramor and Transformedia LLC will not be liable to any reader of this book in respect of any business, professional, or personal losses, nor will she be liable to you in respect of any loss or corruption of any data, database, or software.

Nancy Mramor and Transformedia LLC will not be liable to you in respect of any special, indirect, or consequential loss or damage.

(6) Severability

If a section of this disclaimer is determined by any court or other competent authority to be unlawful and/or unenforceable, the other sections of this disclaimer continue in effect.

If any unlawful and/or unenforceable section would be lawful or enforceable if part of it were deleted, that part will be deemed to be deleted, and the rest of the section will continue in effect.

(7) Law and jurisdiction

This disclaimer will be governed by and construed in accordance with US laws, and any disputes relating to this disclaimer will be subject to the exclusive jurisdiction of the courts of the United States of America.

(8) Our details

In this disclaimer, "we" means (and "us" and "our") refers to Nancy Mramor, PhD and Transformedia, LLC, Pittsburgh, PA, USA.

WHY GET REEL?

Before you click the remote one more time, let me tell you that media is one of the top three things that shape your life. Let me also tell you that this news could be the best news you have ever heard, if you know what to do with it! Think of the power you will have to make decisions! After your parents and teachers, the television, Internet, and movies shape what you think, who you become, and your level of happiness. It is also one of the most powerful teachers because it reaches you in a receptive state, often without letting you in on what it is teaching. Ask yourself if you are

- feeling anxious, restless, unhappy even when you reach a goal you thought mattered;
- a parent who struggles with the messages the media gives your children through TV, the Internet, and video games;
- a single woman or man who struggles with finding love;
- in your twenties or thirties and finding your identity ;
- in midlife and re-finding your identity;
- a married couple that chooses TV watching over other activities too often;
- a parent of a child who is glued to the TV, computer, and video games;
- an avid reader of self-help books or wish you were;
- ready to really look at your dreams and consider revising them in ways that will turn them into realities;
- buying things to feel better or eliminate boredom;
- interested in having a more fulfilling life;
- ready to bump up your happiness;
- an incurable Trekkie (*Star Trek* fan)

- an addict who craves Chris Noth in *The Good Wife* like Carrie Bradshaw used to do; or
- a high media consumer who really enjoys viewing and wants to keep watching but enjoy it even more.

Then perhaps you are in the right place at the right time to *Get Reel*.

To understand how *Get Reel* could give you the power to run your life, understand that your TV, movies, and the Internet do not change your perception of reality by itself. The creators provide the content, and they produce what they know you will consume. They also present information in such a way that you continue to consume. You are all partners in crime, viewers, producers, and consumers who drive the content. But the way in which the content is driven can shape the way that you think and live. So who's in charge of your beliefs, you or your TV/computer? Right now, the TV/computer screen with its seductive convenience and twenty-four-hour availability. But in the end, it will be you, most of the time. And when it's not, you will know how to take back control. Ready to produce your own life?

Get Reel is the most illuminating life-changer for exposing what you have learned and how you can learn from the vast menu of fascinating viewing choices while filtering out messages that will hook you into a false decision about life. You get to become the decision maker and determine what you want to absorb and what you could do without. When you have read *Get Reel* and completed the activities in the book, you will be a wise consumer who is unlikely to absorb messages unconsciously that you don't need. Think of yourself as a detective who solves the mystery of what lies beneath the programs that you watch. Discover your inner James Bond, Ace Ventura, Dick Tracy, Patrick Jane, or Sherlock Holmes. Wearing the appropriate trench coat while reading is optional.

Your first discovery is that TV and Internet are still the main influencers among the media vehicles. You can view TV on the Internet, your phone, in your car, your office, just about anywhere at any time; you can be under its influence. To consider this point, ask yourself:

- Do you have to get home in a hurry to see your recorded edition of your favorite show?
- Do you abandon your family during NFL football games or reruns of *Sex and the City*?

- Could it be that reality TV is more real to you than getting to your son's soccer game on time?
- Do you believe that reality TV is real?
- Are you tuned into your favorite cable shows on your electronic devices?
- And would someone like Rick Warren, author of *The Purpose-Driven Life*, be disappointed in you?
- Has television and media overtaken you and directed you?

TV is a powerful force for information, education, and entertainment. If I interviewed you, you'd probably tell me that you don't believe everything you see on TV. But if you think that you've largely avoided its influence, or that you don't have an influence on what you see on TV, I would invite you to continue viewing during the lengthy commercials until your favorite show returns. Or as Ace Ventura, Pet Detective would ask, if he's not back in five minutes, wait longer.

Too Much of a Good Thing?

Television and the media are great. Radio, TV, print media, and the Internet are fun, entertaining, educational, and full of surprises. What would you do without them? You would not know about the history of the prehistoric man. The sounds of the great composers would be unknown to you. You would not have opportunities for access to every type of fitness routine. If you are living in Iowa in January in the middle of a snowstorm, this could be important to you. TV,

 When immigrants came to this country, what did they do to learn our language? Watched TV! And your children watched *Sesame Street*.

On November 10, 1969, *Sesame Street* premiered on public television. In the first year, according to Lee D. Mitgang, author of *Big Bird and Beyond*, the show

- reached over half of the nation's 12 million three- to five-year-olds;
- was translated into seventy languages; and
- was seen in 140 countries.

Children learned how to count and fell in love with a Big Bird, who enriched their lives and their minds forever.

in particular, brings these things home for you, even when you can't or don't want to get out. If you are an Elvis fan, TV is your Graceland.

Times Have Changed

Will Smith on *Fresh Prince of Bel Air* and later Angus T. Jones, as Jake on *Two and a Half Men,* became your favorite teenagers. You learned to love the characters you watched, and they became like family for you; you looked forward to seeing them and missed them when you didn't. You longed for them in the way that viewers used to wait to see if the evil *V* aliens would continue to peel off their skin, revealing computer-generated innards.

The power of TV and the media to influence is seen in this affection. When people feel like family to you, you're more forgiving of them and overlook many of their faults because of their strengths and their importance in your life. Overlooking the foibles of Lucille Ball was all part of the fun. More recently, Charlie Sheen's womanizing in *Two and a Half Men* was a humorous foil to his dysfunctional mother. You laugh, love, and hang on to the edge of your seats to find out what your "family" will go through this week. And Ashton Kutcher handily took over Charlie's role as heartthrob. *Modern Family* has come to the screen with a variety of family characters more various than ever before. Perhaps you detect similarities between your kids and the character of Manny, who always sees the wisdom in any situation before your uncle Melvin or aunt Mildred. *Good detective work! You have uncovered the first clue to producing your own life.*

In the seventies, the TV business office was occupied by Mary Tyler Moore, whose antics and relationship with a boss, whom she called "Mr. Grant," brought women into the world of work. Fast-forward to the world of *Murphy Brown*, where Candace Bergen (often viewed through the lens of her painter) played a gutsy journalist with a very funny problem of finding a secretary. *The Office* paints a new portrait of the cubicle space and its many colorful characters. The drama *Mad Men* showed what really happened in a sixties advertising agency's office and brought you full circle into a new "reality" while gaining critical acclaim. You "bought the farm," the DVD package and the ideas in the show.

If you have been around long enough, you have fondly watched television characters morph from one stereotype to another. Early TV role models were often unattainable—too beautiful, rich, smart, lucky, and funny to ever be you—and yet you still desired their lives. You watched characters that you could not be and, at times, compared yourselves to the heroes on the screen. When you were little, you dressed up like Spider-Man or Cinderella. If you are still doing that, please get in touch with me!

The shift in character types in the seventies raised more eyebrows, however. When new types appeared, they were mocked with the appropriate amount of irreverence that made you see the bigoted, stereotyped, or unrealistic views of the exaggerated characters you viewed. Norman Lear was a leader in this domain, bringing to life the reality that TV characters flush toilets, fight among themselves about human rights, and lose their grocery carts in the parking lot. Archie Bunker of *All in The Family* would sing, "Those were the days." The characters were human, like you.

Look at the changes over time in the roles of domestic workers. First there was Shirley Booth as *Hazel,* the wise, older woman with the heart of gold who ran the family. In the eighties and nineties, Will Smith played the funny guy for the straight yet stuffy butler in *Fresh Prince of Bel Air.* Even later, we watched the maid, Rosario, dominate Megan Mullaly as Karen on *Will and Grace.* Times have changed. The changes in us move the changes on the screen forward, and the changes on the screen move us forward. What is acceptable and unacceptable behavior is quickly flashed on the screen, and we automatically absorb it. I just learned some new Internet lingo by watching *America's Got Talent,* and the lingo of the Internet world shaped what was said on TV. Technology is affecting what is presented in all other technology.

As a media psychologist for radio, television, and print, I would say that the vast majority of people have gleaned some learning from TV that they could do without. Worse, they probably don't even realize it because many of television's effects can be subtle and insidious. My friend Kristie is always trying to have a flatter stomach. She is proud that her preschool daughter tells everyone she has "rock-hard abs." She is not sure why, but she believes that it will make her happy; she does not realize that TV told her it would. If you think your husband should look something like Brad Pitt, that you should be sipping coffee in a boardroom like Bill Gates, or that your abs should resemble Christie Brinkley's, then perhaps you need a reality check instead of a reality show.

You and Your TV Set: Why You Need to Get Reel

If you are unhappy or dissatisfied with your life and relationships, or even just too hard on yourself and others, it may be that the standards imparted by TV, radio, print, and the Internet have become standards that you measure yourself against without even knowing it. These may be self-measurements that the media is reflecting back to you, or you may be gathering them into your consciousness from the media. Either way, or both ways, you may be unconscious of the measurements you have or where you got them. While you are aware of such things as the hard chair on which you sit or the hot coffee you drink, the messages on the TV are below the level of consciousness. Messages about stereotypes of beauty and success become real goals in your mind if TV has as much impact as research supports. You accept that the cashmere sweater on TV shopping truly goes with everything and that Kim Kardashian's perfume will make you smell *something* like her and give you a chance at building a bank account akin to Kim's. But the price that Kim pays is that her full-body photo, in living color, is on the side of the perfume delivery truck. Ask yourself if you're trapped, like Kristie, who wants rock-hard abs and does not even remember why.

When you are trapped, the natural reaction is to continually reach for the thing in the trap with the belief that it relieves stress and relaxes you. Once you are trapped, there is little questioning of what the trap is; you just act it out, searching for whatever the illusive dream is for you. Much of the dream keeps you in a trance-like hypnotic state where you have no choice. When you take on the short-term pleasure of satisfying the trance, you lose the long-term pleasure of living. You are in an addictive loop of seeking rock-hard abs or face cream or the cashmere sweater. If you stop seeking the thing in the trap, you may become uneasy and unable to relax; you may be addicted. It happens when you allow your environment, in this case your TV/Internet, to tell you what you want. I recall a clever automobile commercial where a woman is looking for a new car, saying in a trance-like voice, "They told me I should like beige." She then wakes up from her trance and buys the car in the ad. So did she awaken from her trance or just take on a new one? Clever marketing indeed!

The effectiveness of TV's power to influence has long been known. Through your senses, you hear, see, and feel the "truth" of the televised messages with the filter of the camera, makeup, and lighting. Does Meryl Streep look as good the day after the 2015 Golden Globe Awards as she did the night before? As an avid Meryl fan, I hope so, but then illusions created by makeup artists can be powerful ones. And if you decide that you want to break these illusions in your own life, then you have come to the right place. You will learn to become aware of them, notice how they influence your life, and reset them to those that serve you and reflect the real you.

Why do you watch? How do you learn (without perhaps intending to) from the pictures in the box? How do you become who you are based on TV viewing? Consciously, you attribute power and expert status to those seen on TV simply because they *are* on TV. The lawyer on your screen promising to get money for your accident damages must be able to keep his oath. Why else would he be on TV? How many products carry the motto "As Seen on TV" to gain credibility? Consider, while waking from your trance, that Mickey Mouse is also on TV and make your own decisions.

The Power of TV to Affect You

In the 1960s, early in TV history, Marshall McLuhan wrote about the power of the media to influence people, telling us that we become what we observe. His consideration of the media and its effects on us played out in later research on the power of TV to educate. Albert Bandura's theories of learning explained why the models with which you surround yourself could be a source of either good or harm. He proposed that you actually become involved in the emotions of the characters you watch and develop a desire to model yourself after them. How does this work?

Statistics from 2009 indicate that Americans average four hours and forty-nine minutes of TV watching a day. If you watch the morning and evening news each day for an hour each time, that is close to half of the national average. Add in a couple favorite shows, and you are there!

You have ingested the national average of TV.

You vicariously experience the romance of Jane Austen's characters, the victory of Mickey Rourke in *The Wrestler*, and the oft-misguided antics of Paris Hilton's nightlife. You may unconsciously adopt certain ideals, behaviors, and mannerisms of the characters, their images, and their lives. It follows, then, that you measure yourself by your ability to live up to these ideals. They have, in fact, *become* your ideals. Your desire to emulate the characters you see becomes your belief about what is right for you and others; you seldom question the truth of your motives. You merely live them out in a hypnotic trance that could be a real block to your goals in life. You have been hypnotized into accepting ideas by your subconscious that have bypassed your conscious filter and gotten under your skin.

Add Internet time and texting time, and you have a trifecta of media use. Certainly this causes both positive effects as well as some concerns. Health concerns related to televised images and watching too much TV are related to higher body weight. According to an *American Journal of Public Health* study, adults who watch three hours of TV a day are far more likely to be obese than those who watch less than one hour. One of the factors is not that the TV causes weight gain but, rather, that inactivity does. Dr. William Deitz, pediatrician at the Tufts University School of Medicine, suggests, that you can increase activity simply by turning off the television. Even 49 percent of Americans admit that they watch too much TV. In

2011, the American Pediatric Society determined that more than two hours a day of viewing is likely to have an impact on weight gain. Are you likely to reduce your viewing time? Maybe and maybe not, but perhaps, instead, you can examine the role that TV plays in your life. TV can be one of your best friends rather than one of your greatest deterrents in life. It can be your Batman instead of your Joker.

Viewing Can Lift You Up or Tie You Down

As you examine the role of the TV, movies, radio, and print media, you can see how you have truly grown up with media in mind.

The adults you saw and read about as children inspired you with their wit, wisdom, and prejudice, tilling a fertile field for a young imagination. You may have wondered the following:

- Could you really fly like Superman or jump like Spider-Man?
- Would you have friends like the ones on *Friends*?
- Were the seventies as much fun as they are portrayed in *That '70s Show*?

As you channel through *Get Reel*, you will see just how much power these images have for you. You have integrated the messages from the past and present, and they are parts of who you are, whether you know it or not; they shape your behavior. You can even feel free to channel surf through *Get Reel* and read the parts that are most relevant to you, first. If you are a notorious remote control surfer, this will appeal to your need for instant gratification, fostered by your "faster service" Internet provider.

Get Reel proposes that who you are is partially the product of television and other media. Research shows that after parents, teachers, and significant role models, TV and media characters are the models that you watch and emulate most. Yesterday's Barbie doll is today's Hannah Montana. *The Girl from Uncle* has been promoted to the role of *The Good Wife*. Yesterday's stay-at-home mom is today's career woman, and how you think you should carry out the new role is reflected in ideas on your screen.

One of HBO's first series, *Dream On*, portrayed a man who grew up with TV as his babysitter. No matter what occurred in his life, he would make associations with his early viewing experiences through flashbacks. The memories usually show the characters in penny loafers or saddle shoes, but the plots are the same as his life experiences. It is the same phenomenon as people referencing real-life triggers to TV shows or movies. When waiting for a table in a restaurant, you may say to your friends, "Remember 'the one' about the couple on that show who had to wait for a table and all the things that went wrong?" Life reflecting TV and vice versa is such a common experience that *Friends* reruns are called "the one about …"

 Since you are identifying with the stars of the show, you should at least have a say in the matter. So how do you decide that even though your abs are not rock-hard, that you don't need to own the latest ab curer, since the one you have has become the coat rack and the new version will probably have the same fate? How do you decide whether you even want rock-hard abs, for that matter? "You, too, can have rock-hard abs like supermodel So-and-So" is a typical remark that does not challenge whether the choice is yours; it assumes what you want. It is time to challenge these messages. Critical thinking, conscious choice, and global support are the tools. If you believe that it is not constructive for your child to see smart-mouthed kids running their families while living in Poughkeepsie, New York, then it is probably not good for kids in Sydney, Australia, either. Even Matt Groening, producer, pokes fun at Bart Simpson's role. Good call, Matt!

I see a similar phenomenon as a psychologist. Then, however, it is not conscious. People ask me how they can make their illusions and trances come true. They suffer in pain as they try over and over to create a perfect life and become the images they see in the media. I sometimes ask my clients, "Are you living a life of subconscious flashbacks? Have you accepted that what you see on TV is what is and what should be?"

You Are Getting Sleepy

To prove the hypnotic effects of TV, I will explain a bit about how it works. Later, I will explain how to detect and break the trance. Hypnosis is a wakeful state of focused attention and heightened suggestibility with lower awareness of what is going on around you. The ideas you take in while in this state are called trances. But once you know your trances, you can change them; you have the opportunity to awaken from your trance and begin to take charge of your mind and your life!

Associations are usually a type of hypnosis. Once you have made them, they stick. That is why, if you are trying to quit smoking and smoke while drinking coffee, drinking coffee is likely to bring up that association, thwarting your efforts to quit. There is a cure for that, and you will learn it soon. On TV, for example, you have formed an association with the music that shows up to open the program or to change scenes. The music keeps you in the associated state of enjoyment that is paired with the show. These sounds are called anchors, auditory anchors to be exact, and you will hear more about them and what to do to empower them soon.

Can you wake up and find the way to conscious viewing? You can, but only if you want to run your own life. The old adage, "question authority," would seem appropriate. As the author of the book *Spiritual Fitness*, I wholeheartedly believe in living a complete life that includes opportunities to laugh, cry, pray, and just watch TV sometimes. A colleague of mine once admitted to me that she watches *Star Trek* reruns to decompress and let the pressures of the day slip away. Why do her cares slip away? Because she stops thinking about her work, her concerns, her money issues, and just about everything else while she views. Isn't that a good thing?

Milton Erickson, an expert on modern hypnosis, told us that life is consecutive hypnosis.

Every single one of us is hypnotized by the images fed to us by our experiences and our culture, believing them as hypnotic trances without examining whether we like the trance or not.

Sounds a bit like a deep state of relaxation. But it is not. While personal issues may go away, you are in a receptive state that allows the programming to simply flow into your mind, uncensored in a TV-induced hypnosis in which you take in the messages without much of a filter. It's like buying a subliminal hypnosis CD by Hypnodog, a canine stage hypnotist based in Wales, all the while that you view. Under the influence of a master such as Hypnodog, you would be the prey, and if he can hypnotize you, he will have you at his mercy. "You will feel very interested, yes, very interested in buying many more CDs." Maybe you can get a refund on these embedded ideas.

Clearly, I am not one of those people who say things such as, "I never watch TV," or, "My children aren't allowed to watch TV." I once met a few baby boomers that didn't even own a TV set while raising their children. I commend these modern-day ascetics for living up to their personal standards. But if living a full life means watching TV, I am fine with that, too. Surely there is redeeming value in the Fitness Channel and the History Channel, as well as public television, even for the discerning viewers. Yet, even those channels do market research to discover the preferences of their viewing audiences and give them what they want. While out of town, I watched a Bob Dylan concert recently on public television that never aired at home; our local PBS station aired an opera. Even different commercials and programs are shown in different locations. It is a two-way street of taking on media messages and giving the media the messages we want to see from them.

Media is not just TV/Internet. Most movies eventually appear on TV/Internet, too. And the concepts relayed through TV are also

- in movies;
- on the radio;
- on the Internet, iPad, Xbox, and all technology;
- in print; and
- forever in your mind as you wake up humming the theme to *I Love Lucy* after fifty viewing years.

How can you resist overload and getting trapped in the trance, not knowing what is true? Oprah's popular magazine tells you each month what Oprah knows for sure. I wish I could be so sure myself. Experts in other magazines have told me that "Fat in the diet is essential for weight loss" and that "Fat should be removed almost completely," all in the same week. What are consumers to do?

Become critical listeners, viewers, and readers. By critical, I do not mean to judge or criticize but instead to question—to compare the message with what resonates with the best part of you. See if there is a real match, not just a match with what the paid expert says is true. Then decide if you want to use one of the trance-breaking and resetting techniques in *Get Reel* to live and view more consciously. Become your own TV spy and produce your own life by detecting its effects on you and deciding if they are good for you. If they are, then sound the applause! If they aren't, you will still have fun breaking the trance and producing your own more successful trance or none at all. You'll hear more about that in the exciting conclusion chapter.

Even research that is presented may have to be viewed critically when it is used to support a particular view. Statistics can be used in many different ways, so "studies show that ingesting shark toenails improves skin tone" may mean a study with a group of twenty-five Aboriginals with great skin tone despite continual sun exposure. Of course, this is an exaggeration, but it does point to the need to evaluate the research, look at who is funding the research, what their motives may be, and how it all affects you, the consumer.

James Poniewozik stated in *Time* magazine that we are consuming the opportunity to window shop. He cites the popularity of shows about the over-the-top rich people as evidence that if you can't have, you can at least watch others who have. While watching in surprise, you get to disapprove. You may even feel better about your own overindulgences with credit cards since you aren't nearly as guilty as those *Real Wives of New York City* who are having dog parties at the Hampton Hound.

I couldn't argue about Poniewozik's cited motivations for viewing. I might add that you like to be surprised, and certainly programs about another group of wives, the *Desperate Housewives*, gave you that chance. It was like an opportunity to open a surprise package each week, knowing that whatever is in the box will be a prize.

To detect what gift/trance you are getting, ask yourself these *Get Reel* questions.

Look forward to the coming attractions of prescriptive RxTV, quizzes, activities, and games in the chapters. Your RxTV will bring the power of TV to you and away from the messages so that *you* are the one making the choices for what you will believe and how you will live your life. Top Ten Cs of Conscious Viewing will assist you on your journey to changing old trances.

And the SpyTV exercises will walk you through you how to be a detective, giving you the power to

- detect the trance;
- accept or release it; and
- replace or respect it.

These three tools will give you the freedom to catapult your way to your dreams or just get there at your own pace.

Especially, you will find ways to be a detective in the rest of your life. Just think, you could change the ideas of other people, academic environments, and friends that have taken root in your consciousness, applying the rules to TV trance breaking to the rest of your life!

V I was struck one day when an elderly woman in a restroom confided to me that every situation in life has its equivalent in an episode of *Seinfeld*. She made her remarks after finding herself short of paper in her stall. If you are a *Seinfeld* watcher, I need explain no more. At that moment, we were members of the same club.

As you navigate your way through TV, I invite you to take this risk-free opportunity guaranteed to change your life and make you happier. (Sound like a commercial? Did you just buy into that promise?) The point is that you are so used to hearing certain words that you accept them as common. But if you can catch yourself almost buying into the common phrases and instead pull back to question them, you have begun to awaken to the joys of television—perhaps minus the potential damage.

So what are the hot topics to watch for (*drum roll, climactic music in the background, visuals of people on vacation*)?

- Why *Get Reel*?
- How Are You Hypnotized by TV?
- Politics and the News—Is Bias Inevitable?
- Love and Sex as Seen on TV
- The Family–How Has TV Morphed Yours?
- Money and Advertising—How You're Hooked
- Suspense/Drama/Violence—Yours and Your TV's
- Supernatural and Spiritual TV—Is It for Real?
- Choose Your Trance: Real Conscious Living

In the chapters to follow, I dare you—no, double-dog-dare you—to take a look at what you believe has driven you to become who you are as a result of TV and other media exposure. As you look at your actions, goals, and words and examine them in the light of television exposure, you may laugh or cry, change or stay the same.

Your first SpyTV assignment is to *get curious* about how you might change while watching TV from the comfort of your home or computer. Get your trench coat on and don't tell what is or isn't underneath it; it's not a time for too much information! Begin to allow your curiosity to bubble up as you open yourself to how you can *detect the trances* that drive your life. If this sounds scary, don't be surprised. The brain raises an automatic fear response to new ideas. As you continue to learn more about the ideas, they will begin to feel less threatening. Consider feeling the fear and moving ahead anyway. If you watch any crime shows, law shows, detective shows, or police shows, you have tucked away lots of ways to *detect* scary things, so you already have strategies at your disposal. Continue reading to find the perfect way to begin your personal path to producing your own life.

Your first C for this section to get you started is *curiosity. It will take a while to make new choices. Just begin to get curious about how it might happen.*

CHAPTER 1

WATCH TWO SHOWS AND CALL ME IN THE MORNING

Do you know how to break your trances and create new ones? Is the suspense keeping you on the edge of your seat? Then follow me through Trance Breaking 101 as I expose the techniques that build and support trances. As with all good courses, there will be quizzes, the key points will be emphasized, and you will be encouraged to think for yourself while reading.

Get Reel Pretest: Seven Questions on TV Trance
- Are you ready to learn about TV hypnosis and when you are most likely to believe a TV image is real?
- Is it time to consider how you filter what you see, automatically omitting what you don't believe?
- Do you know what happens that changes your behavior when you are viewing at a football party?
- Do you make the people on the screen your heroes?
- Can you be addicted to TV? And if so, what can you do about it?
- Do you know why you connect to some TV messages and not to others?
- Do you know the power of the messages on the screen that you take in unconsciously?

How You Buy into the Trance, Drink the Kool-Aid

In November 1978, Jim Jones convinced massive numbers of people to commit revolutionary suicide by drinking poison-laced Kool-Aid (actually FlavorAid but now remembered as Kool-Aid) as a result of his pathological trances about the world, life, and religion. The reference to drinking the Kool-Aid is now used to describe how a massive number of people buy into a trance and behave destructively. While your trances are much less destructive than Jones's, the principle of massive numbers of people buying into destructive trances is not.

Background Noise

Your brain is involved in ways you do not even know. A study done by Gerald Echterhoff at Jacobs University in Germany noted that subjects who had witnessed videos of people performing certain actions remembered doing those actions themselves! Does this mean you are likely to remember shooting someone after viewing *CSI* or *NCIS*? No, but it means that the image stays in the brain, making you unsure if it is a real memory or a viewed one. The memory sticks. And you will need more than an eight-ounce bottle of Goo-Gone to get rid of it.

The brain has something called *mirror neurons* that cause you to feel empathy for the hero. Because of empathy, if the director has done the background work to make you care about the hero's outcome, you hold your breath to see if the brave but outnumbered hero escapes the howling, bloody-toothed villain. Empathy evokes mirror neurons and integrates the memory into the brain. The unpleasant side effects of empathy include scary images, false memories, and internal replaying of TV shows and movies. New theories dispute mirror neurons, but the principles apply. We learn, feel, and become through vicarious viewing.

Emotionally charged, brutal, and violent images are the most likely ones to stimulate mirror neurons, so the images are more likely to become a part of your memory. Nightmares can result, and it does not stop there. Those who watch more violent TV store more images and irrationally tend to be more fearful of the outside world and of crime. The result is that they stay home more and watch more TV, adding to the arsenal of existing violent images in the brain in a vicious cycle.

Can conscious viewing halt this memory storage? Can you tell your brain not to hold the memory of the twenty-six people getting gunned down on the subway? Well, you have a bigger brain than Hypnodog if you can avoid playing with everyone you see when taking a walk. So try to sit back, remember that it is just fiction, hold out on feeling bad for the nonexistent hero, and remain conscious that this is not real. Does that take the fun out of it? And what is the difference between watching consciously and watching unconsciously? Once you become conscious, you will just notice that the director has done a great job of developing the hero's character, rather than that the hero is in deep trouble.

You Remember that You Are Watching TV

The cost of not doing so is having greater stored memory and lack of control regarding how those images connect to those already in the brain. So if you've seen enough mass murders, then a new one may hook into the others and store them in a way that makes you more afraid in general. To redirect your brain off *Sunset Boulevard* and take a new route, begin to unravel the ways that TV produces the trance. After all, it is their job to make you remember so that you watch the show again or buy the product. And it is not unfair; it is their job. You usually love the shows that draw you in, give you warm feelings, and take you for an adventure or appeal to your mind and emotions. This is how it is done.

Let's talk about the power of *association* that forms the trance.

You have associations that are uniquely your own. Take, for example, the name Sandy. What do you think of when you hear that name? A girl in your neighborhood or someone who beat you out of your only chance to be a Mouseketeer, like Britney Spears? Your association is uniquely your own. Now think of the name of someone you truly do not like. What associations do you make with that name? Selfish, dangerous, rip-off? Do you experience a strong physical reaction when you hear the name? Does your facial expression change and twist? Do you start to look like Jim Carrey as *The Mask* or Michael Keaton in *Birdman*? This is the power of association. The important thing to remember is that if you have formed the association, you can break it. It is a subconscious association that you take for the truth now, but if you do some detective work and make it conscious, you can break any connection you have formed when the association no longer works for you.

In the series *Lie to Me* that ran on the Fox network, Cal, a rough-and-tough body-language expert, assisted police and the FBI in reading the signals that told him whether a suspect was guilty or innocent. Your body language is so revealing that any association you have will come to the surface under the examination of an expert viewer. This is the power of associations. Does the woman accused of murder look down or to the side when accused? Does she cry during her denial of the crime or after? You have behaviors that reveal your associations that cannot be hidden, and most of them are unknown to you.

So what difference does this make for you? All the time, whether the medium is aural, visual, or printed, you are receiving associations that will hook you. Sometimes the connections are researched ones that have been found to produce specific reactions in watchers, such as babies or sexy women, but these associations usually don't have anything to do with what you are being sold. Commercials that pair a baby with dog food or a sexy woman with a car, a refrigerator, and even with orange juice really have no connection, but once the pairing is made and in the

 You also connect more to the things you already believe. If you think the current president is either the best or worst in American history, then you will form strong attachments to comments and pictures that support your view.

subconscious mind of the passive viewer, there it is! A trance! You may find yourself making *Confessions of a Shopaholic*.

You do this all the time, whether you are reading, watching TV, having a conversation, or listening to a debate. You latch on to what you already believe. This *filtering behavior* becomes more likely if you have just had an event in your life that raises your awareness of a cause, problem, or solution.

Saturday Night Live and many other shows have relived the Bill Clinton affairs to amused audiences, yet there are some who don't think it is funny. What you take in has a great deal to do with what you think before viewing! My friend Joanne's uncle Frank, a Clinton supporter, told her that he was not interested in what happened in Bill's bedroom, just his politics. Bedroom? It happened in the Oval Office, but Uncle Frank's existing opinion omitted this detail.

Watch out for this filtering behavior if you are buying a car; you may be likely to buy the car that someone like Salma Hayek sits on if you aspire to being a sexy brunette, or the truck owned by superstar Kenny Chesney if you are a fan of country music. It could be a problem if what you really need is a van!

The key point is that of *salience* or importance. If you see something in the media that has current importance to you, viewing gives it much more importance. Take, for example:

If desire for fame is salient for you, reality shows can really hook you. Lifestyles are often sold to you more directly with "reality" shows that follow famous or infamous families, such as the Kardashians, the top earners of the reality families, or the Osbournes or individuals such as Justin Bieber or Lindsay Lohan. Why? Because you, as a consumer, can either get hooked into pursuing the beautiful lifestyle or you can satisfy your need to do so by vicarious viewing. Either way, the lives of others are of interest to you, and viewing satisfies that need, much like a teenager with an iPod downloading the latest CD by Coldplay or Lady Gaga.

Todd, a graphic designer in a large packaging firm, was just told by his nutritionist that he should start taking fish oil capsules. If a health-care practitioner just told you to take fish oil capsules, you may become glued to ads and their claims that support the doctor's recommendations. If your son was just knocked off his bike by a drunk driver, then promotions for Mothers Against Drunk Drivers are likely to get your attention.

If you are channel surfing and glide past the shopping channel, and they happen to be selling the patio swing that you were just pricing this week, you are more likely to view and buy. The same applies to drama; when your life is overflowing with highly charged events or is lacking in any drama, you may be more attracted to dramatic programs—hence, the long-running popularity of soap operas. You ask, "How did Kelly manage when her husband left her for the butler? Should I do what Kelly did?" Since you move in the direction of what you attend to, these considerations could be self-defeating.

Is vicarious viewing really possible? Following the completion of my research on the topic of how you learn from TV, I produced and aired radio and TV programs based on the results of the study. The results, shared internationally, showed that the universal effects of TV could be brought to consciousness. Subsequent work in the media gave wide exposure to powerful ideas about TV and why you take it into your mind. The purpose of this work was to be a part of the solution. And the problem was identified by early research on television effectiveness; it was conducted to determine if children who watched physically aggressive programming were more likely to act aggressively. The results found that they were.

Young children presented with a punching bag were more likely to hit it after watching aggressive shows on television. There is also a theory that you release angry impulses by watching vicariously such as during a boxing match. It releases your need for expression and may serve the purpose of keeping you from acting out aggressively. There is other research to suggest that you may actually act immediately or later, especially if the aggression appears to be justified. In other cases, acting out is only mildly correlated with viewing. The behavior often fades if the person does not already have strong aggressive tendencies or immediate opportunities to act. If they do, the opposite may occur. Whether TV plays a positive or negative role through televised aggression is often determined by the situation and predisposition of the viewer.

So what else happens when you watch TV? Are you more likely to punch out the person who eats the last double-bean burrito while viewing a boxing match? Not necessarily, because you *participate*. As viewers, you identify with the characters and adopt their behaviors, looks, likes, and dislikes. Movies and TV give you a "you are there" feeling. You are shown only the producer's intended focus to maintain eye contact and sustain attention. This prevents distraction and keeps you engaged. Since attention leads to learning, you are now perfectly positioned to learn. The principles in success and motivation theory are that those things to which you give your attention will increase. When driving your car, if you focus off the road, you drive in the direction you are facing. Seems pretty obvious? What you pay attention to determines your direction. Does this mean that after seeing how successfully Gloria, played by Sofia Vergara on *Modern Family*, entertains by screaming that you will do the same? If you do, you will wake up quickly when her husband, Jay, played by Ed O'Neill, does not come to the rescue. You must remember that Gloria says she was a native of "the murder capital of Columbia," so her behavior is relative yet funny. For you, a more restrained approach would win you the family Emmy (Exceptionally Mannered Mother of Youth or Especially Mature Man of the Year).

Do you take in the images deliberately? Sometimes you watch to learn, but, at other times, you attend involuntarily. *You watch through inertia because you are already watching.* At other times, the images become more powerful because you participate. *Once you are attentive, you begin to synthesize the information.* Questions posed by the mind during viewing keep attention sustained as you wonder how plots will unravel, who is the real murderer, what method of triggering recall will be used next on *Drop Dead Diva*. Associations are likely to occur, but you can break them if you can detect them.

I overheard a group of Ohio viewers in front of a large restaurant TV screen asking several questions during an episode of *Flash Forward*, a 2010 series about the world's residents getting a view of their lives six months into the future. The view occurred during a two-minute-long unconscious state. Questions were posed such as, "Well, if he doesn't remember anything, why is he chasing a future vision?" "If she's married, and she sees her future self having an affair with a guy, why is she paying attention to him?" The program was effective. How can you stop viewing until the questions are answered? Too bad they are now still asking the questions. The show has been cancelled.

Notice as you watch, not just how the plot keeps your attention *but also how the style of shooting and presenting keeps you hooked until the end.* To accomplish that, editors use

- cuts;
- zooms;
- colors;
- rapid scene changes;
- visual appeal;
- interesting sounds; and
- unbelievable provocative flashes of half-naked people. (Okay, not all producers use these, I admit. I was just trying to see if you were paying attention.)

All keep your attention and guarantee continued viewing. If the program becomes boring and you take your attention away to do something else or change the channel, you are unlikely to go back to watching. In order to maintain attention, the need for fascinating programs is essential. Whether watching is voluntary or involuntary, there has been evidence at least since the seventies that you give yourself over to the images without questioning what you see.

> The use of voiceover is one example of how media keeps your attention. Did you ever notice that sometimes you are watching the screen and there is someone talking in the background about what you are watching? If that isn't good salesmanship, I don't know what is. As the woman uses the wonder mop, the host is telling you that you will never have to struggle again. This is an example of voiceover. The end of struggle is a powerful motivation, and so there it is! Another association! You must buy the wonder mop so that you can stop struggling.

We also know that *viewing with peers* is likely to keep you watching longer. As you monitor others' attention, you gain clues as to what your own behavior should be. The context of a sports bar capitalizes on this concept. Get everyone out to watch the game together, and they will continue watching longer and drink and eat more. Clever marketing, indeed! The outcome of watching more TV with peers may become complicated with age. Multi-award-winning writer Harlan Ellison has written about a group of old women who dressed up to watch soap operas because their "friends" were coming to visit, believing that the characters were real. Does TV cause senility? No, but if you start talking to your TV, seek help.

On the plus side, you like *to model yourself after good guys or heroes.* You like the idea of being a superhero and saving the world. But what happens when the good guys have bad secondary habits and characteristics, such as bad language, smoking, or slimy hair? Since kids idealize rock stars and the likelihood of becoming one is slim, they *model their secondary characteristics.* When Michael Jackson began wearing one glove, dress codes in schools were broken all over the country by students who tried to emulate Michael. The same behavior reappeared when he died. Now you know the answer to the question, "Why does my twelve-year-old son want to dye his hair orange and pierce his mouth?" Because someone he idolized did the same thing. They adopt the secondary behaviors of the hero or tough guy and leave the building hopping to Superman and the chasing to the police. This saves a selected few from buying electric guitars or getting hurt trying to moonwalk. But for children, the most susceptible viewers, attitudes and behaviors are continually forming. After parents, peers, and classroom teachers, TV is one of their most powerful teachers.

Curious about this research, I decided to find out how children learned from TV for myself. I designed a curriculum for elementary school students that would show a video on stress management, provide a teacher-directed lesson to support the points made in the video, and then give students brief, daily practice of relaxation techniques. The results proved to be powerful. Students' measurable signs of stress had gone down significantly, and, in some cases, academic achievement had increased.

Why was this study important? It demonstrates the power of television to teach. If we can teach children to lower their symptoms of stress with positive coping skills, the ramifications for illness prevention are powerful. Other supporting research shows that when people learn to use relaxation skills before surgery, it has a positive effect on health. In my work, I have seen children learn to manage and reduce levels of stress in six weeks that took adults six months to achieve, given similar training. Based on the connection between stress and disease, the earlier you learn to minimize the effects of stress, the better. See how you can use the powerful tool of the media to create better health in children? You can share positive characters and ideas for children and adults to model and emulate. The question then becomes, positive by whose standard? Since everyone has a *filtering* mechanism, the characters are usually based on widely accepted standards of what is positive. But the associations that you or your children form can be the ones that you find constructive.

Let's further explore the ramifications of the heroes' actions on TV. When someone behaves positively, rescues the damsel in distress, and is rewarded in some way, you are much more likely to learn bravery. The effect of the behavior often determines whether you embrace the action. But if the bold rescue results in getting blown up, you learn not to do something really stupid. You also tend to like and follow role models who remind you of yourself, or the self you want to be. What constitutes a good role model or hero has changed too. The idea of rescuing the damsel is still very present in programming but has come into question. In *Cinderella Ate My Daughter*, author Peggy Orenstein describes takes Snow White as an example of a fairy tale character, a non-assertive princess carried off by a prince, who is attracted solely by her beauty, to live in a happy ending dominated by him. People from small towns, those with dark hair, or characters that also like to sing in the school glee club have more influence with you if you are like them. Marketers use this point to direct their characters and advertising. If the person on the screen is like most of the viewers of a particular show, or like someone they want to be, then there is a match. You continue to watch or buy, and the program is a hit. The success of the show *Glee*

Name That Trance

Name as many of the causes of trance as you can. Stop reading and do this now.

Did you remember association, filtering, peer viewing, models and heroes, participation, and addiction? For each one that you recalled, you are one step closer to living a life of awareness.

is partly based on this concept while the rest of the show's appeal is based on acting and talent. But if you fantasize about having or being Lea Michelle, see the section below.

Can You Become *Addicted* to TV or the Internet?

If you are addicted to TV and other electronic media, you may feel like a mouse trapped in a maze, addicted to the cheese and unable to venture out. As with all addictions, you stay with them to avoid insecurity or pain. Once trapped, the usual reaction is to reach for something familiar that you associate with temporary relief and then ask yourself why you are still dissatisfied.

The path to addiction is a slippery slope. Your interest in programs may move from

- Stage One—Loyalty. You can't watch *24* because you have to watch sports at that time. Your favorite player would be disappointed if you weren't there.
- Stage Two—Attachment. You know you are attached when you need your fix of a show. For example, if you can't make it to your best friend's fiftieth birthday party because you have to watch *WWE Raw, Smackdown,* or the *Victoria Secret Fashion Show*, you are attached.
- Stage three—Addiction. If you *are* addicted, wouldn't you like to know? Do you have at least three of the following symptoms of TV addiction that lead to salivating or to comments such as these?

  1. Using TV as a sedative: "Oh but it's so soothing to see Judy make love with Rudy eight times a night."
  2. Indiscriminate viewing: "What time is it?" you ask after an undetermined amount of *Frasier* reruns.
  3. Feeling loss of control while viewing: "I really should be paying the Netflix bill right now."
  4. Feeling angry with yourself for watching too much: "If I had only spent the last year writing my book about Swahilis."
  5. Inability to stop watching TV: "I really want to think up a new prank to play on my cubicle buddy, but …"
  6. Feeling miserable when kept from watching: "I don't care if it *is* your son's wedding day, I'm missing *Parking Wars*."

According to Rutgers University psychologist Robert Kubey, millions of Americans fit into the third category. If he is right, then conscious viewing may be the answer, as it may loosen the addiction and turn it into a mere preference. And preference is where *you* keep the power to choose. You become conscious by simply paying attention to what you are doing, without judging it as bad, and discerning what is and is not good for you.

You may feel upset about missing the episode that reveals if the actress who fell in the bathtub is rescued in time but be able to reframe the importance of knowing the outcome right now and go to your son's graduation. You can always stay up way too late tonight to watch it.

With Internet addiction, the draw is the continual opportunity for entertainment, connection, or escape. With prolonged technological social networking minus face contact, feelings of empathy, ability to read body language, and understanding emotional intensity do not develop. And Internet Gaming Disorder is responsible for compulsive game playing to the exclusion of other interests. If you identify with stage three above, then you might consider if the Internet is your drug of choice.

SpyTV

Now for the SpyTV portion of this chapter: Can you *detect* one association that you formed that you would like to break? For example, if you decided that letting close friends in on your most personal secrets is undesirable after being betrayed, this is an association; telling your secrets is associated with being betrayed. What if you see actors on *Friends* and *Seinfeld* letting friends' secrets "out of the vault?" Your association has been reinforced. Now let's say that this association is self-destructive and gets in the way of forming trusting relationships. In the *accept or release* stage of your detective work, this would be a big one to *release*.

So will you *replace or respect* it as having value? I can almost hear you telling me how finished you are with attracting people you can't trust and can see you stepping up to *replace* the trance. Prepare to change your association that connects friends and mistrust. Be stronger than *Iron Man*. Think of as many times as you can when your friends or family did not betray your trust. Think of times when you told employers or colleagues personal information. Think of as many times as you can when your trust was not betrayed. Think of friends who told you their secrets, and you kept them.

Prepare to break your first trance with *the trance breaker of curiosity*! Picture a time when you were betrayed and begin to ask yourself what other images might be better of times when trust was well placed. One at a time, get curious about the old mistrust image and how it might be released by recalling all of the safe times and allow those images to flush out the old association. Continue until the new images feel stronger than the old one. Any time that you feel the old association come in, change the association by getting curious about what could replace it. Flood the new images like you were on the *Titanic*. Replace your thought and continue to reinforce the new association. You first have to *get curious*.

Now *detect* an association that you formed from watching TV that you really like. Maybe you saw the talk show where the person with the Internet addiction owns up and changes his life. Maybe it reminds you that by taking responsibility for your own life, that you can make changes, too. Maybe you even went out and did something differently as a result. You have a positive association with owning your own problems and making changes. This is great. *Accept* this association. Continue, each time that you take charge of our life, to remind yourself how well this works and build strength in that association. *Respect* the way it benefits you. Continue to get curious and make the constructive association, adding more strength to the positive connection.

It is possible to view consciously, with new eyes, recognizing the messages you are taking in and deciding to choose which messages to keep. At the point of recognition, you have a choice, and you have just raised your ability to recognize what messages are being projected. You now have the option to change the association if it is an embedded one that does not work for you. The next time you feel like you can't live without knowing if the murderer is really the victim's music teacher, feng shui consultant, cable guy, trash collector, or water meter reader, you can redeem yourself with choice. In the chapters to follow, you will examine specific messages in the media with the promise of freedom to choose to *accept or release the message*. You will be introduced to a set of guidelines known as the Top Ten Cs of Conscious Viewing that will free you from old programs and give you back your life. Then you can move toward what really makes you happy, toward the personal illusions or realities that make you happy and away from the fictional illusions that don't. A sneak preview is available below.

Top Ten Cs of Conscious Viewing

1. *Curiosity.* Begin to wonder about the power of TV.
2. *Change* what you do daily. Don't tune in automatically.
3. *Consciously* watch something you already watch. What are some underlying messages of the show?
4. *Consider* whether the messages are constructive, destructive, merely entertaining, or are good messages for you and for your children.
5. *Cut* out one thing to watch this week. Choose something that you have already identified as not feeling good or having a message that is not empowering.
6. *Choose* three things to watch consciously this week.
7. *Calm* down. It will take a while to make new choices. Cable TV wasn't built in a week.
8. *Check* out how you feel as you watch. Watch the TV Guide Channel. Sort the options.
9. Note *consequences* for the characters. Are the misbehaviors okay if all works out well?
10. *Chisel* away at a global community, in a bottom-up fashion that tells the industry what you really want. If *Dallas* can make a comeback, your favorite show can, too.

C—For now, why not change what you do daily? Don't tune in automatically. Stop and think.

For more up-to-date information on *Get Reel* for this chapter, go to:

http://drnancyonline.com/category/rc-media-and-rxtv/

http://drnancyonline.com/category/rc-health/

http://drnancyonline.com/category/current-news/

CHAPTER 2

POLITICS AND THE NEWS: THE FACTS, MA'AM, JUST THE FACTS

I love the news. I love that it is available twenty-four hours a day. I love that, at any time of the day, I can hear any political party express its views with conviction and without fear. I love that I can catch feedback of the president's addresses or follow a celebrity faux pas at any time. I love that I can catch it on the Internet and that the home page of my server even points out the highlights, much like the front page of a newspaper. I love that I can get the headlines delivered to my computer every day from the *New York Times* or Pittsburgh's local *Tribune Review* or *Post-Gazette*. I love the unbiased presentations on the local news reports here in town. What I don't love is politics. Yes, it is necessary but, as a psychologist, I know that whenever one person has to be right, then one has to be wrong. Usually in right and wrong, there is a perceptual filter, bias, or trance that you have absorbed from experience and/or the news. The message of the filter is that someone really has to be wrong.

Politics is a touchy subject. I won't tell you my political affiliation because I don't have one. I am what they used to call a GDI. If you were alive in the sixties, you know what this means; the last word stands for Independent. I am an independent, not because I am indifferent to the direction of the world but because I know that if I enter into any news broadcast with bias, I will not hear what is said; I will be too busy deciding if the information matches or contradicts my bias. Defending my position makes it impossible to hear what was said, as I would be coming up with mental arguments why I do not believe anything that does not match my bias. Instead, I try to hear each person right there, in real time, and figure out how what I hear resonates with me, with what I know, and with how I perceive it at that exact moment. And my perception is only as clear as my own freedom from bias. Even people that I discern to be terribly destructive sometimes say wise things, and I want to be free to hear them. Free—there is another word that is so important to people. Freedom.

"Don't Quote Me"

In my book *Spiritual Fitness*, I have a chapter called "Don't Quote Me." I wrote this chapter to raise awareness of the static in your perceptions through which you view the world. I call it the static on your screens. If you have ever tried to watch a TV channel without good reception, you know how difficult it is to see the true image behind the static. You also know that you sometimes don't see what's there and that you may misjudge the actual image. These *misjudgments* are forms of

- bias;
- trance from life experience or misinformation;
- personal mythology; and
- the static in our perceptions caused by trances that do not fully allow in the reality.

You can begin to unravel the misperceptions from the truth as you look at the beginnings of television.

In the Beginning

Watching a TV clouded by static was not the intention of Philo T. Farnsworth, the founder of television. Philo began laying out his vision for what television could become. Above all else, television would become the world's greatest teaching tool. Illiteracy would be wiped out. The immediacy of television was the key. As news happened, viewers would watch it unfold live. No longer would you have to rely on people interpreting and distorting the news for you. You would be watching sporting events and symphony orchestras. Instead of going to the movies, the movies would come to you. Television would also bring about world peace. If you were able to see people in other countries and learn about our differences, why would there be any misunderstandings? War would be a thing of the past.

Evan I. Schwartz reported Philo's intentions in his book, *The Last Lone Inventor*. Clearly Philo had a vision, and a powerful one, in projecting the potential of television. Perhaps he did not envision cable TV and the need for huge amounts of programming that would meet the interests of so many different kinds of people and the opportunities of advertisers. Perhaps he didn't know how vastly used his invention would become. Maybe he knew that science, spirituality, history, and the alphabet would be taught through television. I doubt that he would suspect that networks would carry such a varied schedule of crime shows, that some news programs would carry political bias, that stories would be made more interesting through elaborations and reenactment. I wonder what Philo would say if he saw TV today.

In the televised news, we see much of Philo's desire for people to learn about others in other countries. He believed that the outcome would be human understanding of differences. Certainly there are times when this happens. But the view of the same news from each country is different. Each country presents its views of the other country's events from within its own perceptual framework. While Americans are awaiting news on the revisions in health care, China is urging us not to spend so much money so that our dollar is devalued to the point that it affects China's economy. The British Broadcasting Corporation reports on China's desire for more restraint in our spending to that end. Collect viewpoints from other countries with which America trades, and you have a full perspective. You see different points of view, same topic.

Perception vs. Truth

In the nineties, 13 million Americans watched a morning news program on one of the three major networks, ABC, NBC, and CBS. Enter Fox News, CNN, comedy news, and others. The proliferation of individual programs that address politics offers a full gamut of points of view. Who am I to say that they express views rather than facts without stories or bias? Just a

Why is the truth so widely interpreted? Because of the stories we attach to what happens. If four people are killed in gunfire and you attach a story to it, then it turns into "Four innocent children are gunned down by Iraqi militants in search of American soldiers." The story is formed by your perception of a country's political viewpoint and events in history, as well as the interpretation of history that you have been given. The story, not the event, becomes what *really* happened.

conscious viewer who noted a journalist praising political party A that was celebrating the approval of a bill, while suggesting that political party B's comments on the events were creating headaches for Washington. I think I heard opinions, biases, and a suggestion that freedom of speech caused a headache. Maybe it does, but I think there is some opinion attached to the reporting. John Lennon might be disappointed that everyone isn't modeling his ideas expressed in his song *Imagine* of a world with "all the people, living life in peace."

I remember a time when a young, red-haired female reporter was telling a story of a flood. She was dressed in a yellow raincoat, knee-length boots, and was holding a large, dark blue umbrella over her head with one shaky hand, shivering in the cold rain. It was dusk and I imagined that she would rather be at home. I heard her voice shake in a high-pitched tone while she explained the extent of the damage, including descriptions of cars that were totally submerged, houses with windows leaking muddy water into living rooms and family rooms, and roof tiles blown off of buildings. She opened with, "Where I am standing ..." I began to feel sorry for the flood victims and for the cold, shaky reporter in the thick of the mess. I was fully taken in by the report. Then I decided to stop accepting what I saw as truth. I turned on my conscious viewing skills and noticed that while the reporter was reporting flood levels of up to four feet, that her puddle was just a few inches deep. Just as I was beginning to wake up and question, the camera angle shifted, and I saw that she was in a shallow pool out of the way of the flood damage. Although embarrassing for the reporter and the cameraman, it illustrates my point.

Wow! I just took you through brief hypnotic language. Let me break it down for you. In much the same way that television programs do, I painted a fictional picture with a soundtrack: specifics about the reporter, a description of her voice, details of the flood, and some hypothesis about her emotional state. She had a media-induced image as the faithful, well-informed servant of the station, risking her own comfort and safety. Had you been watching, you might have had the same experience. I created a scene for you in the same way that the station did. It was much like a scene in a movie; it was scripted with a designed set, an actress, and emotional content. You may have become interested or even sympathetic with the lead character, the reporter, and have become involved in her story. If so, then the trance was a successful one. Now it's time to wake up from the trance.

While such "reenactments" present an extreme example, on a smaller scale, the news is more interesting when it is an experience. Making it one keeps you interested and informed, both good things, but while interested, you may also be entranced.

 When I stayed in Europe one year to speak at the International Behavioral Medicine Conference, I watched an international channel. I will not mention the city because, other than the international channel, I have no complaint with this wonderful city and do not want to create bias. In other words, I don't want anyone to take this personally, creating a new myth about this great town. There was a filler video between programs that included short clips of different large cities from around the world. First they showed London, then Paris and the beauty of their countrysides and towns, happy people, and beautiful weather. Then they showed New York City. I was appalled; in New York, the only images shown were of a drunken nondescript man, lying on a sidewalk while litter blew up around him. It was shot at dusk to increase the sense of darkness and the absence of light. Clearly there was an intent to bias.

Do You Have Any Power for Change?

If you built a trance, political or otherwise, and recognize that it may be clouding your vision, then you can dismantle it. Take, for example, my cat, Katie. She used to enjoy sitting on the stove. It gave off just a bit of warmth, and she would cuddle up on it and purr. One day she jumped up while the stove was still hot; she jumped off and never jumped back on again. Instead of learning not to jump on the hot stove, she learned to avoid the stove altogether. Trance-based bias is the same. You have a bad experience with something and avoid it on a permanent basis. Katie has not yet dismantled her belief, but you can.

I am not saying that you should avoid joining a political party. If joining and supporting a political party or candidate feels constructive for you, go ahead. After all, if strong opinions and stands did not exist, there would not have been a civil war that ended slavery, and women's right to vote would still be an unresolved issue. But take the blinders off; you're not in Kansas anymore.

Longtime national newscaster Walter Cronkite shared his thoughts about journalism with the public. "If they're preordained dogmatists for a cause, then they can't be very good journalists; that is, if they carry it into their journalism." Perhaps Walter may be right. Every political presentation can't all be right—the portrayals of the Democrats, the Republicans, the libertarians, foreign countries, women, men. How these individuals are slanted and presented clearly shows some bias on the part of the sender of the message, and some trances for you to examine.

One motivation to join political parties is to obtain the feeling of being part of a group, which is a powerful, sociological need, one that politicians often use to personal advantage. Sociology tells you that you want to be a part of a group, whether as a member of the third grade, your family, the soccer team, or the young Republicans. It is part of your make-up and not likely to change. Politically, you have probably experienced disagreements or maybe even knockdown, drag-out fights with others who are not a member of your party about issues that affect you. When there are differences in opinion within groups, it can help to have a sense of humor as displayed in the show *Family Ties*. It showed the abrasive nature of Michael J. Fox's Alex Keaton, a Republican in a family of Democrats, who fought for his right to make a lot of money—a stereotypical portrayal of a Republican.

V I receive a lot of political e-mail, citing chapter and verse of bills before Congress. They generally ask me to contact a congressman to stop the bill. The documents are usually half-truths, misinterpretations, and generalities used to inflame the reader with the injustice of the party's attempt to control the government. Does this also happen in news reporting in the newspaper or on TV? Hopefully not. But if you are a conscious viewer, standing on your side but close enough to see the other side, conscious viewing will be less challenging and more freeing. Am I saying that what is on the air is less important than your clear view of it? You betcha!

They all got along, without screaming or ostracizing the different family members, and laughed along the way.

Laws of Distraction

Even the character of Alex Keaton knew that the basis of the two-party system is to keep a balance of power, something we certainly need. But in order to stay in the majority and move your agenda forward, you have to be right, and someone else has to be wrong, and no one wants to be wrong. This continual struggle to be right takes up a lot of politicians' time that could be spent working together. Nothing new in that idea! (It often happens with couples, too.) But there is a law of distraction, like the one often used with children. When children stand in front of the TV, blocking your view, you distract them with a toy on the other side of the room, and they forget to notice the TV. I heard about a scandal involving a group of media journalists deciding together to squash a story about one party by making something up about the other party for distraction. Is it true? I don't know, but because it is true to what I know personally about the laws of distraction, I might just consider that it could be accurate. If it is relevant or salient to my personal experience, it is more likely to become embedded as a part of my truth. This is usually true when viewing. But it doesn't have to be.

Be a Part of the Solution

Is conscious viewing a solution to the problem? Can we get on with moving the country forward and minimize the time spent on Bill Clinton's personal life or Michelle Obama's wardrobe? While these issues may or may not have merit, they take up moments that you could spend trying to seek solutions rather than dispel rumor. I have heard that simply sending out a rumor is enough to make people believe it. Perhaps some of the individuals involved in politics have heard that, too. Will we ever stop having these two-party differences? It is unlikely, based on the nature of man. We are a duality of positive and negative, back and forth, and so we are likely to have a dual-party system. We will always have the good guys and the bad guys. Who's who depends on where you stand. The challenge is to avoid spending too much time at the far end of an issue, creating so much distance that it does not allow for a view of the other side. This is conscious viewing. It is even conscious living. And before you are done with *Get Reel,* you will know exactly how to do so, if you choose! You'll be able to discern that even your troublesome mother-in-law/boss/hair dresser/lead character in a soap may be right at times.

> In a *Time* magazine article by David Von Drehle in the September 28, 2009 issue, he gives examples of the many ways that liberals and conservatives tell the same stories. He asks if we should trust the "corrupt, communist-loving traitors on the left" or the "greedy warmongers on the right." He proposes that the media are unlikely to share stories about things they don't agree with; it is a harsh take on how the spin dictates the "truth" and how evidence is used to support a personal point of view

When reporting became more biased, it was without excuses and fully out in the open. Shows that expressed specific points of view did so purposely. And I want that when I am looking to see what liberals or conservatives are thinking but not when I watch the local evening news. Then, I just want to know what happened today. If I want a heated discussion, I know where to find it.

Then, after the shooting of Gabrielle Gifford, President Obama requested that parties not blame one another for inciting the shooter. He did not seem to want to see heated blame sessions in the media or in your homes. He asked that people work together rather than allow the shooting to cause division. My subjective opinion of his request was that there should not be blame because, among other things, there could be retaliation, and the whole thing could start a ripple effect that could not have a happy ending. In my practice, I have seen that crimes *can* trigger a copycat effect, resulting in similar crimes. But my opinion was more of a personal one, driven by my survival instinct. The desire to stay alive and keep loved ones alive shaped my ability to consciously agree with him.

I don't think that desires to protect your lives, families, or property from extinction is a trance; it is a basic instinct. Survival is no joke, but often the news is. Programs like *Jon Stewart's Daily Show, 2014's Last Week Tonight with John Oliver* and Stephen Colbert's *The Colbert Report* poke fun at what happened that week and even find a way to be funny when speaking respectfully of the pope. They even managed to have a rally on October 30, 2010 to spoof rallies.

But sometimes in humor stands bias. When *Saturday Night Live* spoofs the week's news in their opening skit, there is a definite opinion about what happened that week. You can laugh at it even if your perspective does not match their opinion, when watching consciously. Politicians even spoof themselves on the show. But it requires conscious viewing in order for your sense of humor to survive.

Survival keeps popping up here, and often the news predicts our very likelihood of survival. We hear about approaching hurricanes, tornadoes, and huge traffic accidents. You hear the terrorist-threat predictions and information about gunmen on the loose. Survival issues can be presented on the news in a way that either lessens your fears (i.e., swine flu vaccine becomes available) or enhances them (i.e., US dollar likely to continue to drop). Either way, interest in information about your survival will remain constant. Belief, on the other hand, can change; it is even highly likely that some of your beliefs will shift over time. And you can involve your whole self in the change so that it sticks! I hope that you are *becoming curious* about how this works right about now.

Strategies for Change

When the brain is presented with a new idea, it becomes afraid. It steers away from the belief and returns to the old accepted belief. One way to introduce a new idea is to continue to introduce it until it becomes one of the old ideas that found a comfortable place to reside in the brain. In order to embrace new ideas, you have to make them feel at home through repetition. If you want to learn to dance, you have to practice the steps.

Sometimes, words are not enough to cause awareness. They didn't work with Lynn. Sometimes you have to learn by consciously observing your own mistakes. My former colleague, Lynn, had an eye-opening experience with bias. She had a very strong, positive opinion about a politician named James. She actually found him to be a top-notch lobbyist and attractive, graceful, and handsome as well. Why? She had a crush on him, and his charm had overridden any perception of fault. One day she looked out of her second-story office window and saw a group of people gathered outside her office. She wondered why she had not been invited to the event. She noticed an awkward, chubby, balding man cutting a ribbon to break ground for a new project. When he looked up, she realized that he was her dream man, the one that she had considered so handsome and perfect! After she recovered from the reeling sensation of seeing the truth, she realized that she had an experience in suspended bias, when her belief was temporarily halted and the surprising truth slipped through.

When you don't know whom or what you are looking at, you see it for the first time and view it with your mind, heart, and gut, without bias. You see what is there. Had my friend Lynn seen James cutting the ribbon from the vantage point of the ground, she might have seen him as graceful and attractive. Sometimes it pays to rise above your perceptions, view from a higher level—literally and figuratively—and see what's really there.

Turn Your World Upside Down

How do we suspend bias to live without hypnotic trance or myth perpetuated within us by sometimes unknowing and even innocent people? Let me give you an example. Betty Edwards wrote a book called *Drawing on the Right Side of the Brain*. It was a book that showed you how to shut off the language in your brain and just see what is in front of you. In this state of right-brain stimulation, you lose track of time and space and just observe what is there, then reproduce it. As an artist, this is a valuable tool because if you are drawing a dog and thinking of what a dog should look like, there will be constant chatter: "This does not look like a dog's leg; it should have more curve, less curve, be shorter"—fill in the blank. We all know what criticism sounds like.

Since I was teaching workshops at the time on right-brain left-brain differences and how each dominant type can get along with the other type, I went to a workshop to learn Edward's method. First, everyone took a photo from a random pile and tried to reproduce it on a flip chart with varying results. After judging some pretty bad reproductions, everyone took another random photo from the pile. But this time we turned it upside down and just drew. The results were astounding. Others and I in the workshop who had no artistic ability were able to reproduce lines that truly looked like the photos simply by suspending language, judgment, and bias about ourselves and the photos. When you are in this state, you experience what Mihaly Csikszentmihalyi calls flow, a state where there is no time and space, just openness to the experience and a willingness to see what is possible.

Edwards suggests reproducing a picture of something by turning it upside down and drawing just the lines that you see—the shadows, the forms, without any language to tell you what you are drawing. Just put down what is there.

Can the concept of inversion *turn your personal worldview upside down*? Perhaps it can by watching and listening without static on your screen. Suspend, just for a time, everything you previously believed or held to be true without question. The next time that you view a newscast, listen to the chatter in your head. How much of it is bias, and how much is perception? And with the perceptions, what is an innate part of you, constructive and unlikely to change, and what is a negative trance? Was this exercise easy for you? Fantastic! If not, the cure is just around the corner. Notice I am using the same technique used by the news. "Coming up, the best way to get rid of stink bugs/hair on your neck/pesky neighbors/cracks in your old ceramic cups/other dilemma.

Confusion does that; it is a powerful tool to wake up and take notice that a change in thinking might be necessary. It shakes up your existing belief such that you can't stick to it and have to reexamine what is true. Confusion precedes much new learning.

My friend Linda's niece, Emily, is a younger, less experienced version of herself. Her mother used to have difficulty telling them apart, and her father never could. In 2014, she attended school at Penn State University and majored in business. This is where the similarities ended since Linda's career choice was much different, as a teacher of handicapped children. Her grandmother, who lived to be one hundred years old, used to say, "Both choices are the right ones if you are choosing from the heart." One day, we were having a discussion about a presidential election in which the potential First Lady was being questioned. Some of her past remarks caused her trouble, because they were angry in nature. Emily took the side of the potential First Lady and seemed to be excusing and dismissing the remarks as meaningless, even though they were directed at specific groups and contained strong opinions. The opinions of the woman were opinions that my sister had chastised in the past when expressed by other politicians. As I pointed out the inconsistency in her views, Emily got angry. Her face flushed, her voice raised, and she began to look directly at me. Clearly she was angry with me and at herself for being caught in the confusion. Confusion reigned where clear trance had previously existed. She had become a conscious viewer against her will and was angry to be awakened from her trance.

I did it again! I used hypnotic language to engage you in my battle with someone named Emily. Does Emily really exist? No! I don't even have a sister. I *did* have a hundred-year-old grandmother, but that is where the similarity ends. What happened is that I created an image of someone and told you about her unwitting conflict when faced with awakening from her trance. Confusion does lead to learning.

Don't misunderstand. News is essential, exceptionally presented, widely researched, and carefully crafted. Some of my best friends are literally newscasters and producers. But even they ask themselves, "Is politics different from fictional television?" They create an image of a person, using image consultants, public relations people, and makeup artists, and then they tell their story. Our hope is that the image that is created is a reflection of the true person inside, only bumped up a notch. And often it is just that.

Confused? If so, it's a good thing. As I've said, confusion precedes learning. So in order to confuse you further and give you some temporary distance from your view, ask yourself the following questions in the Political Viewpoint Quiz text box and see the RxTV prescription below.

Get Reel Quiz: Political Viewpoint

1. What is one political point of view that I believe to be true?
2. What would be true if I were wrong?
3. What would be true if I were right?
4. Who would be affected if I were wrong?
5. What would happen if I took a different view?
6. What would happen if I took no particular viewpoint at all and just decided to experience the issue at each and every moment?
7. How did you feel doing this exercise?

RxTV:

✓ List the emotions you felt doing the quiz.

✓ Were you angry, confused, interested, and able to see another point of view or annoyed, critical, and unable to see another point of view, etc.?

✓ However you approached it and whatever you experienced, ask yourself if this is your usual approach to life. Do unexpected challenges make you curious? Angry? Adventurous? Miffed? It may be a pattern that can help you to see your response to having your bias challenged. It may even be how you respond to life.

Now this next suggestion may be challenging. I know that I said this book would be fun, easy, and effortless. Did I lie to tap into powerful marketing strategies? No, I am still asking you to have fun. As a matter of fact, ask yourself, "How much fun can I have doing this next exercise?"

Get Reel Activity: Viewer Participation

Get comfortable and sit back with your eyes closed. Think of a current political situation on which you have some view, perhaps involving a person you don't like, or something someone said to you that agitated you because it challenged your position. Think of how you may have felt as I brought up the very names of Bill Clinton and Michelle Obama. Then think of my friend Susan and my colleague David. David hates the smell of mayonnaise. He once said to me, "I could ask a woman I loved to never ask me to eat mayonnaise and even hope that she would, but I would defend her right to eat it."

I am not suggesting that I agree or disagree here; I am simply giving an example of someone who knows how he feels but allows others to feel the way that they do. Now notice something else. How did you feel about the words "mayonnaise" and "defend her right to choose it?" You have a right to your response. Just notice it.

RxTV:

√ Is mayonnaise an issue that triggers a strong emotional response in you? Probably not!

√ If not, is there another issue that does? What is that issue?

√ Are your reactions based on personal experience or on sympathy toward others who have had a similar experience?

√ Notice any bias or any "making wrong" or "making right" thinking?

√ Now ask yourself if there is any static on your screen that you want to clear away in order to get a fuller view of an issue.

When you are finished, see how you feel. You may hold the same view but with perspective. You may hold the view without negative emotions. Any possibility can occur, but you may notice a shift of some kind. If there is no shift, try the exercise at another time with any issue. Detachment allows you to clear your screen for a long enough time to suspend the belief and allow you to be objective.

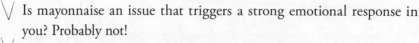 Celebrity has become intertwined more and more in politics, and it is not likely to change. While celebrities are crossing over into politics, the reverse is also true. Barack Obama became a hero on January 14, 2009 in *The Amazing Spider-Man* comic books, even before his inauguration on January 20. Ronald Reagan crossed lines between celebrity and politics but was not fortunate enough to have a London musical named after him. *Obama On My Mind* opened in March 2009.

As you awaken, remember that semantics are powerful. The words that are chosen to describe events carry a powerful punch that can impact you all the way through. When you hear the words "smear campaign," you may develop a reaction immediately. But if the words "honest questioning" are used, you may have a totally different feeling. People with different perceptions and points of view tend to use both phrases to describe the same thing.

Celebrity News

Some actors attack views they find wrong or champion views they hold dear and gain more attention than Mary Sue's mom or Johnny's dad. On September 10, 2010, this fact played out in everyone's favor when the stars came out for a cancer benefit. Marcia Cross and other stars, in jeans and T-shirts, encouraged you to call and pledge money for cancer research.

Now more than ever, celebrities have taken on political causes. Is a celebrity any more important to a political cause than you are? If they are very well informed on an issue, see all sides of the situation, and use their name to lend credibility or draw attention to a worthy cause, celebrity can be a valuable thing. Some question whether they need to present their political views in other arenas, changing the subject during awards ceremonies and interviews about new movies, however.

Pop culture is a part of the daily news. Information technologies spread that news faster and more furiously. Jennifer Aniston, George Clooney, Matt Damon, Tom Hanks, Oprah, Halle Berry, and others have stepped forward to support political causes and candidates. Since people we see on TV are given importance, the opinion of a celebrity may drive some public opinion. Importance is a judgment that people make. It can cause a rock star's opinion about a news item to be more important than John Doe's. Further, what items become newsworthy and which do not can be shaped by the attention that both journalists and celebrities give them.

Producer Barry Levinson did a TV special about the role celebrities play in supporting certain positions. The special seemed to make the point that when celebrities take political positions or magnify a position, they may cross a line. Levinson quoted JFK and present-day celebs that spoke to the public about the power of the media to influence. His exposé gave a bigger picture of the issue of celebrity in politics while Ellen Burstyn reminisced about a time when politicians spoke respectfully of one another. Levinson noted that Hollywood got behind Al Gore and his TV special on global warming and made it more of a household word. Even the pope weighed in on the issue in 2015.

News commentators were described as TV actors on a screen, by celebs. In the same way that Humphrey Bogart was profiled as the tough guy, news reporters are cast in the roles of trustworthy sources. I noticed that truth was discussed as "image creation" in the Levinson special.

Good Guys vs. Bad Guys

The media can create heroes and villains, because we want them. We gravitate toward struggles between the forces of good and evil. The myth of the hero and the villain is one that is present in many cultures and time periods, making it a universal one. The storytelling format of the day's headlines was noted in *Entertainment Weekly's Special Oscar Guide*, in which Ken Tucker posed that the news plots were addictive, proposing that media creates heroes for us to admire because it is human nature to create heroes. Everyone wants someone to look up to and emulate. Unfortunately, at some point, if you have not succeeded in emulating them, you want the hero to fail so that you don't feel so bad about yourself. The JFK of Camelot became the unfaithful husband seduced by Marilyn Monroe. The theme of the unfaithful husband shows up again in the popular show *Mad Men*. You see the themes of hero turned villain when the whole character of the person is exposed and the hero falls.

Many scriptwriters, because of the popular myths that permeate all cultures, read Joseph Campbell's writings about mythology that address the hero and villain. The *Oscar Guide* even makes reference to the normal guy turned hero myth in comparing Spider-Man to Obama, who rises from the role of a child from a single-parent home to the president who puts on the suit jacket. It raises the question of whether there are any *real* heroes. Those whose character remains constant are usually held up as heroes, but viewers get bored with them and want a constantly renewed plot where the hero masters new challenges in new ways or falls on his face.

Conflict of Interest

Are you turning your back on your heroes today? A Yahoo survey indicated that news stories people searched to read on the Internet were not the same ones chosen by TV news stations for their broadcasts. The fact that the journalists selected the stories reported on the news may suggest a certain bias about the importance of the event. Then which details of the events are reported is a reflection of the perceived importance of those details by the reporter and editor. Was the event provoked? Did the soldier deserve to sustain the injuries? Is the ethnic origin of the soldier important? Reporters in different cities have reported news events very differently. Both of these things are influenced by perception and static or the lack of static on the screen. Reporters are aware of the interests of the station and may have to consider how to position a story based on a multitude of factors.

The way that the media presents information plays a critical role in how parties in conflict view one another and can either inflame conflict or promote peace and understanding. The Peace Appeal Foundation notes that because the media plays a critical role in how parties in conflict view one another, they ultimately affect whether they choose to seek peace or inflame conflict. Some say that we are deliberately being misled, but perception is everything.

The principle of perspective is illustrated in the varying descriptions that people give of crime scenes. I have read that a professor of journalism at New York University asked a man to rush into his classroom, create a scene, and speak unintelligibly. Then he asked the students to describe what they had seen. The descriptions were conflicting at best, including differences in what happened, the appearance of the man, his clothing, and what he said.

You are becoming more conscious now that you are reading *Get Reel*, and you are likely to notice that you are viewing politics through a filter of your own bias. Perhaps you will now listen more openly to arguments about health care at family gatherings while having turkey and stuffing. The time is right, and you are ready to take out your mental magnifying glass and use your SpyTV skills. All commercial breaks are over, and you are ready to find out how to "Get rid of stink bugs/hair on your neck/pesky neighbors/cracks in your old ceramic cup." So how can you change your kneejerk reaction to anyone telling you what the government needs to do about Medicare? *Detect* your reaction to bias, now that you are more aware of it. Then *accept or reject* it. Finally, *respect or release* it after you set up an alert system to notice the bias. This alert system is called a new anchor or new association. If you respect it as useful, then you simply keep it. If not, you can release it and set a new anchor and a new perspective. You are really beginning to produce your own life at this point!

> ## SpyTV
>
> *To set a new anchor* or association for a time when you noticed biased reporting, ask yourself, "What's wrong with this picture?" Remember what you *heard* and *saw* and how you *felt* about it. Really recall the memory. Close your eyes and relive it. Then give yourself a key word that will bring this memory to mind whenever you want to be open to noticing bias. Something like "Wow" might be good because it recognizes that someone just tried to put something over on you. The next time you consciously find yourself being taken in by bias, just repeat the word "Wow" for a wake-up call. The more you use an anchor, the better it works. So keep your eyes and ears open for opportunities to "Wow" yourself out of a limiting trance. You have just set an anchor for recognizing bias. Congratulations!

Then begin to think critically and ask yourself as you view *consciously*, the C for this chapter, what trance you want, if any at all. See what trances are floating out there and choose to say yes or no, or create a more positive and powerful one or none at all. Remove some of the static from your screen. Russ Kick, editor of *You Are Still Being Lied To*, compiled a series of articles and research reports that suggest that crucial stories are ignored or suppressed. He finds many stories with "holes in them" are the stories of the day. He includes a report by the Disinformation Company that even suggests that the seriousness of real dangers is suppressed, and the importance of insignificant dangers is escalated. You may wonder, is terrorism down as opposed to whether the swine flu or the bird flu is really a present danger? Consider whether you believe this. Consider consciously.

Get Reel Activity: Trance Changing

Try this exercise. Think of someone with whom you have politically disagreed lately, possibly a newscaster, a friend, or a world leader. Do *not* choose a violent person or someone that you have extreme emotions about. This is just an exercise and is not intended to get you distressed.

Now recall the conflict. What did you say? What did the other person say? And if it was a televised event, what did you say to yourself? Now see the whole thing with your eyes closed, with you and the other person out in front of you. Tell yourself that the way you feel now is the real you and that you will be back to it in a moment. Now see yourself go over and stand in the other person's shoes. Just stand there and see how you feel, what you sense, how you think, what you become aware of. Then come back to yourself and remind yourself of your own real feelings. Now, see if there has been a shift in your understanding.

RxTV:

√ The more conscious you can be, the more likely it is that you will expand your vision in a way that allows you to enjoy your viewing experience as well as the interactions that you have following the program.

√ As you expand your worldview, you expand your compassion, understanding, and ability to make choices that are right for you. They will not be based on misinformation or biased reporting. They will be based on your own gut reaction about what is true for you. And you will fare better in conversations about elections.

I will remain in the two-and-a-half-party system as a member of the half. I received an e-mail this morning indicating that a plan had been set in place for millions of people around the world to gather at the same time tonight to pray for world peace. It was the second of such events this year.

Creating such a plan involves a larger world view. And that is an example of conscious living.

So the SpyTV for this chapter is to set a new anchor called "Wow!" that you use when you *detect* bias or truth and *accept or reject it*. And the *C for this chapter:*

C—*Consciously watch the news and other programs.* Are there any underlying political messages in the show? Or are they doing a great job of telling it like it is? If they are doing a good job, tell them so. E-mail or write and let them know. They work hard, and they deserve it!
And what you want and tell producers that you want is what you will get.

For more up-to-date information on *Get Reel* for this chapter, go to:

http://drnancyonline.com/category/rc-media-and-rxtv/

http://drnancyonline.com/category/current-news/

CHAPTER 3

TV GUIDE TO LOVE AND SEX

Your TV really wants to have a great relationship with you. As with all good relationships, you both want a say in what happens. However, there is one consideration that must be made to guarantee an equal partnership: you must both make concessions. And you, the viewer, must concede by giving up the idea that love on TV and movies bears any resemblance to love in real life. Let me help you.

Once upon a time, there was a burst! And you thought there would be a happy ending. Not so. Sleeping Beauty has awakened from her trance. How about you? This wake-up call may be a harsh one, but it will change, for the better, the way that you relate to a partner in real life. You will stop creating the ambivalence that you see in the characters on *Castle, The Mentalist,* or even reruns of the *X-Files.* You will be free to create your own happy ending that may not resemble what you see on TV.

 When I was in talks with production companies in Germany about syndicating my doctoral video into a series, they told me it was too American. When I asked what they meant, they said that it had a happy ending that was too sweet! I recalled the many foreign films that I had seen that had no ending at all, leaving the future to the viewer's imagination.

Most people could use more love in their lives, and you will have it once you stop expecting your partner or potential partner to "read the script." And what is the script? It is the expectation that your perfect partner will be as romantic as Hugh Jackman in *Kate and Leopold* or your ex-boyfriend and tell you they love you as much as you want to hear it. They will commit to you without compromise and will know that they should do so, just like your mother always knew when you were dating behind her back. Usually the script is unconsciously written in your mind after absorbing images from books, TV, movies, and people who present the illusion that they have perfect relationships. No wonder so many people have unrealistic expectations of their partners and relationships fail as often as they do on *The Young and the Restless*. Let's detect the plots/myths, so you can see them as clearly as Mark Harmon does on *NCIS*.

Relationships as Seen on TV

So what do we know about relationships "as seen on TV"? Few real observations about love play out in the movies and TV, although there are exceptions. Mostly there are universal themes that produce fascinating, happy, or dramatic endings. After all, that is why you watch them. The goal of a good love story is to draw you into the passion and make you care about the outcome of the love affair. To do this, great love stories send the first mythical message that we will discuss: *You have to battle great adversity or conflict if you want to be together.* But you ask, "Can't you fall in love and just enjoy the ride?" Rarely in the shows and movies that end up on your TV screen. The path to love is usually a rocky road that even Ben and Jerry could not match.

Carrie in *Sex and the City* took six seasons to couple with the love of her life. In the series, *Family Matters*, Steve Urkel pined at length for Laura Winslow. Unfortunately for Urkel, it was not until *The Big Bang Theory* that the nerdy guys became cool. Nora Ephron's love stories ended without too much muss and fuss. Remember her movies, *When Harry Met Sally*, *You've Got Mail*, and *Sleepless in Seattle*? The course of love was not smooth, but no one gets killed or drenched standing in the rain or rejected for too long. In the end, most everyone is happy.

The happy ending is just one of the illusions created for your viewing pleasure. You watch, you feel good, you expect great things from life, and if they don't happen, you can always watch TV for more happy endings! Expectations about love are usually unrealistic because you have viewed everything from sadistic love to perfect love and a lot of flawed love in between. But these plots are as old as time.

Many plots include, in this order:

- *Quest* for love (the call to seek the object of your desire).
  This is the love ya, need ya, gotta have ya phase.
- *Overcoming obstacles* to love through great adversity (famine, war, death).
  It's the phase where King Kong climbs a building to get to his ladylove.
- *People to help you* in your quest (tin men and lions, classmates, teachers, old spouses who are now ghosts but still want you to be happy).
  Think of this as the *Drop Dead Diva* with allies phase.
- *Darkness* in the form of scary monsters or temptations along the way (the other woman, man, bad neighborhoods to drive through, feats of strength to prove). The "*Frankenstein* wanders in search of his bride" phase is at play here.
- There is a *final conflict* to overcome just when you thought the lovers would unite (they are about to marry someone else, the lover loses the phone number, trips on his or her way up the plane runway, gets shot).
  Mel Gibson as the man who knows *What Women Want* "may not succeed after all" phase when Helen Hunt delivers a surprise rejection just before giving in.
- Reaching the *goal* or not, like Steve Urkel with his love, Laura Winslow, in *Family Matters*. Usually the "or not" part occurs in a series that is not in the last season of broadcast. Better to keep the lovers in the *overcoming obstacles* phase to keep you in the viewer's seat. And *Drop Dead Diva* really keeps that coming!

Somewhere, Somehow, Some Way

No story is more recognizable than the quest for love, money, or success. Far away, there is a goal worth more than rubies, and the hero must risk everything to have it. Think about your favorite TV shows and movies. The character of Liam on the popular soap *Bold and the Beautiful* ate his shoe to prove his love after making a serious mistake with his girlfriend. The movie *Somewhere in Time,* aired every Valentine's Day, is considered by many to be the most romantic movie of all time, and most of you know how that ends! In love, the *quest* begins with meeting the soul mate and experiencing *obstacles* and challenges to connecting with them. Some obstacles include the following:

- The object of desire is married to your sister/brother/mother/a vampire/a loser/an architect.
- The other person does not like the hero (potential partner) right from the beginning.
- The object of desire is unattainable in some other way (distance, they are really just a ghost, they are a man pretending to be a woman, they are grounded by their parents, they are too young, too old, not old enough).

The suspense love stories, more than the comedies (or in Shakespeare's day, the tragedies), emphasize the message that love has to be difficult. The final episode of the 2014 season of *Downton Abbey* left the character of Lady Mary caught between two suitors, with neither knowing who had the inside track. Viewers were comparing it to the tension of the 1979–80 *Dallas* series that ended with a question: who shot JR? *Dallas* was so popular that pop culture invaded politics. Jimmy Carter remarked that he could get elected if he knew who shot JR, and a session of the Turkish parliament was suspended to allow legislators a chance to get home in time to view the first *Dallas* episode of the next season. It was the most watched show in the history of TV. Could it have the same effect for *Downton Abbey*? Are viewers desperate to know whom Mary will love? The times have changed. Most of the characters on *Downton Abbey* realistically have post-traumatic stress disorder, following charges of murder, suspected murder, sexual assault, unrequited love, and blackmail. But I know that my friend Linda watched her first episode ever of *Downton Abbey* to find that Tony was ahead in the race at the time!

Quests for love have been a TV theme that the *Seinfeld* show captured with all four of the main characters. Jerry, George, Elaine, and Kramer all dated new people each week and failed to establish any kind of long-term relationship. The new partners lasted a few shows at best. The character of Elaine, played by Julie Louis-Dreyfus, courted love in her relationship with the mechanic, Puddy. Their on-again and off-again relationship was on and off more than once in the course of one airplane flight. Even in her later show, *The New Adventures of Old Christine*, Julia Louis-Dreyfus watches as everyone around her finds a mate while she looks on, has short-term romances, and feels the pain of her loneliness. And yes, it is a comedy! Just like *Veep* in which she tries hard to be the vice president of the United States!

On a more serious note, in the movie *What Dreams May Come* with Robin Williams and Annabella Sciorra, suicide leads Robin and the viewer down a horrendous trail to reconciliation with his wife. You may have heard of people who go through hell to find each other, and that is what literally happens in this movie. *When Harry Met Sally* sends us down the long and winding road to love through mistakes in a much gentler way. Both stories are long remembered, and yet finding love through trial and error (*When Harry Met Sally*) is a much healthier theme to embrace than an unplanned and unpleasant trip to the afterlife (*What Dreams May Come*). Enjoy both of these movies but watch consciously. Harry and Sally's cake with coconut icing on the side won't hurt your viewing diet, but too many hours of visually ingesting horror and pain may. It depends on your appetite and grip on reality. And whether you can tolerate the many changes that occur during the relationships. Often the show is so well done that turning it off is a challenge, despite the images that cause pain.

The pairing of love and longing creates an *association* in your mind. Remember, when you see these two things together, you tend to believe that they are connected and must occur together. You make a decision that the two things are inseparable; love and longing become the new horse and carriage. This association is a type of hypnosis; it is a connection that you don't question. You merely react to the association as a truth. And there is a pattern to it that is sequential, much as the desire, obstacles, assistance, darkness, final conflict, and goal has a sequential pattern. If you have had losses in love, there may be a pattern that you follow that is unconscious too. Yours may be more like attraction, rejection, more desire, feet kissing, more rejection and finding out she's in love with your best friend sequence. But really, it's not your fault because this is a common movie theme, too!

While there is truth to the fact that you may value more the things that you don't have or that you have to work for, it becomes more embedded through themes often presented while you watch characters' frustrations. Remember what happens then? Empathy. And then your brain's mirror neurons cause you to care about what happens to them and keep you watching.

Speaking of Overcoming Great Odds

In the half-hour to one-hour formats available to most TV couples, the great odds occur when a boyfriend goes through bad neighborhoods, has a flat tire, and gets robbed but still makes it to the prom. Even with couples that have understood but unexpressed feelings for each other, situations when they come close to death to defend each other are common. In two shows with similar themes, *Person of Interest* and *The Mentalist,* the lead male actors and actresses had unexpressed feelings for each other but were willing to take a bullet, go to jail, and miss lunch to defend each other. Most of the relationship tension is played out over a long period of time in several or even all episodes. But if the couple gets together, it spells doom for viewership and a short life for the show, so the tension remains. After all, you wouldn't have been happy if *The Nanny* had gotten Mr. Sheffield in the first season, would you? Almost all crime shows have tension between a male and female lead that waxes and wanes so that your attention doesn't.

The movies you see on TV have more time in one fell swoop to develop plots about love. The happy ending is also more likely in the movies. When the George Clooney movie *Up in the Air* ended in uncertainty, Clooney fans complained while I rejoiced. It was refreshing to see a story step out of fantasy into reality. Life is not usually tied up with a bow.

> In *Avatar*, a man changes life forms, from human to alien, after longing to be with his love. While you cannot morph from human to alien or move back and forth in the afterlife, both *What Dreams May Come* and *Avatar* seem to reflect states of awareness that you can all attain. Is one of these movies a healthier choice than the other? It depends on how you are doing in your own relationships and whether you believe that you have any control over the outcome. Both of these movies deliver a message that you can have a positive effect on your relationships if you believe and go for it. Wayne Dyer would be proud.

Are We There Yet?

You may have noticed that you and some of the people in your life have the same types of relationships over and over again, with themes like unfaithful partners, married partners, noncommittal partners, abusive partners, or people with a large age difference. You do the same thing over and over and expect a different result. This is an example of an association that becomes so embedded as a hypnotic trance that you do not

> A typical pattern would be: you see her shiny, dark hair from across the room, to having her head on your shoulder and then finding her hair on your neighbor's shoulder. Once you see the pattern, you may still not know how to change it, but you have begun the process.

even see the fault of it until it is too late. You have another broken heart from following the same sequence from attraction to doom.

Simply taking the pattern out of hiding helps make it fade. The same is true for the myths you may have absorbed from entertainment.

In life, you often believe that the path to love must be as difficult as it is in the movies. One of the most resistant problems many seem to have is relationship addiction, or the inability to leave a dysfunctional union. Reel life plays out in real life:

- A business consultant from Denver, Colorado, involved in a long-distance relationship, struggled to continue visiting her beau in Cleveland even though she knew he was being unfaithful.
- An author with everything going for him could not leave his wife after she had an office romance even though she was no longer interested in him. He admitted that he no longer loved her, either, but could not break his addiction to her.
- A professor in a five-year relationship dated as many other women as he could and still could not break the habit of the old relationship.

It's time for a walk through the wonderful world of TV and movie romance with your eyes wide open. "Are they going to get together?" and "When are they going to get together?" are two favorite questions that make for a trance about romance from TV. "Is you is or is you ain't my baby," is a question asked by classics Sam and Diane (*Cheers*), Mulder and Scully (*X Files*), Ross and Rachel (*Friends*), Carrie and Big (*Sex and the City*), Buffy and Spike (*Buffy the Vampire Slayer*), and Jim and Pam (*The Office*). If you have to ask who they are, you haven't been watching enough TV romance. The payoff for watching is usually as much tension as Buffy and Spike's.

For a nail-biter with a predictable ending, examine the strategy that I see as the chase in the movie of *Sabrina*, the chauffer's daughter who was in love with the rich, young man her father escorted about town. Let's theoretically apply the parts of a great movie to see how Sabrina Fairchild, played by Audrey Hepburn and later by Julia Ormond in the remake, spent her time as a child up in a tree watching the character David Larrabee, rarely putting her feet on the ground. As the chauffeur's daughter, Sabrina, hid from the Larabees, her brown eyes spying on their comings and goings, pining away for David's attention on their lavish Long Island estate (romantic music in the background, shots of Sabrina in the tree shot from above), she has met the *object of her desire*. Sabrina was just a child to David, and a homely one at that. He passed her by, continually making her want him even more (*obstacle* is Sabrina herself and the separation of social class). He was a handsome, fun playboy while his older brother, Linus, was the serious, responsible son who had moved the family business into the global arena. Sabrina could think of nothing but David; the idea of being with him was the center of her world. Her unrequited love was consuming (*pining*, the usual reaction). Then one day, something happened that would change Sabrina's world (*opportunity* to resolve the conflict, will the opportunity work?).

She was sent off to Paris by David's mother to become a lady. She returned, after two years on the staff at *Vogue* magazine, a sophisticated beauty, her girlish pigtails now a crown of beautifully coiffed curls.

However, the change of scenery had not caused a change of heart for David, and Sabrina sets her sights on him.

A triangle developed between Sabrina, David, and his current girlfriend (*darkness* ensues, you wonder if she will find her way out). You fear that David and Sabrina's romance may never

College students who watch soaps become a high-risk group because they have unrealistic expectations. Unwanted pregnancy is often the result. Research at Northern Illinois University shows that college students who watch soap operas view unwed mothers as affluent, well taken care of by family and friend's support, and without a need to work. You can be grateful that best-case scenario movies such as *Juno* make it a bit more real, but I would estimate the maturity and resources of both of the kids in this movie as better than average!

get off the ground. And it won't, if Linus (starts out as *an unhelpful friend,* ends up being a *helpful one*) has anything to say about it. Now there is *resistance* from an outside source that Sabrina must overcome, a common plot in romances leading to the *final conflict* in this one. Linus thinks that David's girlfriend's business contacts would be an asset to the family and sets out to distract Sabrina. With the charm of a computer printer, Linus has to work hard to stop the budding romance between Sabrina and David, and, in the process, Sabrina and Linus fall in love. David is no longer the object of her desire, but all ends well for Linus and Sabrina after many mishaps, misunderstandings, and near misses. Then she realizes that David is superficial and unavailable and that Linus is her true love. Sleeping Beauty wakes up from her trance. There is applause, the curtain comes down, and the audience goes home smiling. *Happy ending.*

Now what happened to you as you read about Sabrina? Did you want her to have the object of her desire? If you were feeling empathy, mirror neurons in the brain were activated, and you were hooked into staying until the end while storing a mental image of the plot in your mind. It explains why you have to see the end of the mini-mop commercial to find out if the desperate housewife recovers from her slip and slide on the kitchen floor. This brings us to another message that you may have absorbed: *love is limited, unavailable, or unrequited.* Were you taken in by Sabrina's longing, and did you long for her desire as well? Is this a theme that you experience in your own life? You and Don Quixote may be trying to reach the same unreachable star.

The women on *Hot in Cleveland, The Golden Girls,* and *Sex and the City* play these illusions out beautifully. Do you forget, while watching, that this is just entertainment? If so, watch with less absorption beginning now! Use RxTV to remind you!

RxTV

√ View while consciously identifying the message of the love story.
√ Decide how you really feel about the success of the love-seeking strategy and sequence in real life.
√ Decide what you would do, instead, if you reject the character's strategy.

As for unrequited love, research tells us that *limited availability* is an actual motivation to seek a desired person or thing. We see it all of the time in advertising. There is a reason we hear the phrase "buy now while supplies last." The shopping channels even use a counter system: only two hundred of these left. The message is that "There is not enough to go around."

Ask yourself if the sales strategy of limited availability makes things more valuable. Or is it magnifying the truth so that it becomes distorted in its importance in an attempt to get you to buy a video, product, or partner? The answer is both. TV mixes the truth about human behavior with the sales pitch, using teasers to buy *now* or go after that guy you want to date *now*. It capitalizes on your feelings of urgency and creates a sense of limited access in a way that makes them inseparable. Urgency makes it easier for you to develop an association that turns into a trance. When you see some of the true characteristics of relationships entwined with the mythical ones, you end up believing the whole package. Documentaries have been accused of using this strategy. Other options such

Many young lovers' first sexual experiences are portrayed as gentle, positive experiences with a loved partner. However, teens influenced by these portrayals decide to go ahead with sex long before they are ready and may discover that such loving, intimate opportunities are less available at their high school. Life is never as tidy as portrayed on *Dawson's Creek*. The show *90210* made teen sex even more common.

as waiting for someone to notice your worth can take too long in the movies, and you may get tired of waiting. The more immediate strategy of talking a potential partner into liking you (especially effective for soap opera characters) is presented as manipulative yet effective and may succeed for many years before it backfires. The idea that you too can manipulate partners into your life if you are sexy, rich, twisted, original, foreign, sneaky, freaky, or famous enough is quite a trance to unravel!

Sex on TV

One of the reasons that people are often dissatisfied with their love and sex lives is that they have highly unrealistic ideas about these two critical life areas. And where do you get them? By now, you know the answer. While you want to watch a great love story or some steamy scenes, it is important to remember the message you are being told: that you want sex, that it is highly valued, extremely important, and that you can't live without it, so go out and get it. *Fifty Shades of Grey* takes the idea to extremes. Biology might dictate that to be true, and we know that sex increases longevity and brain function. Tell that to your partner now. Go ahead. I'll wait.

The intensity of the need, however, is enhanced on TV to make the resolution more satisfying and more interesting, and that makes for great entertainment. This brings you to the next message: *nothing is as it seems.*

But you might not be interested in a less romantic or steamy story, so the ante is upped to create interest and excitement that keeps you coming back or buying the DVD. The actress on the screen usually does not pay taxes, wash dishes, or have screaming children. Instead, her life is an idyllic one without anything to do but seduce her man, and his is about just being a hunky guy without a shirt.

Historically, in the sixties, there were congressional hearings about sex on TV and what should be allowed. Any show with two people sleeping together was prohibited. If you grew up then, you may have a few hang-ups about your sex life. Obviously, real people slept together, but TV said it was unacceptable. Then Elizabeth Montgomery as Samantha on *Bewitched* broke new ground when she slept with her husband, Darren, played by Dick York. It now seems foreboding that the new groundbreaking character is another Samantha who would later appear in *Sex and the City,* with scenes bolder than ever before. In the eighties, *Charlie's Angels* brought the female form to the screen as three beautiful detectives solved crimes in scanty outfits that perfectly showed off their forms. With nighttime soaps like *Dynasty* and *Dallas,* there were few holds barred; you knew which characters were having sex and which weren't. In 1993, *NYPD Blue* was the first to show actual sex scenes. The American Family Association unsuccessfully protested, and the show continued to air. Lucky for you. If they had won, you would never have seen HBO's *Hung* about a well-endowed teacher moonlighting as a prostitute.

Cable TV brought all types of sexual behavior into the light with shows such as *Real Sex*, which showed every imaginable type of sexual behavior or aberration, from sex in taxi cabs to group masturbation, prostitution, and much more. Jerry Springer, Maury Povich, and Geraldo Rivera brought real-life couples together to talk about their sex lives. Shows like the plastic surgery show *Nip Tuck* dealt with sibling sex. Girl-on-girl kisses such as the ones with Brittany Spears and Madonna led to on-air guy kisses. In 1997, Ellen came out as a lesbian on her show, and cable began a male gay themed show called *Queer as Folk*. The door to sex on TV was opened wider when a show entitled *Gossip Girl* aired. The show suggested three-way sex as a rite of passage for a man.

Most recently, MTV's show *16 and Pregnant* shows the realities of teen pregnancies without sugarcoating and gives teens a good message about avoiding a similar predicament. Pregnancy rates, which rose in 2005–2007, dropped in 2009 after the show started. The fact that these two things occur together does not mean that the show caused the drop, but the fact that the show enhanced the message by holding a National Day to Prevent Teen Pregnancy might. Remember? When there is an opportunity to enhance learning from TV with follow-up activities, learning increases.

Today, phone sexting messages would make *NYPD Blue's* steamy images seem tame. Sexiness is just more permissible in general. Even *Dancing with the Stars* is not a show about sex, yet the dresses get skimpier, and the moves and gyrations get more graphic. And sex on the Internet has become overly available.

Love Cures

If you hold yourself to the high sexual performance standards of TV lovers, then you may feel like a failure. At these times, you are in a vulnerable state as your mind is looking for ways out. You may find yourself in the following sequence or pattern. You see a car commercial that associates a new car with lots of dates, and you buy the car thinking of the same result. You are disappointed when the result does not occur. You judge yourself as a failure without even realizing what happened. You try the next diet product because the woman who lost fifty-three pounds told you how much her boyfriend likes her weight loss. If the diet or the weight loss fails to produce the same result, you again feel like a failure. You resort to staying home and watching TV, and the whole cycle of buying, failing, buying, failing, starts all over. You are behaving unconsciously. This may or may not be surprising to you at this point. Yet you still need to interrupt the pattern. Otherwise, you may find yourself weighing four hundred pounds, driving a used car that was flooded during Katrina, and living on Slimnow.

The myth is that sex is as wild, tantalizing, and brilliantly executed as what you see on the screen and that it is connected to everything in your life. It makes you want more and better sex, just by seeing what is possible. The myth of more and better will be addressed in advertising, but ask yourself if you really need more and better in your personal life. You may or may not, but decide without the trance. The sex in the series *Girls* in 2014 breaks illusions with some pretty atypical sex scenes with unusual outcomes. Viewer reactions are widely varied.

Are you ready to watch TV in a way that will allow you to awaken from your ideas about love? Ask yourself the following questions:

Get Reel: Real-Time Relationships Quiz
- What are some of the great love stories of all time?
- Which are your personal favorites?
- What messages are in those great stories, the ones that you could watch over and over in TV reruns?
- Are they messages that are a part of your belief system?
- Think of a past relationship. What was the belief about love that attracted you to that person and about why it failed? (Example: partners all lie, partners only want sex/I have to date a lawyer.)
- Do any of the movies or TV shows that you have seen carry the same message?
- Is that message universally true, or is it just a belief? (Example: don't date someone on the rebound as it is likely to be unsuccessful.)
- What might or might not be true about love that you believe, that was reinforced by movies and TV?
- What is the sequence or pattern of your relationships?

RxTV:

Now check out the answers to these questions. Are there some romantic illusions in there that may seem like truths? List them and look at each one individually. Are they really true? Are they always true? And do they apply to your own life? Then ask yourself if there is a better trance or belief in which you are more successful at relationships. For example, would you rather believe and understand that

√ you are fine with or without a partner;
√ there is someone right for you; partners are supportive and/or partners are considerate.
√ Then consider the following:
√ If you find yourself involved in a series of mishaps with partners, locate the patterns that they all have. What is it that fatally attracts you every time? The bad girl? The blond? The muscle man? Maybe you even have more than one specific type that gets you in trouble.
√ If you see a pattern, pick one and write about it in a personal ad. For example, "Seeking noncommittal girl who has had at least five boyfriends in the past month. Must be blond and lack medical insurance." Or "Wanted: guy with a great smile, good kisser, who kisses and tells then never calls. Over 5'10" preferred."
√ List at least three different relationship patterns that you would prefer. Choose at least one

> V Polar opposites make for a fascinating yet bumpy ride during viewing, but in real life they are nothing more than codependent, painful, and damaging experiences. Alice, an alcoholic that I knew through her daughter, was always saying that she was going to leave her unfaithful, alcoholic husband. She would leave for a day or two when she found some evidence to suggest that he was having an affair, but when he told her that he loved her, she would return. She was on a continual seesaw of bliss and pain.
>
> Such a ride is addictive because you never know when the loving behavior will come to you, but you know it will come. When relationships are unpredictable and you don't have enough self-esteem to leave and find more in a mate, you stay in a way that becomes an addiction more than true love. You need affection to validate you, and so you stay, because affection could be right around the corner. This is a pattern that needs to be interrupted.

from a movie or TV. Write a new personal ad. For example, "Wanted, girl with a great attitude about life who wants a guy she can be crazy about forever." Think *Mad About You* with Helen Hunt and Paul Reiser. Or "Seeking guy who is willing to wait for the right girl and knows her when he sees her." Think *Serendipity* with Kate Beckinsale and John Cusack. Once you focus on a goal, you will be more likely to succeed!

See what I mean? There are powerful, life-enhancing beliefs that will bring you more clarity and are more constructive. Then, get ready for a real-life presto-chango. Remember the trance that you identified in the quiz? Can you overcome it with one of the successful strategies mentioned above about finding and keeping love in your life? Maybe there is yet another strategy that truly fits for you. Stay tuned for a transformation. And stay tuned to your TV set as well! (Suspense is building, the commercials seem too long, you want to get back to the story, you already checked your text messages, and it's time for the exciting conclusion.)

Would Have, Could Have, Should Have

Get ready for the message that: *there is always a love that got away.* On *Two and a Half Men,* Alan, played by Jon Cryer, has trouble moving on after his wife leaves him. She was the "one and only." Then there are the characters from *Will and Grace.* Grace loses Will, Will loses his policeman love, and then Grace loses her physician husband, played by Harry Connick, Jr. It all takes several years to play out, until Will and Grace's kids meet at college. The instant chemistry they feel is expressed in the conversations they have that rival Will and Grace's. You believe that Will and Grace are likely to become in-laws, even though they were never able to be a couple on their own.

If you were a fan of the characters of Eric and Donna on *That '70s Show,* you were not too happy when Eric went off to Africa after a long romance. There are so many characters that got away, that perhaps this myth is a real one for many of you. But making the excuse that you can't find love because the one and only left you is just that, an excuse and a red flag when dating. The truth is more likely that you haven't healed from the loss or you want to be able to say that you loved and lost, so that no one thinks you aren't eligible. But in reality, the idea that you can't be happy because one person got away is usually a myth.

Have you ever seen the *Big Chill*? I think this is where the myth gets busted. A group of old college friends reconvene for a mutual friend's funeral with the opportunity to pursue their youthful dreams. But once JoBeth Williams finally consummates her thwarted college love, she returns to her real life, and I believe she realizes that what might have been should not have been. Many other *Big Chill* plot twists convey the same thing, with Mick Jagger's sentiment that you can't necessarily get what you want providing the backdrop for some powerful lessons.

Sometimes, the love that got away died. This is especially true on the soaps when an actor gets a movie part and needs to either be working overseas or temporarily dead in order to get the time off. Some of my favorite characters have been dead more than once.

It seems that Liam Neeson awakes from his trance that he will never find another love in another powerful movie aptly titled *Love Actually*. As if Emma Thompson, Hugh Grant, Liam Neeson, and Claudia Schiffer weren't enough, the movie contains so much information about the many kinds of love. It moves from couples to parents, kids and business associates who cross class, race and age differences, that you are entertained beyond measure. The all-star cast and acting are so superb that your attention is held in such a way that a powerful, positive wake-up call about love can be achieved.

I see some new, more powerful beliefs awaken in *Love Actually*, including, "Love may be right in front of you, but you could miss it by pursuing an old illusion," "It's okay for members of different classes to fall in love," and the ever reality-based one that "You might love someone that you don't completely trust." This last group of trances more closely resembles real-life experiences and keeps you in the loop of reality. And in recognizing that, you become a conscious viewer. You might even find yourself dumping your noncommittal partner for the girl who drives a used police car and works as a fortune cookie writer.

Raising Your Consciousness

We've talked about association as the key to drawing the audience into the story and keeping them there. Association is one of the most powerful ways to advertise. A very well-done and effective car commercial that aired a few years ago showed a couple in a high-end car singing a Rod Stewart song, conveying that the couple wishes they knew what they know now, when they were younger, associating wisdom and experience with the choice to buy an expensive vehicle. Advertising is its own theme and has its own chapter! Coming soon!

Love/hate, abuse/making up and trust/betrayal are strong plot associations in many films. Imagine scene six; take two of *Gone With The Wind*. Scarlett (Vivien Leigh) turns to Rhett (Clark Gable) and gives him a look intended to melt his heart so that he forgives her for her unending cruelty to him. Rhett turns away, unaffected by her attempts to change his mind about abandoning her. Oh, the angst! The pain! Sound familiar? Ross and Rachel on *Friends* experience trust, mistrust, trust, and mistrust indefinitely in order to keep them apart. Or consider Kim Basinger's character's naive experiment with the sexy, manipulative Mickey Rourke in *9½ Weeks*. Dreams turn to nightmares with Mickey's character pushing the envelope of sexual trust to a dangerous and destructive place where Kim's character ultimately knows how things will go and that her affair will end, but how?

The thought of Kim Basinger and Mickey Rourke brings up another common plot that is very real. That is the storyline of the person with the *fatal flaw*. Mickey was one of those. And so are the new vampire hotties! When interviewed for the NBC website, I was asked why the new rage over vampire lovers. I agreed with Bart Simpson who thinks it's really cool to be the new outsider while knowing there is no real danger of getting bitten.

The vampire can never be perfect, and neither can anyone else, so there is a clear identification with the new heroes. Shows and movies such as *Buffy the Vampire Slayer, True Blood, Vampire Diaries,* and *Twilight* show a new kind of fictional hero. Young people may be noticing that the characters can be perfect vampires, suggesting the idea that the real-life nerd can be really good at being a tech/sports/science/alien nerd. It is freeing for teens and young adults and very attractive to them. Hence the movie sales and promotions! However, there is some caution in too many empathetic mirror neurons storing vampire images. It could keep viewers wanting more of what they already have.

When examining the sexuality of the vampire, the message is more mixed. They preach abstinence but act in highly sexualized, vampirized, and sensual ways. Mixed messages cause confusion, which causes continued viewing to see how or if the confusion gets resolved. Brilliant. Healthy? Not really. Interesting? Only if you have ever had a successful relationship with a fatally flawed person, like my friend's aunt Sue who married a deaf crocodile wrangler.

What You Have Is Not Good Enough

If you have any doubts about your self-worth (and what normal non-vampirized person doesn't), you are at risk for the illusion that what you have is not valuable. This causes you to undervalue your partner. After all, who would want to be a member of any club that would have you as a member? The illusion that *you have to be perfect to have love* goes along with this myth. The combination of illusions that

- *you have to be perfect;* and that
- *what you have or are is never good enough* is a recipe for a failed relationship.

If you saw this men's deodorant commercial, it capitalizes on the usual commercial pattern comparing your life partner to the one on the screen. It creates the illusion that you would prefer the partner on the screen, moving you toward a product purchase. The very handsome Isaiah Mustafa asks you to look at him, then look at your mate a couple of times, and decide that you would rather have the handsome man and the deodorant. He then gives a verbal command to look down to see his chest and ends with the statement, "I'm on a horse," so that you take notice. Telling you to look down is usually done by moving the camera down the screen, and the horse is usually just a visual suggestion that the virile-looking guy on the screen rides horses. In the deodorant commercial, it is done in a very obvious way, pointing

> out the sales strategy and making you see it while taking you into it. Very interesting! By the time you are done, you are so impressed with the cleverness of the ad that you may feel dissatisfied with your guy for simply not being as clever!

As long as an ad leaves you feeling that you should have something that you don't have, it has accomplished its goal. If you recognize the intended message, you are still conscious and have been entertained as well. In this case, it aims to make you dissatisfied enough with your current guy to buy him a different brand of deodorant. Perhaps advertisers know that women make the majority of these purchases! This is an example of how commercials encourage you to want something more ideal, and if you deserve something better, great. TV has been a wake-up call, as it often is! If not, then watch consciously and don't fall into a purchase or a break-up.

Then there is the trance that: *love is easy, romantic, always fresh, and never tiring.* Everyone is always happy, men are always bringing just the perfect gifts, and there are serenades at the window and evenings in private dining rooms. Women are always beautiful, perfectly made-up, and dressed in sexy lingerie or tightly fitted suits. This is one of the most dangerous illusions because you may feel that a romance that is not this way is not working. These characters look glamorous and desirable, but, again, they are an illusion not a reality. They can feed into the belief that in comparison, what you have is not enough. These programs follow the same pattern of the undying-love-themed shows where the lovers are inseparable. Both are illusions, and if you buy into them, they are also trances. The beautiful people have their hearts broken on a regular basis, as you can see from the covers of *People, US Weekly,* and *Entertainment* magazines. A better middle ground for a real relationship would be Billy Joel's sentiment of "I love you just the way you are."

Fairy Tales at Work

We will end with the message with which we started: *there is always a happy ending*. Ross and Rachel do get together on *Friends* after many seasons of tension. *Sex and the City's* Carrie and Big take several TV seasons and a movie to make it work together. When Matt McConaughey and Kate Hudson as ex-spouses went after buried treasure together in *Fool's Gold*, you kept wondering if their joint purpose would reunite them. Even though the seasoned viewer knows the characters will be likely to unite, a good TV show or movie creates enough tension to cause you to wait until the end. Remember to enjoy the tension, knowing they will reunite, even if they don't until the very last breathtaking minute. But don't imagine this is true in real life. You can wait for someone forever, but if it is over, it is over. In real life, if you decide to end a relationship, be clear and mean it. If the other person ends it, take his or her word for it. If you still feel unfinished, have a conversation and resolve whether there is still more to be played out. But whatever you do, do not sit and wait. This does not create a happy ending and may result in being late for your life.

Let Me Take You Higher

In real life, research shows that

- men need to know that they are getting it right in relationships;
- women need to know that men want them to be happy; and
- women in real time seem more open to receive many types of fulfillment from a man who wants them to be happy while men seem to require more validation that they are succeeding at such a goal.

The best example of TV and real life coming together that I have noticed on this reality of romance is in the comedy *Everybody Loves Raymond*. It addresses what we know about real relationships in a funny way. Ray tries to make Deborah happy (or doesn't, depending on his mood), and she lets him know when he has failed. The meddling mother-in-law, who sides with Ray, makes Deborah's struggle to relate to Ray more complicated. A good show about romance is even better when there is some tension from outside of the relationship. You will see plots that show men trying to make their wives happy with varying results in reruns of *Rosanne, King of Queens, Yes, Dear, According to Jim, The Neighbors* and now, especially, *The Good Wife.* They are a funny/poignant look at some real/fictional life situations.

Hmmmmm, let's see, when was the last time you observed these characteristics in Charlie Sheen's character when he was on *Two and a Half Men?* When was the last time he courted a woman by focusing on *her* needs rather than his own? Do you think Charlie's goal is to make women happy or to punish them because his own mother was a narcissist? The show let you in on the dysfunction and kept you laughing all the way. However, Charlie courted beautiful women all the time and later threw them away. You see a guy who would make a pretty poor partner in a relationship dump women he did not even deserve in the first place. It's only later when he is really trying to get it right that you get a chance to laugh at his clumsy yet unsuccessful attempts to change.

It's Not All Your TV's Fault

Other hypnotic trances about love come from your personal experiences, the examples of your parents, other significant family members, teachers, and by the media. If you were one of the kids who told your mother that you were going to be an artist and run away to Carmel, and you had practical parents, they routed you into getting an MBA and marrying an accountant. In this case, someone told you who you

Remember the discussion in chapter 1, the way that relevance makes a message take hold more easily? If a guy without a job, a house, or any prospects has ever left you, then you know what I mean. The message of a similar show reinforces what you already believed about yourself based on your life experience. Of course, since every situation in life revolves around an episode of *Seinfeld*, let me mention that reversing his belief about dating *did* actually work for Jason Alexander's George Costanza for a while!

were and influenced your perceptions. Have you ever sat back and asked yourself if you "bought" the trance and wondered what the nagging feeling was in your mind that something was missing? On *Desperate Housewives*, Felicity Huffman admitted that although she is again a new mother, that what she really wanted was a career, and she goes for it, risking and losing everything. The movie *The Notebook* also comes to mind, as you watch Joan Allen tell her daughter, Rachel McAdams, that she, too, had a lover in a lower social class that she never forgot. The positive message in these shows is to never let anyone tell you who you are when you already know, even if there is a price to pay. Rebel Wilson's struggle in *Super Fun Night* to sort it out is more than entertaining!

Moment of Truth

Did you watch Gabriel Byrne as a dysfunctional therapist and his varied clients in the HBO series *In Treatment* to look at the real problems of real people? This is fiction, and as a therapist, I can tell you that most therapists are not as confused as this one, and most patients do not act the way that his do. If they did, therapists would need more vacations. Members of the American Psychological Association Media Division even review movies to see if they can come up with any that portray therapists accurately! But if you watch Joan Allen with Kevin Costner in *The Upside of Anger*, you are likely to come closer to the truth. Never was there a more powerful movie, I believe, made that exemplifies anger and trance, and the power of our beliefs and negative emotions to drive relationships toward destruction. I won't say any more about this because I don't want to ruin the film by telling you how it ends. I would suggest that you rent it, find the two and a half hours to watch (the time goes by very quickly), and experience a message about real life in real time. The messages about the real roots and effects of anger and trance on love are explored and played out as they often are in reality. So if you are beginning to make conscious choices, this one is one to choose.

My friend Sophie formed the soap opera habit and identified with the nice girl resembling her own physical appearance, the one who always got hurt and found herself in painful relationships. It was not until she became a conscious viewer that she watched from a distance, became proactive, and attracted a man that was more in line with her interest in working with glue guns.

Q **SpyTV**

Detect the *pattern* in your love life. It can be a success pattern, a failure pattern, or something in between. Then use *choice.* It's time to *reject or accept it.* If you find yourself with great partners, decide they're not perfect, and then get picky and cause small disagreements, you will have to change the pattern at the point of deciding they are not perfect. Since it is at the root of pickiness, it is the point of doom for relationships. What if you *rejected* that pattern and then *released* it for *a pattern of finding the right partner,* deciding that they are good enough and being more *accepting.* This could result in a happy ending with ups and downs. That's an ending that even Mr. Sheffield and *The Nanny* understood!

"But how can I enjoy my life *or* the show when it's just been dissected for me?" you might ask. The magic is gone, and the trance is broken. Sleeping Beauty has awakened, and Prince Charming, as Broadway producer Stephen Sondheim would tell us in *Into the Woods,* is less than charming. As a matter of fact, he indicates that he was groomed to be charming, not faithful! While some say that he takes a pessimistic view of human nature, he certainly makes you laugh until you cry. And the tears may be the grief over a lost illusion. *Pattern interruption is the trance breaker for this chapter,* so take this opportunity to do the SpyTV exercise and break a pattern.

Begin to sort and sift so that you can get back to enjoying your favorite show and your life consciously. What does it mean to enjoy consciously? It means to look at the illusions *and* the truths and notice how creatively your favorite producer has woven them together on the subject of love. Enjoy it immensely. Then remove the illusions from the realities.

RxTV:

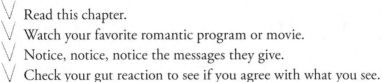

√ Read this chapter.

√ Watch your favorite romantic program or movie.

√ Notice, notice, notice the messages they give.

√ Check your gut reaction to see if you agree with what you see.

√ Choose what you want to experience about love and sex.

√ *Interrupt your pattern* of relationships if needed.

√ Watch TV again, enjoy, and absorb consciously the messages you will choose to accept or reject!

Recognizing some of the true characteristics of relationships in the mythical ones is a process of sifting that brings us to the C related to this chapter:

C—Consider whether the messages are constructive, destructive, merely entertaining, or good messages for you and for your relationships. If you have a pattern of relationship problems, interrupt the pattern. Shake it up at the core when it first begins and go down another path.

For more up-to-date information on *Get Reel* for this chapter, go to:

http://drnancyonline.com/category/rc-relationships/

http://drnancyonline.com/category/current-news/

CHAPTER 4

ALL IN THE FAMILY

What's Your Family Got to Do with It?

New shows are pitched each season, and the TV guide features more reality show reviews than ever, many based on families. You may be consciously starting to notice just how much of your TV viewing is reality based. In the process, you will see how both reality and non-reality TV have shaped the TV family and your own family.

If reality is one of your favorite genres, rest assured it is here to stay. One of the most important things portrayed in both scripted TV and reality TV is the family. Examining the treatment of the family on TV, one can see that portrayals have gone from an unrealistically perfect format to an unrealistically *im*perfect one. Beginning with shows such as *Ozzie and Harriett, Father Knows Best,* and *The Donna Reed Show,* you were shown that the family was one in which everyone got along, mostly, and that they all looked good all day and solved simple problems with simple solutions. Variations such as *The Andy Griffith Show,* which portrayed an unconventional family structure, and *Leave it To Beaver* were mild compared to the reality of the family post-new-millennium. Andy Griffith's unconventional family without a mother has been left behind for shows with two same-sex parents. The problem child called Beaver who got into problems with his homework has evolved into the teen in the center of a drug intervention.

Enter Bart

The Simpsons, the first Fox series to land in the Top Thirty program ratings in 1989, opened the door to the kids of *Family Guy* (1998) and *Two and a Half Men* (2003). Bart Simpson uttered words that challenged his parents and changed the TV family. *Two and a Half Men* featured the wisecracking child character, Jake, as the nephew of womanizer Charlie Sheen. You watched in wonder to see which one of them would be more inappropriate. Later, there was less of a contest. Charlie started cleaning up his act, and Jake, well, the actor left the show due to moral dilemmas over the sexualized scripts. Use it as a conscious viewing experience. Angus T. Jones, who played Jake, had an early life crisis when he became a Christian and questioned acting in or watching a show with such a highly sexualized content. Try not to judge. Just observe and get curious!

The Simpsons, Two and a Half Men, and *Family Guy* show an illogical mix of opposites that don't match your expectations, take you off-guard, and make you laugh. Being taken off-guard is one of the ways to make you laugh. Does it also desensitize you to rude, unacceptable behavior? When you see something over and over, don't you become less charged with emotional response? Does it get worse when the family is a reality TV family? Or are you just enjoying a view on how the other half lives, walking away with your values intact?

Shows like *Two and a Half Men* and *Family Guy* use mismatch humor because the events of their characters would be unlikely to happen, so it's funny. For example, *The Family Guy* theme song pleads its case with lyrics like, "Where are the good, old family values on which we used to rely?" just before using sex and violence in animation to make you laugh or turn it off, whichever you choose. Part of the mismatch

If you watched Will Smith in *Fresh Prince of Bel Air* when the sitcom opened in 1990, you saw Will as a street-smart teen who often clashed with his wealthy relatives. Will was sent to live with them when he got into trouble at home. Then he got in trouble trying to be himself in the new environment. The positive message showed that his behavior, while funny, has consequences; his family lays down the law every time.

is that the kids, and even a dog, get away with strange, age-inappropriate, or rude behavior. As long as you see the mismatch, fine, but many children really can't tell the difference, so careful screening is necessary. Avoid adult cartoon viewing for kids.

Is there anything funnier than the family discipline of Bill Cosby in *The Cosby Show?* Beginning in 1984, for eight seasons, you were treated to Bill Cosby as Dr. Huxtable, a funny man with a typical yet challenging family whom he disciplined, loved, and supported. It is a classic that aired in reruns. It came along just in time to give America a model that would both precede and accompany other family sitcoms to your screen. Bill *was* considering coming back! Yet negative exposure about his personal life resulted in a change of plans but not in the quality of the original *Cosby* show.

Both *Fresh Prince* and *The Cosby Show* had strong female figures who had equal say about managing the children. Contrast that to *Two and a Half Men*, where the comic structure is enhanced by the masculine style of child mismanagement. *Family Guy* is another story. There is not one stereotype that is left unturned. Peter Griffin, the family's father, fantasizes continually, and his wife, Lois, brings him back to reality with the latest family crisis or a seduction scene. Either way, there is not a role model to be seen. Parental advisory suggested.

In 2010, *The Middle* arrived, considered by some critics to be the best new comedy of the year. It seems that in *The Middle* you learn different lessons about family life that could be useful! No one looks great in the morning or knows what to do when their son, Axl, gets a broken heart or their daughter, Sue, is a nerdy wrestling cheerleader. By simply doing their best, Frankie Heck, played by Patricia Heaton, and her husband, Mike, played by Neil Flynn, come out okay in the end. And that is a real message, prime time or otherwise. If these models of the family didn't resonate with you, you could see almost any kind of family that interests you. For example, some ideas about what they may represent include:

- The *Girls Next Door*, Hugh Hefner's show, took you into the world of sex and exhibitionism.
- The *Kardashians* showed what you can do with money.

- What about the *Osbournes*? Decide for yourself if there is a specific projection from this show to you or if you are just watching the family. Use it as an exercise in conscious viewing.

But the family model's morph from perfect to rude to "real" has a meaning, and you should view consciously. Does being told what a family is or does on TV reflect or influence the way that real-life families shift, or does the real-life family influence TV? The answer is a bit of both.

Back to Your Reality

First, let's examine the real-life influences on your behavior and then how TV and real life came together. The sequence goes something like this:

1. Parenting changed after the sixties when baby boomer parents, who make up 28 percent of the total US population, questioned their parents' style of strict, regulated child raising. If you are now a baby boomer parent, as you reflect on your own upbringing, you may feel that you would have liked more freedom and greater latitude during your childhood. Issues of low self-esteem resulting from the typical high-control parents who failed to give high levels of support or praise may loom in your memory.

2. If you are a child of a baby boomer parent, your levels of support to your children became higher while you relaxed the structure and control of your parents' generation. Your desire for more recognition in your own life and the knowledge of how a lack of praise and support made you feel caused a revolution in parenting styles.

3. You may have struggled with forgiving your own parents for mistakes they made. Since most parents are amateurs without degrees in child development, they really did not know any other way to parent. Many of their parents were immigrants who had to concern their lives with survival, not whether their child had enough friends. The effects on your psyche have been deep yet unintentional.

The idea that too-strict rules squashed a child's creativity and self-expression was part of the new parenting trend. When there are few rules or children make the rules, the boundary between who is the parent and who is the child is blurred or

> Many boomers have remarked to me that when they were children, if they got into trouble at school, they would get into trouble again at home. They proceeded to contrast today's values toward discipline by noting that many of today's parents approach the teacher to discipline him or her for picking on their child.

obliterated. The new child is expected to behave as an adult who knows what is best for him or her as well as for the parents. If you want to stop now for popcorn, go ahead. We are about to enter into a new generation. The plot is set, the path is determined, and all that awaits is the outcome.

The result of this combination of factors may have had mixed consequences. In *Growing Up Again: Parenting Ourselves, Parenting Our Children*, authors Dawson and Clark state that without both high support *and* high control, you cannot fully develop responsibility and self-esteem—both traits that make a successful adult. Without the support and control of bedtimes, curfews, and rules along with praise and positive reinforcement, a child may not develop fully. Think about *your* childhood. If you or your parents were in the boomer generation, what did you notice about their parenting, and how did it affect you? If you find yourself growing up again, catch reruns of 2014's *Growing Up Fisher*, a comedy featuring a child raised by a blind father.

> In my therapy practice, I see men and women who have been raised by too-permissive baby boomer parents. Their crisis often is not being able to move ahead at work. They may have a disproportionate sense of entitlement. All of the high self-esteem and lack of discipline have created go-getters who expect to get what they go for. Sadly, they don't understand that the current economic condition might make them simply happy to *have* a job. There is a mismatch between what they were taught to go for and what is available. Should they or can they settle for less? The conflict between what they have accepted as a real goal and the reality of the job market creates a conflict. Whether or not they settle is not the main challenge. It is to mature and change from being an entitled young person into a responsible adult. Those who cannot adjust end up in my office.

The time was ripe for Bart and Jake. By 1989, their behavior did not even seem out of place. Don't blame your television because the times have changed. When cable TV arrived in the eighties, if you were a confused, young adult, you were already unsure of your identity. At that time, cable TV and TV hypnosis stepped into a ready market. Bart showed children an example of defiance that felt like fun; children eagerly embraced it. As parents, you were challenged to respond. You know that the Simpsons are just having fun, now, but what about then? Matt Groening's wit is perfect for adults who view with children and explain the real boundaries of behavior. It will make for more fun, as you will have children who know the rules for behavior.

The issues surrounding the changing child are complex. If you were a typical parent, not only did you want your children to have higher self-esteem than your generation but you did not want them to have financial concerns the way that your parents did. Typical of post-Great Depression parents, you considered shifting your children's focus away from basic survival needs and toward self-fulfillment, spawning the Me Generation. Children have come to feel that they are entitled not only to a hot meal but to a lifetime of self-actualization or at least to having what they want.

So how do you address the roles of children with the interface between real life and TV life? What is known about TV and children that could help you answer this question? Imagine that Matt Lauer is interviewing me about this subject on the NBC *Today Show*. Since you will begin to imagine your own reality by the end of the chapter, this will be good practice for using your imagination.

Matt: Dr. Nancy, you have done research on TV. What do you think? Is TV watching for kids *that* bad? (*leaning forward*)

In the late seventies, I began working with children. By the eighties, many media outlets as well as numerous organizations asked me to give advice to parents on how to deal with the changing times. I recall teaching a workshop where a child interrupted me to make a remark. I responded to his remark and continued with my workshop. He shouted out, "You did not answer my question." I responded, "You did not ask a question!" He sat back and did not say anything for the rest of the session, but I knew that times had changed.

Dr. Nancy: (*matching his forward lean*) TV watching should be done with caution. If programs are age-appropriate and send children messages that you want your children to have, then watching can be entertaining as well as instructional.

Children learn more when an adult watches *with* them and talks with them about the program. For example, what did they see? What message is it sending? Is there something instructional that you need to be sure they understand? Be sure to talk about any messages you don't agree with, such as commercials or shows that associate being "cool" with name-brand jeans or tennis shoes.

Also discuss the consequences of characters' actions. Children are likely to repeat behaviors that have positive consequences. For example, if they see someone break into a building to get something to help someone, they may see the action as positive. Talk about what's right or wrong about such actions.

Matt: So what's the down side? (*serious look verging on a frown*)

Dr. Nancy: (*remaining unbiased*)

- Commercials are one big thing to consider. They pitch junk food, sugary cereal, and expensive toys during children's viewing time.
- Violence—kids can sometimes release their own aggressive instincts by watching TV aggression but are also more likely to act aggressively immediately after viewing if an opportunity arises. This could be an issue if they watch with siblings because there is someone there for them to direct aggression toward.
- Obesity is a national epidemic. Although TV watching does not *cause* obesity while viewing, children are inactive and miss out on physical activity.
- TV can contribute, along with video games and movies, to children getting used to fast-paced viewing. As a result, they may not develop sustained attention span and concentration.
- Modeling—kids become like the characters they watch. Children may repeat the exact behavior of a character or just a secondary characteristic such as clothing, language or makeup. This is both positive and negative because children become socialized through TV. So it is a part of how they develop their identities.

Matt: Any positives? (*checking to see if I am consistent*)

Dr. Nancy: (*remaining unruffled*) Again, modeling. Choose to expose them to good models.

- TV is a good way to unwind, but children need to learn to watch *consciously* so that they don't experience "TV hypnosis," an inactive state where they just take in what they see without analyzing it. Parents can help them learn how to pay attention to what they see, even when they are watching to relax.
- Stress management—children have demanding schedules and need some down time. The rules for making the time productive apply to my previous comment on unwinding.
- TV is one of the most powerful instructional tools available, and so it is a double-edged sword. *Sesame Street* and *Mr. Roger's Neighborhood* were two of the most powerful positive influences in children's TV, and *Sesame Street* was translated into seventy languages! *Yo Gabba Gabba* and *Daniel Tiger* are today's equivalent and are socially conscious, too!

Matt: Can you break down by age group acceptable (if any) amounts of TV watching time? (*appears interested in the answer*)

Dr. Nancy: (*pleased that he wants to know*) It really depends on the child and on the show. If it is *Sesame Street*, watching a couple of shows with your child back-to-back is much like attending a morning at preschool. The American Academy of Pediatrics provides some guidelines for average viewing. You may or may not find them realistic. (*move to on-screen graphics*)

Child's Age	# of Hours of TV Watching/Day
0–2	None
2–4	1–2 hours a day
4–6	2
7+	Still 2!

Matt: (*clinching the interview*) Can violence—and I'm not talking *Pulp Fiction* but just *Sponge Bob Square Pants*—have a negative effect on kids?

Dr. Nancy Mramor: (*staying positive*) Again, kids can sometimes release their own aggressive instincts by watching aggression on TV, which is not a negative thing, but are also more likely to act aggressively immediately after viewing if an opportunity arises. This could be an issue if Susie is viewing with her brother Harry, who just stole her favorite Sponge Bob figure, because there is someone there for her to direct aggression toward. For preschoolers, signs of solving problems using aggression are inappropriate. There are better ways to catch Tweety Bird than using your teeth.

Matt: (*doing his job*) Are there any shows that are aimed at kids that you feel should be avoided?

Dr. Nancy: (*trying not to offend anyone or be contacted by any networks*) The following should be avoided but may be acceptable in some cases *if* they are viewed with a parent who can moderate what is on the screen. (*more screen graphics*)

- Actually, anything violent, including video games and movies as well as TV.
- Anything that promotes any kind of negative stereotype.
- Too much scary stuff or science fiction. *Star Wars* and *Avatar* have powerful, positive messages, but too many horror movies do not and cause trauma and nightmares. Kids also need to learn how to distinguish fantasy from reality at a certain point.

Matt: Do you have any shows you recommend for kids and, if so, why those shows?

Dr. Nancy: (*answering cautiously*)
- I have mentioned *Sesame Street* and almost anything in the "children's block" on PBS. The Disney Channel and cartoon channels have some mixed messages but are worth viewing with a parent.

- Watch out for MTV and VH1—lots of highly sexual scenes and lyrics!
- Great if they watch Discovery and Learning Channels, but documentaries have to be viewed critically. Often even the History Channel may have two documentaries with opposing views.
- Comedies that show kids what is and is not really funny!

Matt: (*looks worried*) *I actually do try to avoid turning on the TV but some days rely on it. Is that okay for my son?*

Dr. Nancy: (*concerned for Matt*) Depends on what he is watching. I would observe to see if he acts differently after specific programs or after *all* programs. He may be a child who is getting too much stimulation from the screen or just from one show.

Matt: (*moving toward closing the interview, noticing the stars of the new reality show* Cheer Factor *are waiting in the wings armed with batons and pompoms*) What are your feelings about DVD players in cars and turning them on for short trips?

Dr. Nancy: (*not noticing the cheerleaders*) No problem as long as you apply my earlier rules. Kids should not watch movies in the car that they would not be allowed to watch at home. But don't forget to play interactive games, like "I see something blue" or to sing "Row, row, row your boat" in family rounds. These types of activities develop skills and social behaviors that TV viewing or overuse of the Internet does not.

Matt: (*wanting to move along, seems tense*) There are a number of books and experts who say that TV is ruining our children. TV can't be *that* bad, or is it?

Dr. Nancy: (*trying to talk faster, so much she wants to say*) There are a large number of books about the evils of TV. Having researched this and *not* been traumatized as a child myself, I would say that

TV has incredible power to teach both positive and negative things. Each month I offer RxTV in my newsletter and—

Matt: We only have nine minutes, Dr. Nancy. Please get to the point.

Dr. Nancy: (*starting right back in with personal promotion*) See www.drnancyonline.com for some pros and cons about TV viewing. In my newsletter this month, I offer TV viewing tips for … (*Matt looks down at his notes and looks up with his mouth open; she knows he is going to interrupt her.*)

Matt: Getting back to the questions, don't laugh, but another concern I have is that if I were to eliminate TV altogether, my kids would be missing out on a big chunk of pop culture. For example, if you make a *Three's Company* or *Brady Bunch* joke, I'll likely understand every reference. And I'm proud of that (LOL). How can I not fry their brains but allow them the enjoyment of entertainment?

Dr. Nancy: (*likes this question*) Where would we be without the *Brady Bunch* or *Three's Company*? Would TV have become more open if *All in the Family, The Middle,* and *Modern Family* hadn't come along, changing the family stereotypes? They are

Notes for Girls and Boys
• As a female child, you saw role models on TV and learned that Marlo Thomas as *That Girl* Ann Marie (1966) and Mary Tyler Moore as Mary Richards (1970) could have careers. You were "Free to Be You and Me," as Marlo Thomas would later tell children in a charming TV special.
• The feminist movement of the sixties let you know that you had choices. Then all you needed to do was to figure out who "me" was.
• Gloria Stivik, played by Sally Struthers on *All in The Family,* was considered another of the first women to break the family mold by speaking up to her parents and husband. Her perpetual student husband, Mike, played by Rob Reiner, exposed you to a new model of the newly married man. He did not have to go out and get a job to support his family immediately if continuing his education was a better idea. Archie Bunker, played by Carol O'Connor, had a very hard time with that, and it was funny yet pertinent. Talk about a reality show!

groundbreakers, and, thanks to Nick at Night and TBS as well as many other channels, we can still see some great shows in reruns.

Matt: Anything else you would like to add or share about TV and kids?

Dr. Nancy: As someone with highly positive (and some highly negative) viewing experience, I maintain my neutrality as often as I can, viewing as an open-minded viewer, determining if I want the message on the screen or not. I recommend the same strategy to others.

Matt: Dr. Nancy, this all sounds like very good advice. Would you like to produce a children's TV show for the station?

Dr. Nancy: Of course, Matt. I'll have *my* people call *your* people.

(*The credits move over the screen as clips from today's news and weather play in the background. You can just barely hear Al Roker laughing with Matt. Natalie Morales is looking professional today in her navy blue suit.*)

So Many Role Models, So Much Viewing Time

In my dedication to offering viewing guidance to parents, I set out to research the effects of television on children. Many of the studies indicated that TV, in fact, influenced children.

My research found that certain factors predict how you define yourself with television as a part of the equation.

- Repeated exposures to your favorite TV heroes reminded you that you could be someone, too.
- If you had real role models in your life and family who modeled the same positive behaviors and values, then the effect of TV and life in combination strengthened them.

- If an adult was clarifying what you saw on TV to help you decide if what you saw was real or not, then the show's effect was more positive.
- Without this clarification, TV hypnosis, or belief in what was presented, became real.

The role of the parents is obvious here as they can make the difference between what children see and what they learn. Parental advisory is a great idea.

Have you noticed the *new* portrayal of children on TV today? You now see wise children, who are the only wise one in the family! Look at irreverent and inappropriate Stewie, an animated American child who speaks with a British accent and has the vocabulary of a well-educated adult, in *Family Guy*. He tells everyone what to do and is surprised when they don't respond.

Contrast that to the character of Manny, played by Rico Rodriguez in *Modern Family*. He is the voice of reason to the hilarious chaos of the Pritchett family. This comedy of the modern family premiered on ABC in 2009 to critical acclaim. It went on to win several Emmy awards for Outstanding Comedy Series, Outstanding Supporting Actor and Actress in a Comedy Series, and Outstanding Writing for a Comedy Series. If you have not seen it, imagine Ed O'Neill, of *Married With Children*, as the family patriarch, married to a much younger Hispanic woman. Their son, Manny, is the sage of the family. He has few lines to say, but the ones he has steal the show. Whether it is the intention of the show or not, his wisdom reflects that of today's wise child who has to make many of his own decisions. Add to the equation the hilarious, stereotyped gay couple, Mitchell and his partner, Cameron, who have adopted a Vietnamese baby, Lily, and many other characters, and you can see why Manny's voice of reason and honesty are so essential to the mix.

Another typical real-life and TV stereotype is the new undecided or financially strapped child who can never leave home. Consider the plight of TV parent and career criminal Tony Soprano in the HBO series *The Sopranos,* who complained to his therapist, Dr. Melfi, that his son A.J. was such a problem child. Dr. Melfi noted that the bombardment of information children are exposed to causes a delay into adulthood. Tony expressed the plight of many baby boomer parents that their children are not doing well. Art imitated life.

In another episode of the series, Tony contemplates whether physical punishment would be more effective with his son A.J. After all, that is how his father treated him. Tony is questioning whether the boomer trend away from spare the rod, spoil the child is any less effective than his wife Carmela's more lenient ideas, which don't seem to be working, either. These are situations and challenges that many parents can identify with today.

Notes For Boys
- The wise children are often boys. Males have come full circle from the wise fathers of the fifties and sixties to the bumbling fathers such as Ray Barone in *Everybody Loves Raymond* and now back to the wise male child.
- The fathers of the wise male children are usually still bumbling, so the natural progression suggests that fathers used to be wise, then became bumbling, but their children will bring back the old model as they mature and become parents. Consider Manny and his dad in *Modern Family.*

Your Family vs. the TV Family: Why Choose the Real Family?

Those who write for TV know that when you feel a part of a family that you tend to continue to watch to see what happens to your favorite family character. You root for that character against the other family members, just as you would for someone in your own family or neighborhood. But what happens if you don't see your family or neighbor every Sunday night at 8 p.m.? Does the bond feel as real? The producers and advertisers may hope not, otherwise you will be sitting on the porch playing cards or volleyball with the neighbors and their kids instead of viewing. After a while, televised characters feel like a part of the family, which is why you become so forgiving of them. In the frenzy toward vampire stories, you even root for characters, such as the vampires in *Being Human* who bite people and turn them into vampires. Remember the thrill as the vampire approaches, taking in the whole screen with its mouth, making you feel as though they are about to bite *you*? Is this a competition? Real life vs. TV? Can real life compete? Yes, because in real life you can bite back, creating an exchange that is real.

SpyTV

Detect the messages in your favorite family show and decide if you will *accept or reject them.* Then as you decide to *release or respect them,* if you choose to release, begin to *mismatch.* That is the trance breaker for this chapter. To *mismatch,* decide what is a mismatch for the message of the show that you would like to adopt. If the message you choose to reject, for example, is that broken families are dysfunctional, decide that modern non-traditional families are different and interesting. Think of a mismatch for the message you want to change and then hold that new attitude!

C—Cut out one thing you are watching that is not giving you or your family a good message.

For more up-to-date information on *Get Reel* for this chapter, go to:

http://drnancyonline.com/category/rc-relationships/

http://drnancyonline.com/category/rc-health/

http://drnancyonline.com/category/current-news/

CHAPTER 5

LET'S MAKE A DEAL

Money talks, and the messages about money are many. If you are Donald Trump, money gives you the right to choose an assistant celebrity on national TV and be boldly honest, at the same time, firing people with abandon and using interesting hand gestures. We are already identifying some of the illusions about money, and it's not only the Donald who makes us think that wealthy people have the right to behave differently.

Research is clear that the goal of attracting a lot of money to the exclusion of other goals does not make you happy, nor does attracting money for money's sake. But on TV, most money messages are not as obvious as the research or the title of the show *Dirty Sexy Money*. It's more likely that the messages are imbedded. That's where the trance comes in. By forming associations, the ideas about money become a part of the trance that you carry, which determine how and what you spend. TV trances about money reflect real-life situations as well as fictional ones, again, mixing things up for your brain to sort. And once again, what you want to see appears on the screen, and what you see on the screen becomes what you want to see, reinforcing the money messages.

Money and Status

Has TV been fair to the topic of money? Mainly yes, it wants you to feel at home. Mostly that's where you watch TV, and it was where you spent more time when the economy turned down. TV became one big reality show.

The trances you saw on TV were yours, not theirs. You and the economy were driving the content.

- Working-class heroes dominated the screen during the seventies era, affected by inflation. *All in the Family* and *Laverne and Shirley,* the first *Broke Girls,* reigned supreme. In the eighties when the economy recovered, you were treated to the upwardly mobile and wealthy, with *Dallas, Knots Landing,* and *Dynasty,* even *The Cosby Show.* The return of *Dallas* in 2012 was predictable based on popularity.
- The nineties recession was paired with *Rosanne,* a comedy about a family struggling financially.
- Homer Simpson, of *The Simpsons,* went into foreclosure in March 2009 in the twelfth-season episode after financing their Mardi Gras party with a home equity loan.
- *30 Rock* in February 2009 showed interns, former investment bankers, who were laid off by the economic crisis. "They have zero real-world skills, but … God they work hard," quipped Alec Baldwin's character, whose remarks were written by Tina Fey.
- In 2009 on *Ugly Betty,* a show about publishing, five publications were shut down the same year.
- *Desperate Housewives'* characters Tom and Lynette Scavo lost their pizzeria related to a poor economy the same year.

Shows that profiled the wealthy did not do well during the recession unless they were realistic.

- The *Confessions of a Shopaholic* movie was not a match for a frugal public. A housewife on *Real Housewives of Orange County* who lived the high life even had to refinance after defaulting on her mortgage. It is reminiscent of the old theme of *The Great Gatsby* age of excess leading to ruin. The movie of the same title did well at the box office in 2013.
- *Wall Street II* in 2010 brought the 1987 Michael Douglas back again as a corrupt financier. The movie premiered as Bernie

Madoff, mastermind of the Ponzi scheme, was taken to task. The movie examines whether greed is really good.

- In 2009, Kelsey Grammer had a brief series, *Hank*, in which he was a Wall Street exec who lost his job and moved in with his working-class relatives.
- The movie *Company Men* showed what happened when Ben Affleck lost his job in corporate America and ended up working with his construction-worker brother, Kevin Costner.
- *The Millionaires Club* was a different kind of show. Financial difficulties forced people to come up with a get-rich scheme—a dream similar to real people who play the lottery.
- The 2014 movie *Monuments Men* profiled the bravery of George Clooney and Matt Damon, fighting to recover the world's art treasures at the end of World War II, at a time when the country was fighting to get back its jobs. Congress extended unemployment benefits.
- At a time when health-care reform was on the table, Edie Falco worked as *Nurse Jackie* to fight against a hospital that wants to get money from patients, while Jada Pinkett Smith of *Hawthorne* took on the bureaucracy that had overworked her. Jada has since moved on to rocking the *Batman* prequel, *Gotham*.
- And the character Dr. Hank Lawson, played by Mark Feuerstein, got fired for putting the health needs of an average citizen before a hospital board member's in *Royal Pains*.

Redistribution of the Wealth

When it comes to money, there is a lot of evidence that TV imitates reality, saying, "Hey, we're just like you, so come see us, turn us on, make us a part of the family." A "We're in touch with you" message makes you more likely to watch. TV makes

Outsourced was set in a call center in Mumbai, India, where an American novelties company had recently been outsourced. The twist of an American manager in an Indian company in Mumbai offered a weekly dose of cultural mistakes and misunderstandings that both Americans and Indians said they couldn't live without.

these real-life financial themes more accessible and asks you to identify with them even more because they *are* realistic models, not far-fetched ones. And this can be a good thing, although conscious viewing is needed. It makes hypnosis and the addiction to the show and any side messages, like commercial messages, more likely. Everyone likes people and messages that agree with them, increasing the likelihood that you will embrace them. And when they are timely, there is a higher likelihood of a positive outcome for the show and you. You may be inspired by the characters who overcome money crises, get creative ideas that are practical, or just feel vindicated and a little less alone with your woes.

Since the financial status of TV characters is often a measure of economic trends reflected on TV, the speed at which we see real-world events show up in pop culture is getting faster and faster. Fantasy mimics reality, with a bit of non-reality thrown in, and, as usual, it all gets confusing. The messages get mixed, and the truth gets muddied week after week.

Finances even rule the availability of the media, as TV, radio, print, and the Internet intertwine. TV, fighting for ratings, is more available now on the Internet, as sponsors see how much less expensive it is to advertise on the net. Flagging TV news shows and magazines end up on the Internet because you don't have to sit and listen on time; you can catch it later. The economy affects the print media because classified ads are now available on Craig's List, Angie's List, and eBay, and Internet radio is alive and thriving. Sponsors have new opportunities for products that appear in the hands of celebrities on programs, such as the reality show *American Idol* and in movies like *Sex and the City II*.

The show *Outsourced* was based on a fictional novelty company, Mid-American Novelties, that even had its own website and T-shirts, and it doesn't even exist! Money, fiction, reality, and humor formed a recipe for success. It made light of the cultural divide and the employees' attempts to sell fake vomit, sex toys, and you-name-it. One episode of *Outsourced* showed the elite business bullies getting taken down by the novelty department by stealing their lunchroom table. If you have ever been bullied at work, they had your attention! This show hit a home run: you learned a bit about another culture and the clash between India and America's spending.

Justice to the Rescue

Viewing money messages can provide a valuable service for you. TV may be your champion, putting the corrupt rich guy in jail for good. It supports your sense of justice, especially if you ever took anyone to small claims court and lost. You get vicarious pride from the courage of the farmer who would not let the bank foreclose on his farm and from the bank robbers who are finally jailed. If a mail order company or online sales associate has ever ripped you off, you feel vindicated when the embezzler with the fancy haircut goes down. And in real-time news, you witnessed the Ponzi scheme that did not work out for Bernie Madoff or his investors.

On TV, the wealthy person is often characterized as a crook who bribed his way to the top and is now a ruthless, controlling monster. Recall Tony Soprano, played by James Gandolphini of *The Sopranos*, with family problems stemming from his illegal and ruthless pursuit of money and power. He wrestled with greed and his aggressive and sexual impulses, losing the respect of his wife, played by Edie Falco, and the safety of his children. The show ends with little closure so you get to make up your own mind about how Tony fares. It gives you an opportunity to project your own ending into the show and tells you a bit about your own attitude toward people who use crime in exchange for money.

Boardwalk Empire looked a bit like a sequel to the Sopranos, but then if a show is successful, you will see ones that look the same. And money is often associated with crime in the movies and TV. The embellished real-life story of the movie *Bonnie and Clyde* is one such example. As you look at the many ways that money is portrayed on the screen, you will begin to sort what is

Remember Nicolas Cage in the 1994 movie *It Could Happen To You* that has been recycled many times on local TV movie channels? He bought a lottery ticket and promised a waitress, Bridget Fonda, that he would split his winnings with her if he was lucky enough to win. Not only was the noble Nick lucky, he was honest and kept his promise to share. The problem arose when his not so noble girlfriend, played by Rosie yours and what are Nicolas Cage's, Donald Trump's, or Ray Barone's ideas about money and become conscious about the dollar.

Perez, got in the way. The wheat was separated from the chaff, and he ended up with the poor waitress rather than the greedy girlfriend. Money brought him a love rescue and happiness. It was a once-in-a-lifetime dream come true. The trance was set, and lottery sales went up.

The Joy of Spending: Money and Happiness

Now jump to the reality of all-day shopping experiences that you can have anytime that you turn on your TV set, guaranteed to bring you ease, joy, and friendship. There's the shopping channel, the full-time shopping channel, the part-time shopping channel, the Home Shopping Network, QVC, and others in various pockets of the country. Home Shopping Network reaches 94 million homes with an annual sales record of 3 million dollars. QVC celebrated its twenty-fifth anniversary with 50 million buyers and 7 billion products, some of which can also be purchased at Macy's, Saks, or Target.

"Treat yourself." "Wouldn't it be fun to get one for your granddaughter?" "Get one in every color," and "Make life easier," are TV shopping hosts' marketing suggestions. My aunt Jo loves to see Jane Rudolph Tracy on QVC offer savings on silver. My friend Stan watches just to see Lisa, the former beauty queen, and my invalid neighbor watches because he can't get out to shop. Everyone has a good time. The deals are good ones, and the offers are generally sound. Quality, value, and convenience come right to your door. It's a lot of fun, except for the extra shipping costs, but most people are willing to pay for the convenience of receiving a package that feels like a gift that you give to yourself.

Is there an effect on your purse strings? Of course, and it can be good or bad! If you can resist impulse buying and watch consciously, you can find ways to save money rather than lose it. Watching consciously involves tuning into the phrases used to sell you the products. Deliberately or not, the trances are thrown in with the true statements to blur the line and create more shopping. By now, you are familiar enough with trances to pick out deceptive or accurate statements from trance-building statements in advertising, so let's play "Trance or Not." In the statements below, write "Trance" or "Not" after the statement.

Trance or Not

Statement   Trance or Not Trance

1. It's so much fun to use.
2. Your daughter, sister, or aunt would love one.
3. It can be used in so many rooms of the house.
4. How many other colors can you use?
5. This can be worn with jeans or trousers.
6. Wouldn't this be nice on a spring day so you can feel like winter is over?
7. This would work on the mantel or on an end table.
8. Think of all the fun you can have with your family.
9. These are great for family gatherings. Get one for every member of the family.
10. This will make your hands feel so soft and smooth.

You are getting more sophisticated by now, so I will give you a clue! Any words that cause an association not already automatically associated with the item are trances! Now take a second look at your quiz and see if you want to change any of your answers.

When you are satisfied with your responses, review the following key: Trances are items 2, 4, 6, 8, and 9, while simple descriptions that are not trances are numbers 5, 7, and 10. The lines are blurred in statement 1, "It's so much fun to use," because fun is subjective. "You can use several in so many rooms of the house" may be true if it is a small clock or a picture frame, but if it's a VCR, someone is trying to sell you an extravagant lifestyle.

To further raise your TV shopping consciousness, awaken you from the trance, and help you make buying decisions, ask yourself the following questions:

Home Shopping

1. Is the item on TV an item that you wanted to buy prior to the TV offer?
2. Have you priced the item already, and do you know what is a fair price for it?
3. If the price is truly a steal, would buying in multiple quantities solve the issue of grab-bag gifts for the holidays, even if it is still only June?
4. Is the item unfamiliar but solves a problem you have, such as storage space, making french fries, or massaging your achy feet?
5. Is it the perfect gift for someone you know, especially if it is something not sold in stores?
6. Can you afford to pay for it, even on the "easy pay" plan?

Or

7. Are your charge cards maxed to the limit?
8. Do you have a problem with impulsive purchases?
9. Do you have several items in your drawers and cupboards with price tags still attached?
10. Did you succumb to the suggestion of the show host that you should buy this just to make your day better?
11. Are you buying the item to get rid of boredom?
12. Do you need the item?

Scoring: For every yes response you gave to questions 1–6, give yourself one point.

For every yes response to questions 7–12, take one point off of your score. If your score is

5–6: Go ahead and make the call, wait for the package with anticipation, and enjoy the purchase.

3–4: Reconsider. Take down the order number and decide later, after the buying impulse has passed, if this is a wise or necessary purchase.

Below 3: Forget about it!

So where is the harm if you scored in the "Go ahead and buy range?" It's pretty much a feel-good win/win for everybody. Except for businesses that used to sell those products and now have become extinct. TV shopping has had a major effect on the local appliance store, the garden shop, and the jewelry store.

Not to spoil your fun, none of these things are reasons to stop TV and Internet buying. But the ease of home shopping on TV and Internet affects the economy and business. The availability of home-shopping shows and infomercials has lowered the profits for retail outlets. Department stores have taken a hit because of TV and Internet shopping and have had to come up with competitive deals that will get you out of the house. Other buying options such as Amazon have done away with small independent shops, book and music stores, and even larger chains such as Borders.

On February 16, 2011, the *New York Daily News* reported the bankruptcy of Borders and the layoff of six thousand employees. While they kept some stores open, clearly times had changed. You can get books, new and used, on the technology of Amazon for lower prices, and Barry Manilow's new CD is available on TV with special gifts attached. The *New York Times* cited the rise of Amazon along with the profusion of iPads and Kindles, the dominance of video games and movies online, as

New technology of a call-in TV show or a one-stop shopping website offers new and seemingly better choices. Just decide if you want to put your favorite local hardware store out of business while shopping at Walmart or Target online. There is a global effect to your shopping choice.

wake-up calls for the book, magazine, and newspaper industries. Whether you read the news online or watch it on TV, there is no such thing as free news; someone has to pay for it. The *New York Times* is charging for an online news feed. Some think that newspapers and books will someday be obsolete and that a computer/TV merger is at hand. But not to fear, commercials are not going away!

Adsociations: Do Not Adjust Your View, This Is Not a Typo

The annual *Year's Funniest Commercials* show is one of my friend Carla's favorites. She looks at the clever, creative ways that products are sold and says, "Bravo!" One friend, a CFO of a large company whose career is in the world of finance, particularly enjoys the creative marketing ventures. While I agree wholeheartedly with my friend about the creative nature of advertising, I want to break it down for you. TV advertising is purposed with the intention of making you buy and making you so interested in their product that you have little choice but to pull out your credit card. In order to accomplish this mission, ads must make associations to things that consumers value whether they exist or not. Hence the Adsociation, the association created by the ad, is born.

Warning Label: You Will Be Adsociated through Pictures, Words, and Actions

You have seen Coca-Cola on *American Idol*, the iPad on *Modern Family*, and Starbucks coffee on MSNBC's show *Morning Joe*. The trend has shades of *The Truman Show*, a movie in which Jim Carey was the unwitting victim, a reality-show character whose fictional wife advertised by holding up household products during conversations with her husband. If you are taking in the trance of some TV shows and are the unwitting victim of adsociation, then perhaps you are a bit like Jim Carey. And leaving the fictional town in which he lived may require as much courage for you and result in a trip to the unknown world outside of Adsociation Town. But I will help you break out if you need to. And it won't require sliding through the ceiling of the White House or running down a broken fire escape.

False Identifications

The surgeon general has determined that obesity is the largest growing cause of disease and death in America. It is due to a lack of physical activity and over consumption of foods high in fats and sugars. Statistics show that kids view fifteen food ads daily during the average viewing period, mostly for foods high in fat, salt, and sugar.

Despite the evidence, food producers are creating false associations to get you to eat more of their product. Unhealthy eating behaviors paired with positive outcomes anchor you to the idea of "eat and feel good." Conscious awareness falls below the radar. Add to that the pleasure centers in the brain that light up each time you see your favorite junk food, and addiction occurs. You are hypnotized once you attach or anchor pleasure to the food. Coupled with genuine pleasure of eating the food, the adsociation makes the anchor more powerful.

Escapes from the Trances That Bind

It doesn't take an advanced viewer to see that viewer perceptions or trances about spending are caused by adsociations. But it's time to look at the adsociations and find out

- which ones are true and which are false trances;
- what the trance convinces you to do;
- how to awaken; and
- what is life after trance.

Silent Adsociations: The Good, the Bad, and the Ugly

Sometimes I watch football on TV. The key word is sometimes, not as an addict or at the risk of alienating friends celebrating their anniversary. There seems to be a natural association between watching TV with a group, such as at a sports bar, and drinking more, according to a study reported by American Psychological Association. Ads for beer showing social drinking during sporting events are playing on this natural association. They are also reminding you to emulate the behavior if you want to have as much fun as the group on the screen.

This leads me to tell you that you or any other sports fan can't buy happiness, but you *can* buy things that are adsociated with happiness. I see people in the stands wearing their favorite player's shirt and number. This is an accurate association—you and your favorite player. Your admiration for your favorite player led you to buy his shirt and either support your team or feel better about yourself by wearing it. In the ad with the football player throwing his shirt to the little boy who is waiting for any sign of attention from his favorite player, you experience the "feel-good moment" and identify with the happiness of having the shirt. The power of having the shirt just increased. Notice the adsociation. And it's an ad for a soft drink! Trifecta! And a chance to see the clever new trance of anchor stacking, coming up next.

Anchor Stacking

Anchor stacking is piling more than one association on an item or idea. In a naturally occurring situation, the happiness trance that you experience from wearing your favorite player's shirt gets stacked each time you wear it and is therefore more powerful.

> Commercials that build on themselves like the humorous Geico ad with the Cave Man or the Gecko ads are stacking positive anchor on top of positive anchor, building their brand and your affection for their sense of humor, ad after ad. You look forward to seeing what the Gecko is up to today as soon as you see him.

- You like to wear the shirt because it reminds you of your favorite player.
- You will feel even better wearing the shirt the next time you have fun at a football party.
- You will associate attention from your favorite player after viewing the ad of the boy getting his favorite player's shirt.

Anchor stacking, or adding layers to trance, is a powerful method of adsociation. You will learn how to use it to your advantage soon.

Holiday ads often make natural associations such as Christmas and Grandma's house, winter and hot chocolate, Fourth of July with certain clothes. These associations are usually not harmful but are still adsociations rather than the naked truth. If Christmas is not your favorite time of year or you don't experience any warmth from your granny, they can actually be a turn-off.

The Good: Real Associations

Some empowering adsociations occur in ads that tell you the truth. Statistics often accomplish this goal. If you hear that the largest killer of women is heart disease and that a way to beat the disease is to brush your teeth twice daily to remove bacteria from the system that invade the heart, mission accomplished. You may be likely to remember the brand name on that toothbrush when you shop in the dental aisle.

Genuine associations often show you the problem and offer solutions. There is a cell phone ad with a woman walking down the aisle to be married while texting, a man spilling coffee while texting, and a parent sitting on a seesaw forgetting to take their turn while texting. They offer a faster phone to end the crime of over-texting. It may use slight exaggeration, but it makes the ad more memorable because it reminds you of you!

Some real associations are clever. Like the ad that associates Hansel and Gretel to a GPS. It's better than breadcrumbs! But the winner of the most honest ad in this category goes to Starbucks for the slogan "Crafted perfectly just for you." It is true. It goes with the visuals of the barista making the coffee, steaming the milk, and adding the toppings and makes you feel special and important. Is the price good for you? Not sure, but it is still truth in advertising. Are you special and important? Yes, but I hope you don't need coffee to know that and can connect to these feelings on a regular basis with or without a slim decaf cappuccino. Separate the message from the coffee, and you have a win-win situation. You get to have your coffee and drink it, too! *Choice* is the answer.

This is a good time to mention that there is a difference between buying goods and buying services. Pampering makes you feel wealthy, so service ads play on the desire to have enough money to let people take care of you. The coffee ad, playing on this desire, causes an association between the goods and the services without breaking the piggy bank. Kudos!

The Bad: Unnatural Alliances

Misadsociations can be bad or just humorous. These are ads that connect two things that are clearly not connected. Sex is big in this category. Sex has been connected with cars, shirts, soft drinks, brand-name items, and many things unsexy. Some ads are just a stretch; you continue to watch because you can't imagine what product will be connected to the walk on the beach in bikinis this time. I saw a diaper ad connected with the psychologist's inkblot test, the Rorschach, and wondered how these two things were connected. I watched to see, and that is the important thing to the sponsor.

Speaking of diapers, one study showed that the most appealing image to ad viewers is a baby's bottom. Can you think of any ads that throw that image into the mix unexpectedly? Sometimes, advertisers play on the fact that they expect you to watch to see what the ad is about and to feel surprised when you do. The activation of the emotion of surprise or any emotion is more likely to cause an association with the product.

The Centers for Disease Control and Prevention call our society obesogenic, meaning that the "environment promotes increased food intake, non-healthful foods and physical inactivity."

Junk food ads are guilty too. Millions of dollars are spent on food before and during Super Bowls. A study reported by the American Psychological Association showed that children consumed 45 percent more food after watching food ads. Adults consumed more healthy and unhealthy foods after food ads. The ads even produced more eating of foods not advertised. The study showed the power of food ads to prime automatic eating behavior and influence more than brand preference. Since there is a direct relationship between TV watching and obesity, these findings are relevant. Not only is TV watching a sedentary pastime but food ads cause more eating.

The Ugly

These ads are worse than misadsociation ads. These ads are lies. An ad for a drink mix that contains chemicals and preservatives urges you to take time for yourself. To do what for yourself? Contaminate yourself?

Understand, I am not suggesting eliminating fast food as an option. There are many choices that are healthier at fast-food chains. You can find some of them in the book *Eat This, Not That*. The problem with the chains is that some of the most popular and promoted items are high in fat, salt, and preservatives. A triple bacon pancake wrapped avocado cheeseburger is unhealthy by definition, whether eaten at home or at the drive-through.

An experiment showed that a brand-name meal did not decompose over six months. Children who buy kids' meals are encouraged to buy "hope," because a food chain gives donations to a cause. Ads for foods high in fat move you toward food-related health problems and then give you hope of healing them but don't let you off the food hook. "Do you want chemo and radiation with that?" might be a better question than "Do you want to supersize that?" Huge food portions aren't healthy.

In 2009, a New York City councilman proposed a ban on fast-food chains within one-tenth mile of any school, and San Francisco has outlawed a fast-food children's meal. Great advertising was not enough to get them to ignore the research. The chain bounced back by creating adult-oriented drinks such as the special coffee drinks produced by Starbucks. According to Josh Ozersky in *Time* magazine, the food chain is close to beating Starbucks at their specialty, based on revenues in six of the last seven quarters of $24 billion since introducing the drinks.

And what about the fast-food slogans? These are really fascinating to see and are rarely ever truly connected with the real value of the food. Although there are ads for healthier fast foods, such as fruit, salads, or yogurt, these are usually presented in a straightforward way for parents who will want a healthier choice while buying the fast food that their children want. Most fast-food ads try to connect the food with a feeling or an experience that is not naturally connected to fried chicken lumps.

The ads make associations with fun, being cool, and even respecting your elders. Associating fast food to these virtues is an unnatural alliance. Check out some of these catch phrases from food ads.

Food Ad Slogans

There are 1,440 minutes in a day—take at least fifteen for you.
You deserve a break today.
I'm lovin' it.
We love to see you smile.
Feel the Joy.
Bigger, better.
Now that your tastes have grown up.
Eat Fresh.
Smile.

The Simple Joy of Temptation

Then there are question slogans that cause an immediate refocusing on the question because the mind wants to answer it. If the answer to the question "Aren't you hungry?" is "Yes, I'm hungry," you have already made a visual association with the burger. Consider the following:

Where's the beef?
What are you eating today?
How do you get more prosperity?
Do you believe in magic?

In an article in *Spirituality and Health*, by Matt Sutherland, dairy products promoted in the "Got Milk?" ads were deemed responsible for the "hazards of milk allergies, lactose intolerance, and adverse reactions to … different hormones and growth factors in cow's milk." The ads associate celebrities with drinking milk by showing them with a milk mustache. Whether you agree with the research quoted by Sutherland, you can see the associations connected to the slogan. And let's not single this ad out because the issues for ads with adsociation are everywhere. But conscious watching means asking yourself, "Is this ad really catering to the product and to a true association about what they are selling?" Then *choose* to buy or not. Even with adsociations, the product may be just fine. Now, look at some categories of ads that will raise your conscious awareness so you don't get hooked, unless of course you want to!

Unforgettable Adsociations That Let You in on the Gimmick

In a car ad, a woman wanders around looking at cars in a hypnotic trance while saying in a monotone voice that she was told she should like beige. She comments on being told that she should like practical cars, as a part of her trance. She then wakes up and buys the car she really wants. It is a switch from one hypnotic trance to another, one that is desired by the car manufacturer and a clever one at that! The location is elegant, and it's been proven that a chic location with a product will cause more spending and a willingness to pay more.

Consider the ad of Betty White rolling around in the mud playing ball with a group of men or talking jive. The setting is used to surprise you and make you notice. The emotions of joy and surprise further attach your interest to the ad.

Now think of the World's Most Interesting Man ad campaign. It features a handsome, mature man in various exclusive settings like moonlight expeditions through a rocky canyon or sitting in a fancy club surrounded by beautiful women. He emulates sophistication, sex, adventure, and maturity, and all of these things are adsociated with his favorite drink, as he tells viewers to "Stay thirsty, my friend." That stacks another anchor on top of his drink—live in the lap of luxury but want more. It's transparent, so it's funny, and you see through it.

Some ads are unforgettable as they try to sell you something and expose the methods to their madness. The Old Spice ad with Isaiah

Mustafa pointing out how his good looks are selling deodorant is a perfect example. "Look at me, now look at your husband," he says. Then he says, "Look down," as he points out that he is not wearing a shirt, something you would have noticed if you were not blind, based on his musculature. You definitely remember the product. A good ad is absurd enough to make an association, help you to see how ridiculous the association is, *and* make you store the product in your mind. It also has you saying to your friends, "Did you see that commercial? It's hilarious," further spreading the word. You do the work for the product with the ripple effect.

Other Tricks and Trades

Special Interests

- Some TV commercials want to sell you their product even if you can't afford things and/or they aren't good for you, or there is some evidence that they aren't good for you. Some say that there is evidence that stockholders in large corporations want to continue the sale of a product, even with evidence of harm from the product. The movie with Russell Crow, *The Whistle Blower*, is about the ways that the tobacco industry kept harmful information from the public. The ads have come full circle, with plans to put aversive images on cigarette packages following research on the product.

Political Ads

- With political ads that sell candidates, ratings go up as pressing issues are televised. During the health-care debate, contentious ad dollars were flowing in swing states. Once legislation is passed, viewing goes down, and advertising stops.
- During the health-care debate, Brian Aiello, principal with Washington DC-based IKON public affairs, quoted research by the Campaign Media Analysis Group, saying that pro-health-care

reform groups made more than $100 million nationwide for the largest issue-related spending in history.

- Pressure to contact the candidates stems from the ads. They appeal to independent thinkers who are still persuadable.

Reconsider the illusion that you must have *things* to make you happy. There is typically a general increase in the stressed financial economy in conjunction with an increase in lottery gambling and drinking while there are no increases in church attendance. This is typical of depressions in the economy. Look at prohibition during the depression of the thirties. And look at where the country is now. Denial is not the answer.

- If they were products, the ads would be pulled for false advertising, but candidates may buy time and say what serves the campaign.

So let's take a commercial-free break where you can *choose* whether or not you want the new healthy trance below. It's safe to indulge!

Choosing the Trance You Want, Keeping the Trance You Build

Imagine a utopia where you know exactly who you are and what you want. Imagine that you have connected the products and services to your goals that will best serve you. You may even be aware that you can find other products that will do a better job and that you are willing to find and accept them. You might be able to see yourself *choosing* these products now. How does it make you feel? Are you feeling proud or satisfied? Or maybe you are feeling secure or grounded by your choices. I wonder if these choices make your career better or maybe your health ... maybe even your relationships, or maybe you just *feel* better about yourself. I wonder if you can feel good about all of these areas after you make or choose not to make a purchase. You may find that you can *choose* more easily now, or that there is a part of you that is getting ready to *make* intentional choices. You might find yourself making these choices easily or making them more consistently.

Perhaps you recently made a wise purchase and then smiled to yourself. Can you see the purchase now? What feelings do you have as you look at your successful purchase? Maybe there are things that you can hear around you as you look at this successful product or service … perhaps even things you were not aware of at the time. As you see, hear, and feel this success, is there a word or phrase that you can associate with this experience? Now write it down and keep it. You have just set a success anchor for purchasing that you can build on for the rest of your post-trance life! Say it each time you make a wise choice.

Landmines to Avoid When Viewing

Mismatching

It's not just products but ideas that are sold while viewing. Have you ever noticed that the waiter living in the efficiency apartment and the unemployed actress in the big Manhattan apartment on your favorite show have very little money yet look and dress as though they do? Characters going on job interviews, clerking till they get a break, or just doing nothing often have high-fashion clothes and shoes, expensive haircuts, and take trips to visit relatives in remote locations. The producer's intention may be just to create a more visually interesting show, but the result, intentional or not, creates *mismatching*. You see a character that you like with little money acting as if they have lots of money, and you may have a number of different unconscious reactions that can become set as trances.

At first, there may be a sense of confusion that the brain tries to sort. The brain is trying to make order of what you see. There is tension till you can decide how the good life and a low income match. You may feel badly if you have a small budget and can't pull off the high-fashion look, resulting in less self-esteem. Or you may tell yourself that if he can do it, you can do it. You recreate the look and end up with bills you can't pay. Watch consciously the next time you see your favorite actor having lunch in a trendy café; what looks like the good life could just be a pretty illusion.

So how do you use your detective skills to break the trance? *Choice.* The trance breaker for this chapter is *choice.* You have a choice. To activate your power to choose, try the SpyTV and RxTV tips that follow.

SpyTV

Detect what is going on in the ad. I like to call out the adsociations as I watch. I say things like, "Can you believe they just adsociated beauty with french fries?" They made you watch, and then you saw their product. Then use *choice.* It's time to *reject or accept.* Then *release or accept. Reject* the image of a cute kid eating french fries. On the other hand, if the ad tells you that taking calcium is good for your bones, and you believe it, then you can *accept* the message. Use your detective skills to decide if their brand is best. *Respect* the connection as a good one. And for some tips on releasing, RxTV to the rescue.

RxTV: Beginning the Break from Adsociations

√ Watch, watch, watch to see what the show is anchoring. Is it good? Bad? Ugly?

√ Consciously view food ads and follow with conscious eating. Give yourself a *choice* by asking, "Do I want this or don't I?" "How will I feel if I eat or buy this?" "What decisions, if any, have I made about this product?"

√ Try some new way of responding to food ads, anything healthier than what you are doing now, for twenty-one days. It seems like a reasonable time frame and is also the amount of time it takes to change a habit. For example, take a few weeks off from foods high in saturated fats or sugars. Just looking up the nutritional information will make you more aware and less likely to be fooled. Substitute something less harmful and healthier.

√ Ask yourself if you even like the sugary drink that makes you do the double chocolate mocha polka, getting you high on sugar. Whether the answer is no or yes, you have slowed down to make an aware decision.

√ Have fun breaking the trance down. Comment to a friend and see how you can de-trance together, and the fun of it will set a new association of fun and trance breaking!

Changing Your Spending

Let's face it. Countries are in debt. And individuals are not far behind. An interesting study at the University of British Columbia teased out some of Americans' views about money that may differ from views in other countries. It may even explain differences in ads seen in the *Top Ten Best Commercials* show that contains ads from all countries.

Getting Past Your Spending Culture

The study, "The Ultimatum Game," was conducted by Joseph Heinrich to determine values about money. Each participant was given one hundred dollars and asked to share it with someone else. You could offer the person any amount, and if they accepted your offer, you each got to keep your share. If they rejected it, you both walked away empty handed.

Psychology varies across cultures, and Heinrich's study illustrates this. Ninety-six percent of human behavior research is done on Americans, according to the UBC study. Based on research that showed that American views about money are atypical of global human behavior, other research on Americans may be skewed in a direction not typical of global human behavior.

The study showed that educated Americans would make an average offer of forty-eight dollars. The study suggested that they might be motivated by fairness or just to make an offer that would not be rejected. The study showed that the other player in the game was typically unlikely to take offers less than forty dollars.

Compare that to the Machiguengas in the Peruvian Amazon. Heinrich found that they perceived the rejection of any free money as absurd. He compared the wisdom of the Machiguenga to that of economists, who also tend to think that there is no reason to turn down any free money. It is just irrational. Other cultures that played "The Ultimatum Game" also differed from the Western culture, with Heinrich suggesting the conclusion that our culture differs from the rest of humanity when it comes to money.

I did a survey of financial experts, CFOs, bank officials, individuals with websites, and some average citizens and compared them to the conclusions of the study. I asked them for their point of view on why they thought Americans would turn down free money. Interestingly, they answered from their political and personal perspectives rather than a financially analytic point of view. Their views were likely a mix of ideas from their parents, their social and financial status, effects of the media, and political persuasions, so they were a good example of typical results. These were some of the interpretations of the study's results.

- The study suggested that Americans are the most individualistic and *nonconformist*. Therefore, they make different choices about money than others. Individualism is one of the key values that differentiates Americans from many other more group-oriented cultures, according to Rhonda Coast, cross-cultural specialist.

- Some survey responders said that Americans are *capitalists* who don't want to settle for something if someone is getting more, citing people and organizations that go out on strike and won't settle for a two percent raise when they want a four percent raise. *Greed* factored into these opinions.

- Others said that a lack of familiarity with *socialism* was the reason. Americans are not used to sharing the wealth and resent systems where there is wealth sharing. Rhonda Coast, however, indicates that this is not a matter of being unfamiliar with socialism. She explains that Americans are individualistic and achievement oriented. As a result, they believe that each individual should always strive to be better. Better includes earning more money and accumulating things, which shows success. Americans tend to accept large differences in income levels because of a belief that "If others can achieve that, so can I—if I just work hard enough."

- Still others said that Americans have issues *with fairness*. If someone does not want to share equally, their sense of fairness is compromised, and they don't want to participate. This view was very popular. Coast equates fairness with equality. "More than 25 percent of the US population volunteers in some way to give others a fair and equal opportunity."

- Some thought issues of *pride* were involved. If someone was not going to treat you as an equal, they were trying to make you feel inferior, and, therefore, participants did not want to play that game.

- Some saw Americans as *aggressive* when it comes to money, yet some did not see it in a bad way.

- The *perception of value* of free things, even free money, is reduced. "If it was worth something, why would it be free?" was the thinking of these responders.

So maybe Americans are greedy, proud, obsessed with ideas of fairness about money, and nonconformist in their spending. And the media may drive those motivations or reflect them. The roots of acquiring and wanting money have many causes.

And how willing are Americans to give money away? A survey of charity appeals looks at a different point of view. Ken Pope, in *USA Today*, spoke of infomercials for causes and pleas during religious shows. He found that the degree of one's charity depends on happiness more than wealth. He cites a Gallup poll done for the Charitable Aid

With happiness as the driver for charitable giving and the US ranking number five for giving worldwide, there may be a reason you are not as happy as other cultures. A look at what causes Americans' happiness will take you to, among other things, what you are told that you should have and be in order to relax enough to be happy. And once you begin the pursuit, it can be a slippery slope. You end up keeping more than you give

Foundation, with the USA listed as the number-five nation for charitable giving.

American attitudes are specific to the culture and drive getting, spending, and giving. But the perception that free things lack value plays right into some of the advertising offers on TV for free things—that are never really free.

Maybe there is an urgency to sell products that causes too much free money to be tossed around in Western culture, reducing the value that people place upon it. Perhaps there are so many "free TV offers" that really include memberships and subscriptions to things you don't want that are hard to cancel once you agree to them. Maybe buying a "free for thirty days" product on the phone results in an automatic delivery every thirty days indefinitely until you go through the inconvenience of canceling the item completely. Or perhaps you are tired of calling for the free item only to be kept on the phone for another five to ten minutes to hear about all the other things you can get for just a few dollars more. Consider whether "free" is worth the price. Studies support charging for things, even a small amount, because the item with a price tag on it has more perceived value to the consumer.

These TV sales techniques work because people are likely to continue to allow automatic shipments long after they are tired of the product because of busy schedules, the complications of long phone calls and automated attendants used to stop shipment of a product, or because of disorganization. All in the name of "free."

So if you are true to your checkbook and to your authentic self, *choose* whether to turn the volume up or down. Maybe you'll watch or not. Or just be a conscious viewer and sit back, notice the trance, notice how many ways the trance is perpetuated and if it is good for you. It may be a lot more frugal to watch the eye candy on TV than to purchase that box of overpriced creamy dark chocolate that comes with automatic delivery. And it won't contribute to the obesity epidemic with which TV is constantly associated.

The C for this chapter as well as your trance-breaking tip is: choose. Choose three things to watch consciously this week.

For more up-to-date information on *Get Reel* for this chapter, go to:

http://drnancyonline.com/category/rc-media-and-rxtv/

http://drnancyonline.com/category/rc-business/

http://drnancyonline.com/category/current-news/

CHAPTER 6

REALITY TV UNPLUGGED

What Is Real about Reality TV?

What is reality is an existential question that has been asked for centuries by some of the greatest minds in the world. What is reality TV is a similar question in many ways. What is real and what is illusion takes on a complexity in TV that is truly a reflection of the producer and his or her artistry. So relax and buckle your couch-belt; you are about to discover what is real.

Reality TV takes many forms: documentary, science, history, weight loss, games, celebrity reality shows, sports, talk shows, contests for everything from talent and beauty to cooking, finding the most valuable antiques to shows about your storage unit, your mental health, and your parking space. The possibilities for reality shows are almost unlimited, with many different themes, actors, and subjects. They change continually to maintain your interest and your desire to answer the unspoken

V A secretary from Chicago recently referred to her favorite reality character's dilemma about what to wear as a serious problem. A miner from Atlanta reported that he enjoyed watching his favorite reality show gal "accidentally" caught in a compromising video. Then I overheard two colleagues discussing the love lives of "Housewives of their Favorite City" reality show and being genuinely concerned about them. It seems that they are imagining that reality TV is real. It's a slippery slope into believing the shows' messages and catching the characters' trances. Yes, I did call them "characters"—excellent catch! You noticed that something didn't seem real, too, didn't you?

question, "What's next?" Three-minute previews for TV shows and movies are proof that you are asking yourself such a question. The problem is solved before you even know it is there. Times have changed since it took three minutes for your TV screen to warm up when you turned it on! The tables are turned: reality TV is really turning you on. And if it has succeeded, then you are probably experiencing excitement, sweaty palms, anticipation about upcoming episodes, and rushing to the water cooler to discuss who will be waltzed off of *Dancing with the Stars.*

And Why Do We Watch It?

Karl J. Paloucek, writing for *Channel Guide* magazine, answers the question of why we watch so much reality TV. His take on the answer may explain some of the reasons for the changing family in society and the current reality. He indicates that early in our history, we sat around fires at night telling stories and that TV has done a good job of taking over the storyteller role. His challenge is whether we really need that many stories and vicarious living. In the case of reality TV, the viewing is truly vicarious and invites you to be a partner in celebrity kitchens to whip up crème brulée, to go to the everglades to search for wildlife, and to go to the pawnshop to find out what Aunt Mildred's brooch is worth.

 Paloucek proposes that TV watching may be like eating; we're not really hungry or in need of nutrition but are seeking sensory experience. If you crave sensory stimulation, you may find yourself either bored or anxious in the absence of TV and may crave a dose of *The Voice,* a reality vocal contest, and veal parmigiana both at the same time. You want to have your Hostess Twinkie and your *Top Chef,* too.

Reality Goes High Tech

A major new TV reality is that now you are watching on your laptop, iPad, phone apps, DVRs, Netflix, and independent apps, creating a phenomenon called "second screen" television. Neilson surveys show that up to 85 percent of participants use a tablet or smartphone to watch TV at least once a month. So while you need a TV to create the reality in the first place, TV is becoming the middleman. The reality is that you can get an app for Major League baseball, TV networks, or Disney with the capacity for tweeting or posting your reactions to the show on Facebook at the same time. Some iPad apps reward users with points for usage that can earn you an exclusive opportunity to access a special online account, movie tickets, or even makeup. If you're willing to take their quizzes about what you've seen, you get extra points. What's ironic is that by the time you jump through the technical hoops, you could be further removed from the reality of your child's baseball game, meeting of Women Over/Under Forty, your recommended dose of exercise, local celebrity look-alike contest, or dusting your fake plants. *And because you were more attentive to viewing in order to pass the quiz to win points for the trip to Balooka, you were more entranced.*

A child recently told me that her mom was so engrossed in TV after school that she had to complete her book report on *Winnie the Pooh* alone. And if A. A. Milne was writing about Pooh today, the plot might revolve around Pooh tagging Tigger's latest photos of Eeyore using his new app on Facebook and Eeyore tweeting about the pleasure of the honey pot. If you are a parent, hearing this may make you feel as guilty as the latest suspect on *NCIS*. But a storm that takes out your TV cable still can create withdrawal symptoms if you don't own the accompanying technology. You may go to bed early, unable to sleep without your daily dose of drama. Your TV watching may have become a habit, then an addiction. You may be unhappy without it. But is reality TV what you crave?

Tracing the Bottom Line

According to a Harris Interactive Poll, reality TV is only the fifth favorite genre of TV shows. There were no reality shows in the top fifteen TV programs that people (of all ages) listed as their favorites. So why are there so many reality shows? Because they satisfy a need to believe that it's real.

What do they satisfy for you? Well, you could be the next American Idol. After all, it happened to that guy from your hometown. And 60 million voters came out to vote to prove their interest in 2012. Or you could win the prize money on that game show or even get the home makeover. It happens to ordinary people, and everyone has a chance. There is vicarious satisfaction in seeing someone just like you get something you want. You may have even said to yourself, "That could be me.: If you have watched *American Idol* until the end, you care about who wins and have a favorite. The point is, it makes you *feel*. You keep viewing, and everyone is happy: you, the producers, the stars, and the sponsors. You can now relax, knowing you are not alone.

Much of reality TV is an escape, a word you have heard before in *Get Reel*. Once you have paid for your TV cable, you can get away from life without paying for designer bags and nights at Latest Restaurant, or watching Scary News. The difference with reality TV is that you can escape into other people's lives by leaving your own life behind. You may even feel that you are better off than the person on the screen. After all, you are not in the group of *Hoarders* who can't get in their front doors because of the stack of *Mad* magazines, dating back to their origin. You may think that your life is bad, but at least Simon Cowell is not buzzing *you* off of a talent show, making *you* feel like a big loser. But living vicariously may keep you from living your life up close and personal.

Once Upon a Time, There Was a Queen

So where did it all begin? With the first talk show or game show? I recall as a young child watching one of the first game shows, if you can call it that—*Queen for a Day*. Most of you will not remember this show or will have blocked it out of your mind. Good choice if you did. It was a show that profiled two women who became "queen for a day" by telling their life stories of misery to see who was the most miserable. The applause meter (or if you are becoming a conscious viewer, maybe the producer) would decide who was the most miserable, and she would get a prize. The dubious winner would get to wear a queen's crown and cape and cry while she received her new washing machine or other gift. If you are smiling, so am I, but this really happened in 1956, after *Queen for a Day* moved from radio to TV. People still remember feeling miserable afterward. It reinforced the message that miserable people get rewarded and magically rescued—reminiscent of the fairy tale *Cinderella*.

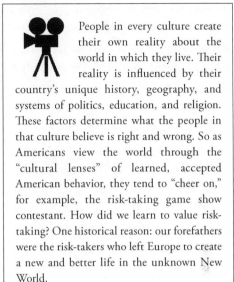 People in every culture create their own reality about the world in which they live. Their reality is influenced by their country's unique history, geography, and systems of politics, education, and religion. These factors determine what the people in that culture believe is right and wrong. So as Americans view the world through the "cultural lenses" of learned, accepted American behavior, they tend to "cheer on," for example, the risk-taking game show contestant. How did we learn to value risk-taking? One historical reason: our forefathers were the risk-takers who left Europe to create a new and better life in the unknown New World.

Fast-forward to 2010, where you can win a house makeover on *Home Makeover*, a clothing makeover with *What Not to Wear*, or a body makeover on *Extreme Makeover*—all simply because somebody tells you that you need improvement. These shows are appealing because you see someone you know or like obtain a better life. You get to watch as others' lives morph in ways that you might wish for yourself. One of the reasons that you watch, hypothesizes Robert Thompson, professor of media and culture at Syracuse University, is that Americans are fascinated with reinventing. He bases his idea on the fact that we are primarily descendants of immigrants who had to reinvent ourselves in a new country. If he is correct, then more self/house/garage/pet/blender improvement reality shows are inevitable.

Believe It or Not

Want to know what makes reality show contestants believable and creates the trance that what you are seeing is real? Many reality shows are filmed documentary-style, giving the viewer the perspective of a fly on the wall. It makes you feel as if you are there, chopping sugarcane on the island, a part of the viewing audience. But after filming, scenes are edited to create the plot and give the show a story. Along the way, some scenes end up on the cutting room floor and others in the final product. The creator makes subjective decisions about the content based on personal goals for the show, leaving room for slanting, often unintentional, just based on his or her own perception. If you recall from the politics chapter, this also happens with the news. So how do you know if what is presented is reality and what isn't? Does it matter?

Let me give you some guidelines. The late Steve Irwin's *The Crocodile Hunter* shows us what happens spontaneously while following a general outline that is prepared, combining reality TV and planned TV in the same program. But even the animals are sometimes set up. I've heard that in a *Shooting in the Wild* Yellowstone set, the producer chose to shoot film of a captive bear with a hibernation den set rather than wake a hibernating bear. Such depictions of reality can be a good (and safe) thing! In contrast, a game show or competition has less opportunity for such scripting and reveals the reality of the moment. You might assume that a fly-on-the-wall point of view show like *Big Brother* would be unscripted or less scripted, but you don't know for sure. Reality changes when you know that you are under a microscope. After all, didn't you change from sneakers to platform heels when going to a crowded entertainment district at night for an opening of *Hunger Games* or the new *Star Wars* movie?

The Outer Limits

The boundaries of mental health are pushed in reality shows such as *Hoarders, Intervention, Addicted, True Life,* and the talk shows *Dr. Drew* and *Dr. Phil.* These shows help to humanize mental health issues to make them more easily understood. They take them out of the closet and bring the reality of these conditions to light. And believe me, they could not make this stuff up.

The boundaries between reality and comedy also are being pushed. Programming that blurs the line between reality and fiction occurred in *Curb Your Enthusiasm.* The program is an exaggerated (I hope!) version of Larry David's life that is both unscripted and unrehearsed. A general plot is thrown into the middle of the set, and the actors move ahead and improvise. The situations parallel real life, unlike many fictionalized programs that blur the lines and aren't as open about it.

To Tell the Truth

Right now you may be asking yourself if I am biased in a positive way toward the *Seinfeld* show, and I really, really hope you are! I have mentioned it a few times. If you are getting the point of *Get Reel*, then you are reading consciously and wondering if I have a point of view on the show. Congratulations! But if you are truly conscious, you may notice that I still have not answered the question. Have you already made a decision about whether I have a bias?

Truth is, *Seinfeld* has been judged by many in the media industry as the best comedy ever made, so it is a good resource from which to draw. I have watched it more than many comedies and am more familiar with it. After all, I only have four hours and forty-nine minutes of viewing time a day, so I can only view so many comedies thoroughly! In any case, you now have enough information to unravel the mystery of whether I have a bias if you are reading between the lines. I hope you are. It is a skill that will make you a conscious viewer and reader. Perhaps this skill will transfer over into your real life. You may find yourself looking past a guy's shiny white teeth to see if he has a history of serial dating, or a girl's hot dress to find out if she is a serious student of vampirism.

Speaking of real life, I watched the *Today Show* as Kathy Lee Gifford told her cohost Hoda Kotb and viewers that reality TV was not real. She revealed that producers and contestants are told to raise some controversy and tension to make the show more interesting. She informed viewers that reality TV was not simply a cameraman following people around and shooting what was naturally happening. She even challenged a celebrity friend of hers who was on a reality show to admit that it was scripted, as least in part. I was relieved and encouraged. Celebrities were revealing celebrity realities, and it was time to open up the conversation about reality shows.

You could also ask yourself what is real about talk shows. Are the things that happen "naturally" during the interview really natural? Some are. But if you look closely, even when actors are interviewed, you can tell that the surprise movie clips, childhood photos, and new show promos are really not knocking the stars off of their seats. If Matt Damon and Ben Affleck were suddenly reunited for a new documentary about demolition derbies in the middle of *The Tonight Show* with Jimmy Fallon, I'd find myself viewing consciously.

Games Producers Play

In contests, even if contestants are coached, you get to see some reality. It's the same dynamic as when an interviewer leaves the camera on the interviewee too long, hoping they will feel self-conscious and say something revealing about their cosmetic surgery/lover/next movie/last movie. Contest-based reality TV has been a popular form of entertainment for many years and invites you to become one of the competitors. Reality game shows consistently have high ratings and attract sponsors. Early in the game show market, there were programs such as *The Newlywed Game* and *Match Game,* the former for newly married couples and the latter for those hoping to *become* newlyweds. In *The Newlywed Game, y*ou heard how the wife responded when her husband didn't know her favorite movie starring Walter Matthau and compared the spouse's knowledge to *your* knowledge about your *own* partner. It was funny. But only if you didn't get depressed thinking that you and your spouse would be unlikely to win the *Newlywed Game.*

Later, the entertaining game show *Family Feud* focused on relationships within the family. The show, in which two families compete to decide the most popular answers to questions posed to an audience, still airs today. Why? Because you may wonder and hope that your least favorite brother-in-law could remember the most popular sock designer for just one day, focusing on something other than himself. You might think about yourself—*your* coping skills and talents, *your* ups and your downs, *your* family origin. All of this thinking causes you to compare your own life to that of the contestants to see if you come out ahead. Such introspection can be good for you, but what do you do if you come up short? How do you manage the feelings that watching may generate? TV makes you feel. It makes you *compare* yourself to the person on the screen. Skills for managing emotions will make TV viewing a healthier experience. For now, begin with some simple methods by opening up Pandora's box.

Get Reel Game: Pandora's Box

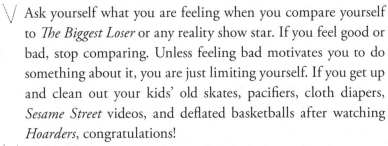

∨ Ask yourself what you are feeling when you compare yourself to *The Biggest Loser* or any reality show star. If you feel good or bad, stop comparing. Unless feeling bad motivates you to do something about it, you are just limiting yourself. If you get up and clean out your kids' old skates, pacifiers, cloth diapers, *Sesame Street* videos, and deflated basketballs after watching *Hoarders*, congratulations!

∨ Notice where in your body you feel the feelings. Check out your heart, gut, navel, ear lobes—all of it! Notice if they feel positive or not.

∨ If the feeling is positive, take it in with a deep breath and feel it fully.

Imagine that you are breathing in your favorite girl or guy's perfume—really breathe it in!

∨ If the feeling is not positive, take a breath and breathe the feeling out with the exhale. Keep breathing until the feeling seems flushed out.

Think of releasing your teenager's old clothes to throw them in the trashcan or tossing an old flame's photo into the Grand Canyon. Feel the relief.

∨ If a negative feeling persists, it is likely that not only did the show generate the feeling but also that it is connected to a deeper sense of insecurity that was there before viewing. Watch two shows with a positive message and e-mail me in the morning. If that does not work, …

∨ Consider whether you can work it through alone or with a friend or if counseling is needed.

One of the emotions that may have surfaced during your delve into Pandora's box is fear. It is often one of the feelings generated by viewing. *Fear Factor* takes reality contests to another level to capitalize on this basic human emotion. Game show contestants are asked to do things that cause tremendous fear, such as hanging from a helicopter or sitting in an isolation pod or an alligator pod while passing poker chips back and forth. It may remind you of your sister or brother chasing you with the boogieman as a child. It was scary and riding a rollercoaster may have been a more pleasant yet still fearful experience. When you can sort out whether it is a fun coaster ride or you are being taken for a ride, raising fears for ratings, you are becoming conscious *("Happy ending" music playing in the background as the frenzy of William Tell Overture fades out, and the whistling wind becomes a cool breeze).*

In It to Win It

Games and contests are a big part of the reality market. While reality TV is still new and expanding in the media industry, the games have been played for a while. Think of a situation, and it could be a reality competition. There are shows for models, singers, drug addicts, island dwellers, and dancers; just about anything could be a reality show. I am waiting for bricklayers to step

And who would ever consider a soap a reality show? You would if you saw *The Bold and the Beautiful.* Producers organized scenes at a homeless shelter to highlight the issues of homelessness. Real people in the shelters were interviewed about their lives there. Producers even integrated homeless characters and/or actors into the program. It's not the first time a soap has addressed a social or health issue, but a live shoot was a sight to see. *The Bold and The Beautiful* raised the issue of prescription drug addiction, alcoholism, transgender issues, and gay relationships, keeping current and politically up-to-date.

forward with "Lay it on me" or "Brick House" themes. Maybe you've even seen Mike Tyson bite off Evander Holyfield's ear. Do you need a network for shock TV so that we can filter all of this to one channel? Some of you would say that we already have a few of these channels. But as viewers get tired of one reality TV show, the Top Ten ratings wane, and new reality shows take its place. Even *Survivor,* the most watched series in 2000–2001, slipped as the years went by to number eleven.

What new ideas will it take to entertain? Perhaps it will take a new twist on the Miss Universe Pageant, boxing, or the Olympics. And your opinion matters in making that decision. Contests have even started giving you a say in how the show ends, with programs like *Dancing with the Stars, American Idol,* and *America's Got Talent,* letting you vote for the winner. Voting gives you a greater sense of involvement and control and involves you more deeply in the outcome of the show. In these cases, it also provides you with outstanding, rocking good entertainment and a chance to jeer at American voters who don't know a good country star from an over-the-top wildly exceptional pop star. You become one of the judges, but you are shaking your head at voters who just can't get it right. Ninety million of them voted during one week for a single *Talent* finale.

Give Me One Good Reason to Watch

So what can you learn from all this that applies to your real life? In my work as a therapist, particularly when using equine-assisted therapy, I can tell you that the way you handle a quiz show or a horse or any ambiguous situation without a lot of rules will tell you how you function in your life. If you sit on the horse and wait for it to decide where it wants to go, you are unlikely to be a leader. If you push the horse using ineffective techniques, you may be a bully who uses force instead of skill. Taking this into account, you are really seeing the true nature of program contestants when they are unscripted and unable to hide their true feelings. And you like to see what is real. It gives you a window into another's reality and a frame of reference for your own life, for better or worse.

> The people and pets that are eliminated on *Survivor, American Idol, Celebrity Apprentice,* the *Kennel Club Dog Show,* the *Miss America Pageant, The Amazing Race, Project Runway, Deal or No Deal, Iron Chef, Top Chef,* or any competition may be coached on how to properly respond to the loss. But only skilled observers like *The Mentalist's* Patrick Jane could probably have figured out how the loser really felt.
>
> The reality show *Intervention* exposes the "elephant in the middle of the room." Family and friends gather to confront a person about

his or her bad habit, such as drinking or using drugs. They surround the person and try to break through the addict's denial that he or she has a problem. The goal is to get the individual to acknowledge that this many people who know and love him/her could not all be wrong and that he/she really does need to get professional help. This is a psychotherapy technique that is not new; however, televising it *is* new.

Interventions have become so common that the word intervention was even tweaked in the second *Sex and the City* movie. Sarah Jessica Parker's character, Carrie Bradshaw, said that her friend Charlotte needed a *friend*tervention because she could not leave home without worrying that her husband might sleep with the sexy nanny. Carrie, who buys too many expensive shoes and may need a *friend*tervention of her own, made this accusation!

This scenario is made funnier by the "club" of women viewers who have seen every *Sex and the City* program since its inception, own the videos, were first in line for the sequel, and attended local breakout parties for the film. This is what I sometimes refer to as the "Seinfeld effect"—a common understanding of a particular program's language and jokes, which has become a kind of "Seinlanguage" by people who so consistently view the program that they form a type of informal insiders' club. By viewing long-term, you become part of the "in crowd" at the office water cooler. To show you're hip, you might respond to a colleague's comment with an often-used *Seinfeld* quote, "Not that there's anything wrong with that," applying it to almost any situation.

Ain't Nothing Like the Real Thing

Media has shaped your words, made you laugh, kept you a part of an insiders' club, and infiltrated your thinking. And reality TV has given you a chance to see real events as they happen.

In one week during September 2009, I witnessed three people admit to inappropriate behavior on national television, with repercussions. Congressman Joe Williams called President Obama a liar and apologized for his inappropriate behavior. He maintained that he had a right to free speech if delivered in an appropriate manner, and although his manner was not acceptable, his opinion was. Serena Williams, tennis pro, yelled at a judge for a call she made that cost Serena the contest. And Kanye West took the microphone away from seventeen-year-old Taylor Swift at an awards ceremony and shouted out his opinion that Beyoncé Knowles had the best music video. He later apologized on the *Jay Leno Show* without clearly saying anything that would explain his behavior.

This is what actually happened during that week. It is not my *opinion* of what happened or the media's "take" on what happened or anyone else's opinion. Our perception of what happened is based on the meaning we attach to what we see, and that becomes our new reality. This new reality depends on how we interpret what we see. But this was powerful television. After watching it, I became more discriminating about what sorts of shows I committed to, because I'd seen, once again, what TV was capable of achieving.

I watched as Dr. Phil commented on these three events on the *Larry King Show*. He was there to give an opinion. His remarks about Joe Williams and Serena Williams were tempered. His opinion of Kanye West was that he was a bully. As a fellow psychologist, I asked myself if I would have said the same. It was a good exercise in conscious viewing for me. It doesn't matter so much what I decided but what you the viewer decided. Did you view these events consciously and decide for yourself if the behavior and the remarks of every newscaster, expert, and newspaper in the country were in line with your own thinking? Or did you objectively decide that you felt differently? If so, then you are developing a *Get Reel* consciousness.

Basically, reality is what *actually* happened. It is not what was devised to lead you toward the *illusion* or story of what happened. It is not what someone thinks about what happened. It is what is concrete, tangible, and what a number of observers would say happened. It is someone turning on a light, walking down the street, blowing up a factory, feeding the homeless. There is no story.

> So by now you realize that *all TV has to have a story.* Even though the cake maker is just making a cake, there is the icing that would not harden, the help that did not arrive on time, the painter who painted the kitchen a horrendous color, the winning or losing the cake contest. Did he really drop the cake when the cat ran across the sidewalk? Get the picture? Without a story, there *is* no story.

When Fiction and Non-Fiction Meet

At this juncture, the plot thickens. You will need conscious viewing skills as you continue to view and read *Get Reel* as well as watch movies and TV. Movies such as the *Da Vinci Code* caused some confusion between what is real and what is not, due to mixing historically correct information with plot elaboration. Confused and sometimes anxious, you wanted to get to the bottom of the story and determine what plot lines were real and which were false.

Documentaries about the film addressed some of the historical accuracies as well as the historical rumors. This is great film making. You are so involved that you want to dissect the film

A physician named Laura told me that in real life she feels like the character Grace on *Saving Grace*—both dark and light at the same time, and tortured by it. Grace's character had helped her to explain her own feelings about herself.

Another woman, a stockbroker named Carol, watched *Hot in Cleveland* and decided that her own life was not so bad after all. She was a middle-aged woman who was divorcing with hesitation, but after seeing Jane Leeves, Valerie Bertinelli, and Wendie Malick starting over, she felt empowered. She knew that their reality was not hers, but the courage of the characters reminded her that she had her own courage.

This brings us to another critical question for conscious viewing: does the show bring out the best or the worst in you? For example, does it remind you that you are brave, powerful, and deserving, or fearful, tenuous, and unpopular? Does it make you understand yourself better or just make you feel worse about yourself?

and learn more. Other viewers were motivated by religious concerns about the film giving false impressions of the church. Again, the movie involved you and made for relevant entertainment by causing you to ask questions. Some viewers were motivated by anger that the author of the story, Dan Brown, would dare to create such a book and movie. But no one was indifferent. Brown had caused a stir. And that is good programming. It is also conscious viewing! By engaging the viewer to discover the truth, the gauntlet was thrown down. You became engaged in a scavenger hunt for the truth and were consciously aware without even realizing it was happening.

In the case of the *Da Vinci Code*, caring about the truth caused the conscious search for the truth. Do you have to care if a show is telling you the truth to view consciously? Maybe not, but if you have had an experience such as curiously viewing the *Da Vinci Code*, you have developed the skill of *getting curious* and can use it whenever you like. And you will most likely apply it without effort since there has been a shift in your viewing habits by becoming a proactive viewer.

Try using your newly enhanced curiosity on this challenge. So far, the feedback networks get is about the number of viewers who watch a show. That should be enough, you say. If you watch the show, obviously you like it. But how do you feel afterward? Are you addicted to the show? Do you come away and experience problems sleeping? If you don't like the actions of a reality/fiction show contestant and can articulately explain why, let the networks know how you feel about the acts and performers chosen. Then watch consciously. Begin to think of yourself as a proactive viewer. To move you along into consciousness, try the reality game Let's Make It Real.

Let's Make It Real

When you play this one, writing down your responses makes them more real. Or take the quiz with others and discuss your results. It will help you to integrate the information. The first question is also a great conversation starter.

What is *your* favorite reality show?

√ Why? What do you like about it?

√ What kinds of stories does the show employ? Do the main characters do something positive that you would like to do? Do they sing, make cheesecake, dance, whisper to dogs, become models?

√ Do they do something that you would never like to do and would only experience on TV?
Do they treat each other badly, become mean girls, and eat worms?

√ Or do they do things that you would never really want to do but secretly enjoy seeing others do? Do they ...
  - have extravagant homes that require a fleet of servants to manage?
  - sit in a boardroom with a powerful executive?
  - travel to dangerous places, sky dive, sail across the world?

In other words, what needs are these shows meeting? What do they tell you about what really matters to you? How you can get more of that in your life?

RxTV for Finding the Reality in the Reality Shows

√ Notice the messages on the screen, both obvious and subtle. The Stooges don't need to hit you over the head with a rubber hammer for you to see that all have a story attached.

√ Be aware that as you watch and discover the messages, it comes more easily with time and is more effortless. Look forward to having a "Eureka! I think I've found it" reaction at least a few times a week. Eliminate anything from your viewing schedule that encourages a trance you don't like.

√ Try stating in one or two sentences what the messages are for shows. If you are stating things like, "Crime doesn't pay," "I would have to have a home gym to get killer abs," or, "This show is biased toward straight heterosexuals/gay pregnant women/mountain climbers/square dancers," then you are on track.

√ Notice how the message makes you feel: positive, negative, or neutral. If you're doing the hip-hop happy dance, keep viewing. If you feel more like the guys in the movie *Hangover*, reconsider.

√ Make some decisions based on your observations. Those decisions can include the following: continuing to view, changing the channel, not watching during that time slot, making a substitution for a current show or viewing habit, or doing something else that makes you happy. It's okay to watch *New Girl* or *American Pickers* instead of the fifth crime show of the day.

√ Share your thoughts about shows with others whom you respect. Use them as a sounding board to get more ideas about

I once experienced bias directed toward me from die-hard fans of a city that had just lost the World Series of baseball. I arrived in their city the next day.

When they found out I was from the city that had won this national sports contest, they would not even speak to me! I was one of those @%^$# fans! The city will remain nameless, but it was clear that the reality contest had become personal, jumping off the TV screen into their lives and mine.

It was time for them to take off the blinders and for me to simply withdraw, turn off the baseball game along with the fans, and live consciously. Once *you* start to view *your* TV screen consciously, you will have the skills to view your life the same way—if you choose to do so.

the messages and biases in the TV programs and movies you watch. If you have a savvy sister or brother, ask them what the message is behind the *Kardashians*. Let me know what they say. I still am not sure.

√ Speak up. Contact the networks and give your opinion about the programming they are showing. They want and need to know to keep viewers watching. If you want a new season of *Sex and the City* or a new boyfriend for Zooey Deschanel, say so.

√ View consciously and ask yourself, what is reality and what is staged reality? Are those eyelashes really the ones she wakes up in?

√ What is presented to cause you to take a point of view? Is the bully cop getting set up to look like the killer of the short, underweight woman wearing pink? Know that he will *not* be the one to go to jail; it's too obvious. Are you seeing backstage clever remarks from one of the competitors of a talent program? Could these remarks increases the likelihood that you will like his oversized hat/beret/bald head/ well-trimmed beard so that you will vote for him?

√ When are you unsure of the message and feel confused, decide whether to watch or not. If you are unsure if the message is pumping up your happy endorphins, you may decide to watch later when the answer becomes clearer to you.

Once you've played Let's Make It Real and you know what you want more of, go out and get some of it in real time. These are the times when you know that TV has heavily influenced you. At these times, you don't need to watch more consciously or read anything about conscious viewing. That is when you find yourself comparing yourself to a character and identifying so strongly with them that their fate has an effect on your own. If you are depressed when your *Bachelor*

Can real life compete with reality TV?

Examine the first family reality show to seek an answer. In the early seventies, PBS followed the Louden family around Santa Barbara to examine the workings of an American family. Then in the 1979 movie *Real Life*, character Albert Brooks, a producer, wanted to make a meaningful, successful film. He based it on the Louden family as a reality series, showing the technology used to create the Louden's experience to let the viewer go behind the scenes.

or *Bachelorette* ends up with the wrong match again and watch faithfully to see not if but when he or she will wise up, then you are too entwined, and the show has affected your mood. You may think of yourself as the girl or guy on the show who always gets overlooked, if you resemble them in some way. On the other hand, when you find a character that perfectly emulates you and helps you see yourself more clearly, the effect is a good one. Should you find yourself shifting your wardrobe to meet your aspirations because a *Celebrity Apprent*ice does the same, you are getting it.

Blurring the lines is necessary to get you to identify with the character or not. Either way, you choose to root *for* them or *against* them. It's TV. It is okay. Just be aware that you are being pulled in. In the past, you may have watched characters you hated to see if they were going to get theirs today. But now you are becoming more conscious. If the ruse no longer fits, you are automatically turning the channel.

Network, Paddy Chayefsky's 1976 satire on network television, could not be more relevant today. He hits the mark with his portrayal of a network dedicated to ratings at the expense of dignity and integrity. Faye Dunaway, almost as if a futuristic robotic model of the human of the future, and William Holden, a vestige of the values of the past, play the leads convincingly. And Peter Finch plays an anchorman who is losing his sanity. He tells us that he's mad as hell and he's not gonna take it anymore, in a statement that has become universally known. With variations, this statement has appeared in commercials and TV as recently as this year.

Finch's character defies the network and the need for manners to voice the sentiment of many Americans. Ironically, the network keeps his ranting on the air, as everyone is interested in seeing not only if Finch's character will survive but also if the network will televise it. The ratings skyrocketed. I knew at the time that they were foretelling a future that could approximate reality. Manners were out the door, and ratings were in. I felt full of gratitude for the newscasters I know who are full of integrity and mismatch the motivations of Chayefsky's characters.

The Price of Letting Go Is Right

Begin your detective work early. Look at how you are responding to *Get Reel*. Be your favorite spy. What are you personally *detecting about TV?* Now that you have become aware of the ways that real events are presented, how reality is shifted to make it more interesting, and how fiction and reality blend together, do you accept or reject it? Consider it? Feel confused and try to read on to figure it out? Get confused and stay confused? Give up? *Accept or reject it?* What you are doing is likely a reality check on your life and on how you will choose to use TV. The level of consciousness that you use here may be a clue to who you are and how much *friend*tervention you might need. These are the same questions you can ask as you consciously view. Are you a serious addict unable to let go of your ideas or habits about TV even when they become transparent? How much of this information are you really considering? If you *accept it, then respect it.*

SpyTV

Star of Your Life: Retrancing with Substitution

Just for fun, create your own reality show with you as the star:

∨ *Detect* a trance that came from TV exposure. Decide if you *accept or reject* it. If you *reject it*, then *replace it.*

∨ Decide what trance you are replacing and what trance you might prefer to *replace* it with. If you think you will never be successful, maybe instead you could choose one thing with which you believe you might be successful. Then see how it could change your life. Ask yourself how substitution of this and other trances could create a perfectly real life.

∨ What is in your perfectly real life?

∨ What do you look like (remember, this has to be real)?

∨ What are you doing?

∨ What is your level of happiness and life satisfaction?

∨ What is the condition of your health? Describe it.

∨ What have you accomplished and *who is there with you?*

This is called a life vision. You have just created a vision of a life worth moving toward. You can almost hear Howie Mandel telling you, "And the winner is *you*!" It's enough to make *Kojak's* Telly Savalas revise his usual inquiry to "Who loves you *back*, baby?" Now watch shows, make friends, read books, and take actions that support your vision.

If you are hooked on TV, you need an intervention. The doctor is in. Dr. Nancy's RxTV for this problem is to enjoy TV but be careful that you don't cut off friends, work, or family to sit and feed your addiction!

Have I dissected reality shows too much for them to be entertaining anymore? Rather I have opened up an awareness, shared by Oliver Wendell Holmes, former Supreme Court justice, that once the mind is expanded to new boundaries and bigger ideas, it never returns to its original state. Watch all you want—but with an expanded point of view. And now that you have done the work, it is time to play.

By now, you may have decided what is good for you and what is not. Substitution is the trance breaker for this chapter. It's important to have substitutes for the things you leave behind so that you don't fall back into watching the same, old programs. So let's visit the top reality show genres that are good for your mind, body, and spirit. They all make great substitutes.

RxTV:

V Let's not leave the topic of reality without visiting the comfort TV of the Food Channel. When you need a warm fuzzy or hot cup of soup, where do you turn? To the many, many shows on the Food Channel that offer you tips on how to cook and entertain, where to find the best diners in the nation, and much more. Chocolate crème brulée and artichoke soup are the new killer detective and hopeless heroine story. Just watching someone cook for you is soothing to the soul. The shows are nurturing, sometimes funny, and often throw down the gauntlet for cooks at home. The cake-baking shows will let you in on how they make a cake into a pool table or an Eiffel Tower. There is no danger to your psyche in these shows unless they make you hungry or spur a strong sense of competition.

V Re-boot in order to use one of your lifelines if your appetite for food calls.
- Do something else for ten minutes; it reroutes your brain.
- Drink water or tea.
- Change the channel.
- Call someone.
- Go outside. Don't take your technology with you—no iPad, phone, or laptop.
- Breathe deeply.
- Phone a friend.

V You might also: Play cards. Stretch. Take a walk. Do something nice for someone. Do something nice for yourself. Grow a plant. List your goals. Go to the grocery store and smile at someone. Read one of Don Miguel Ruiz's books, read my book, *Spiritual Fitness*. Do nothing. Sit, breathe, and relax each part of your body one at a time. Be happy at rest. I think you get the idea.

V The exercise channels offer exercise that includes aerobics, yoga, belly dancing, kickboxing, Pilates, and just about anything else you might want to try. Channels like FitTV and cable on demand network's library of sports and fitness channels offer twenty-four-hour fitness for the physically inclined. Spending time working out with your TV will balance the time you spent inactively in front of it. Add Wii to your TV, and your exercise options are endless.

V Often it is fun to vicariously watch someone you fancy yourself to be, even if only in your dreams. It may be a lot of fun to watch *Who Wants To Be a Millionaire?* before going back to work and earning a paycheck. You have vicariously enjoyed becoming a millionaire, and the viewing statistics for the show prove it! It was the number-one show on TV in 2002. It is harmless, fulfills a need to be wealthy by imagining what it would be like, and allows you to return to your life without selling the farm or relying on your new invention for husking corn to bring in money.

V And remember to use the trance breaker for this chapter: substitution. You know that when you are changing a bad habit that you often substitute a good one to make the change stick! You eat carrots instead of chips, walk to work instead of walking to the mini-mart for chocolate gobs, go to websites about health instead of sites of cooking-show hosts, famous for buttered potatoes with gravy that come with an increase in your health care. Or eat everything in moderation and break any addictions.

The reality chapter's C is:

C—*Calm down.* It will take a while to make new choices. Cable TV wasn't built in a week. You may have to think about substitutions for shows or viewing habits that you are using now until you are ready to make new choices. Pay attention to any illusions in real life that may have come from your TV reality and take the advice from the Moody Blues' "Knights in White Satin": "You decide which is right and which is an illusion."

For more up-to-date information on *Get Reel* for this chapter, go to:

http://drnancyonline.com/category/rc-media-and-rxtv/

http://drnancyonline.com/category/rc-health/

http://drnancyonline.com/category/current-news/

CHAPTER 7

CSI: CRAZY, SCARY, INTENSE

Today, watching television often means fighting, violence, and foul language, and that's just over who gets to handle the remote control. Once the set is turned on, prime-time crime is a killer idea by any standards. So buckle your seats because drama is the one genre where cautions are far greater than in any other. There are more dramas on TV than ever, and that's because, as you know, you are watching them.

Prime-Time Crime

You've secured the remote, are surfing through the channels, and come to something mysterious that catches your eye. The corpse/bloody photo/dismembered head/missing person appears in front of you, and you wonder who it is / why they were murdered or kidnapped / is this really the end. You continue watching out of curiosity and become hooked into figuring it out. You start biting your nails, eating more popcorn or pretzels, and start a conversation with your sister, spouse, friends, or yourself about who is the real villain. The criminal is identified, but there are ten more minutes left in the show, and you are savvy enough and conscious enough now to know that this is not the person going to jail. Or they think they have the real criminal, but one more time he/she slips through their fingers. There is a surprise ending, and you enjoy being taken off guard, marvel at the clever writing, and come back next week for another wild ride. This pattern of a quick start, a high point of tension, some confusion, and a surprise happy ending are very, very popular these days!

There is predictability to every good suspense and drama show on the airwaves, and that is what makes them good. Beautiful people track dirty deeds in less than an hour and with a finality that feels like closure while closure is elusive in real life. You still have undone laundry, your desk is

 Ninety-eight percent of American homes have TV sets, which means the people in the other 2 percent have to generate their own sex and violence.

-Franklin P. Jones

covered with multicolored sticky notes, it's spring/summer/winter/fall and you still have your Christmas tree or Menorah/artificial tulips/outdoor sunflowers or fall leaf wreath up. You have no idea how you will get all of your work done tomorrow while on TV the closure is neat, tight, and clean. But the real crime is that no one is the wiser about what is happening to you while you watch. Research to the rescue—there are clues to the damage that can occur during viewing.

Studies show that a daily immersion of multimedia stimuli is changing your brain. When a high level of media intake is combined with excessive work demands, you may experience symptoms of an ability to only partially pay attention, techno-brain burnout, identified by difficulty with thinking, desperately multitasking, or compulsively ingesting multi-media on TV, computers, smartphones, or iPads. By now, you probably know that the simulated world of media-generated images is just the reel world, not the real world. But if you are having challenges in this area, check to see if you are experiencing any of the symptoms.

There's no need to depart from the reel world into TV rehab; just notice when or if these symptoms occur while you seek closure on the reel screen. You know when to turn the channel before you get caught. And because suspense in TV dramas is important for keeping you until the end and there are many things that have not been revealed. So get the trench coat out again *a la* Columbo and find your hat and sunglasses, as you become the investigator who unravels the suspense shows' mysteries. You can shave your head like *Kojak*, live in a trailer like Jim Rockford of the *Rockford Files*, or have a personal secretary who helps you solve crimes like *Perry Mason*. Perhaps you will model yourself after Matt Dillon on *Gunsmoke* with a cowboy hat and holster. After all, it was the longest-running drama on TV until *Law and Order* came along. You can be as clever as *The Closer*,

Paddy Chayevsky would say that television is not the truth but rather is an amusement park. With a good reality check in place, decide how much drama and suspense you really need and how much you choose to create for yourself.

The Mentalist, or John Reese on *Person of Interest*. You can follow *Law and Order, NCIS, CSI,* or *Boston Legal* reruns to see how the pros solve crimes. Maybe you remain silent like Jake did in *Touch*, but whatever your personal style of getting to the bottom of a good drama, you are truly hooked by these shows.

What Makes Good Drama?

The dramas you view are clearly defined by the culture and the generation. They are intelligent, moving, suspenseful, exhilarating, sometimes scary, other times confusing, always with hidden outcomes and surprise conclusions. But there are many options when it comes

When *As the World Turns* moved from TV to the Internet after a twenty-year run, with a final show watched by ten million viewers, the handwriting was on character Erica Kane's wall. Actress Susan Lucci was now free to be her own character, as are you. Then she found her role recreated for *Hot in Cleveland*.

to the genre that stirs the mind and keeps the blood rushing, accompanied by nail biting and wide-eyed startle responses.

The Many Flavors of Drama

The only people I know who don't watch a lot of drama are the ones with enough of their own. They either get their quota from high-drama or high-stress jobs or their personal lives rival Elizabeth Taylor's. Those who do watch a high level of drama may either be lacking in activities that will create their own real-life drama or those who just love the adrenaline rush. The rest of you fall in the middle, but you all appreciate the wide variety of succulent choices to devour. And there are so many options!

Drama by definition is a serious theatrical production designed to elicit an intellectual, physical, and emotional response. You have to wonder/care/ dislike/like/fear what is happening on the screen, and with drama, you do. The big reveal here is that suspense often includes a crime, identification of the usual suspects, investigation, more or new suspects, and resolution. The better the show, the more surprising the resolution. A variation is that the criminal is revealed, but the hour is spent with the hero/heroine trying to prove the suspect's guilt. You get involved as a backseat sleuth, with powerful, well-presented programs that entertain and stimulate. You took pride in figuring it out before *The Closer* did.

But the concept of drama that holds you in suspense until you discover the ending can also trap you into watching the juicer commercial to discover the secret food for weed allergies or the number of attachments on the master sweeper. Just today on my Internet home page, I saw a promo for a homespun video about a cat and a frog gone wrong. For a second, I wanted to know what happened, then remembered that I have a life. Suspense is a trap into which you fall naturally, as someone starts to say something and stops midsentence, as you catch someone outside the house and have to find out who is there, or receive a package in the middle of the day that must be opened. Suspense is part of the richness of life that comes with certain warnings. And with TV, there are ratings for the warnings. They are:

Early Drama—ED (usually a safe viewing option)
Most Popular—P (come with various other ratings)
Drama and Suspense without Crime or with Less Crime/ Violence—S
Suspense with Crime and Violence—Rated CV

Coming up after the end of this paragraph, soon to be discovered, are some dramas that scream for ratings. Stay tuned, as the suspense is building … *Commercial break … Wait for it … suspenseful music …* Okay, go!

Early Dramas—Rated ED

Early dramas, like family programming, adapted along with the changes in culture reflected by the fifties, sixties, and seventies. Shows with ED ratings begin with *Dragnet*, the first radio drama that transitioned to TV and is now in reruns. The hero, Jack Webb played by John Randolph, was a national icon. He didn't crack a smile or show you the dead body, but he didn't need to do so; the audience loved it. The early dramas could really get your attention with well-written scripts and great acting and were not likely to cause you to wake up screaming in the middle of the night searching under the bed for the murderer/thief/man from Mars/slimy thing.

Mannix was an unpretentious detective who thought that his way was better than a computer's way. He had not yet met the 2012 heroes of *Person of Interest*, whose high-tech machine is one of the show's most critical elements. In 1965, Bill Cosby on *I Spy* was the first black performer with a role equal to his costar, Robert Culp. Then along came the ladies, as women's rights evolved. *Honey West* starred Arlene Francis as a female private detective and Diana Rigg's character, Emma Peel, in the *Avenger* earned a high level of popularity onscreen. But Angie Dickinson, as a feminist *Police Woman*, was an out-of-the-box cultural response to the women's movement. She was the first heroine to have an hour-long show, inspiring others such as *Wonder Woman, The Bionic Woman,* and *Cagney and Lacey*.

> Australian-born Shane Brennan, scriptwriter for *NCIS and NCIS: Los Angeles*, doesn't think that Americans are more into crime shows than people from other countries. The number of shows with foreign translations supports his opinion.

By the seventies, you could choose from multiple heroes in shows like *Charlie's Angels* (three clever women), *Starsky and Hutch* (two sharp guys), *Macmillan and Wife,* and *Hart to Hart* (married couples with a rapport so strong that even Prince William and Kate might be envious). But singles like Buddy Ebsen as *Barnaby Jones*, Don Johnson in *Miami Vice*, Telly Savalas in *Kojak,* or Erik Estrada in *Chips* held first place as heroes.

Heroes with personality evolved into downright funny guys, with Peter Falk as the confused detective *Columbo*, Robert Blake as *Beretta* with a talking bird, and the funniest, Bruce Willis with Cybil Shepard in *Moonlighting.* They were later replaced with the neurotic *Monk,* played by Tony Shalhoub, and Shawn Spencer in *Psych* as a fake yet highly observant psychic detective.

Most Popular—Rated P with Additional Individual Ratings

Elements of a drama may now include varying amounts of one or more of the following ingredients: suspense, crime, mystery, violence, romance, humor, medical examiners, terror, or monsters. The menu can be broken down for your viewing selection, based on what your time, drama tolerance, and stomach can endure. The amount of violence and intensity displayed in drama has increased with time, so consider how many violent images you want on your brain vs. how much comedy/social interaction/documentary/ images you want to store for future recall.

Most popular dramas are getting the most attention because they are culturally relevant, well written, and they really keep you in your seat, despite the violence. So spy on the best of the best and detect the reasons for their charms. Then you can decide how long to view and when to stop to avoid TV rehab. If you're not paying attention when your boss/spouse/ chef/waiter is talking to you or you are trying to frantically eat your Fruit Loops, talk on the phone, and find your lost iPad, then you are due for a healthy dose of non-technology-based real life. For the rest of you, let the games begin. Many that are no longer on the air are available on video.

At the top of the list is *The Sopranos,* a series that revolved around the New Jersey-based mobster Tony Soprano played by James Gandolfini. Tony's challenge, as I see him with a therapist's eyes, after running the crime family, was work-life balance and how to keep from falling for his therapist, Dr. Melfi played by Lorraine Bracco. I still recall the therapy session when Tony knocked off a few people, and Dr. Melfi reflected that he must be feeling very angry. The good message of this drama, as the series came to an end, was not whether Tony gets what is coming to him but when it will occur. *The lure of a show about a power player also draws you into the consequences of the dark side.* Rated CV.

The Good Wife stars Julianna Margulies as Alicia Florrick, whose husband Peter Florrick (Chris Noth), a former state attorney, was jailed following a very public sex and corruption scandal. *How timely.* Rated S.

NCIS with Mark Harmon is eternally popular with *NCIS LA* and *New Orleans* versions taking us to new heights of crime and drama. In 2011, *NCIS* was voted America's favorite television show. The series was the most-watched television series in the United States during the 2012–13 TV season. Rated CV.

Game of Thrones is based on the bestselling book series *A Song of Ice and Fire, Game of Thrones*. It tells the tale of two families, fighting to reclaim the throne, accompanied by a large cast, and by a popular setting, theme, and acting. *Since it also is rated CV for crime and violence, if you watch, do so consciously.*

When her family loses everything, Emily Thorne takes up residence in the Hamptons and is looking to exact *Revenge* on every single person responsible for ruining her life and to enjoy doing so. *You'll need to sidestep the message of the end justifies the means.* Stay conscious and be cautious with kids, especially if your teenager tells you that he had to step on the cat to get to his iPad.

Boardwalk Empire took you back to the 1920s during prohibition to meet Nucky Johnson, Al Capone, and Lucky Luciano. *If you take a stroll down the* Boardwalk*, watch for violence and the usual corruption.* Also rated CV.

Taking a break from crime (mostly) is *Downton Abbey*, a highly popular BBC drama set in the early 1900s through World War One. You will meet the aristocratic Crawley family and their servants from Yorkshire, England, and follow the dramas of both. *It's pure entertainment as long as you don't forget to take out the trash or show up for your wedding rehearsal.* Rated S.

Breaking Bad was the story of Walter White, played by Bryan Cranston, a struggling high school chemistry teacher who was diagnosed with advanced lung cancer. He turned to a life of crime, producing and selling methamphetamine, intending to secure his family's financial future before he dies. *Again, the cause justifies the means shows up in this series, so view consciously and consider letting Big Bird entertain the kids until it's over.* Rated CV.

In *Homeland,* you meet American Marine Sgt. Nick Brody after eight years as a POW in Iraq, held by suspected members of Al Qaeda. After he's rescued, CIA agent Carrie Mathison suspected that he has turned and is plotting an attack on American soil. She finds her answer, and the drama about terrorism continues. *It's current and politically charged.* Rated CV.

Mad Men takes a prize and an unlimited number of awards, epitomizing the fifties and sixties in a prestigious New York City ad agency. You watched Don Draper, a mysterious and talented ad executive, reveal his dark side. *Be sure not to go too far into the darkness with Don and enjoy this show with high viewer ratings.* Rated S with crime.

And the crime show *Empire* is breaking records! Taraji P. Henson, as Cookie, is a new favorite crime ex-wife, following her role in the suspenseful drama show *Person of Interest.*

Drama and Suspense without Crime or with Less Crime/ Disturbing Images (DIs) and Dead Bodies (DBs)—Rated S

Here you found shows without terror, monsters, or heavy violence. Highly rated shows in this category are *Mad Men, Downton Abbey, The Good Wife, West Wing, Friday Night Lights, Glee, Brothers and Sisters, Queer as Folk, The Wire,* and *Smash.* Honorable mention goes to the *Newsroom, Necessary Roughness,* and, of course, *Boston Legal* for variety, humor, acting, scripts, and social relevance.

CSI is seen in nearly thirty countries from daily to multiple times weekly. American shows seem to be more popular than Americans; the show is also popular in places where America is not. Major cities in Syria enjoy *CSI: Miami* multiple times each week.

Medical dramas fall into the suspense without crime group, beginning with *Marcus Welby, M.D., Dr. Kildare,* and *Ben Casey* of the sixties, giving way to *St. Elsewhere* and *General Hospital,* a daytime drama that survived soap opera death row. *Grey's Anatomy,* a long-running hospital show, includes a lot of personal drama and satisfies a need for a powerful nighttime soap, if that's your interest. Speaking of high-interest shows, you had *Perception* with Eric McCormick, or the brilliant *House* who healed the latest mysterious illness. You can safely watch these shows, mostly in reruns with a few look-aways and a caution on the medical shows if you are squeamish about surgeries, stomach gashes, bullet wounds, or broken limbs.

> Dramas contrast with dramedies, such as *Six Feet Under,* and *Drop Dead Diva,* a show in which the now-dead heroine is inhabiting a lawyer's body. In 2013, the diva's dead boyfriend's soul inhabited the body of a criminal on death row who she proved innocent. Try to keep up.

Dramedies

Shows with both drama and comedy include some that fall into two categories—both dramedy and usually one other. Again, here you will find *Boston Legal (S), Drop Dead Diva (S),* and *The Librarians (S).* The rest of the best include: *The Mentalist (S), Psych (S), Harry's Law (S), Desperate Housewives (S), Political Animals (S),* and the ever-popular *M.A.S.H.* These dramas had staying power, since comedy is the favorite genre of a large number of people. And *they take the edge off of the drama, away from heavy breathers to give you a healthy breather.*

> "Television has done much for psychiatry by spreading information about it, as well as contributing to the need for it."
> – *Alfred Hitchcock*

Suspense with Crime and Violence—Rated CV

All suspense with crime and violence obviously comes with a *warning label* and a long history on TV. You will find many more DBs (dead bodies) and DIs (disturbing images). Legal shows sometimes belong in the CV or S category with offerings like *The Closer* and *Suits,* a Wall Street style drama with high-fashion stakes.

People who watch forensic and crime dramas on TV are more likely than non-viewers to have a distorted perception of America's criminal justice system, according to new research from Purdue University. Popular legal shows might influence how TV influences viewers' attitudes, according to Glenn Sparks, a professor of communication. They found that people who watch criminal justice shows routinely are more likely to overestimate the frequency of crime. Susan Huelsing Sarapin, who did research with Sparks, reported that TV crime viewers who watched a great deal estimated two and a half times more real-world deaths due to murder than those who did not view heavy crime shows.

The next step for these researchers is to determine how attitudes and beliefs formed by watching crime shows translate to actual proceedings in the courtroom. If an impact is found, there could be major implications for anyone involved in a legal matter. Some states already allow the juror screening process to include questions about their television viewing.

Sparks and Sarapin's study sparked a discussion of "mean world syndrome," where people start to think about the world as a scary place. Some people develop a fear of being victimized. Sarapin indicates that this belief can affect their feelings of safety and comfort.

To determine if you have been left with lasting frightening images that might impact you, ask yourself, "What is the scariest image I've ever seen on TV?" Many involve an image of an undead/monster/serial killer/animated vulture or other unreal image. The mind may be able to dismiss them as impossible, but they still disturb the memory. It depends on how you answered the scariest image question. If you are having nightmares about them, then absolutely yes. Do they out-scare images on the news or non-fiction dramas that could be real

In a recent study, researchers at Indiana University showed people episodes of *24, The Sopranos,* and others, with all the violent scenes cut out. Turns out, the test subjects said they enjoyed them *significantly more* than people who saw the original versions situations? Well, did your "scariest image" answer have anything to do with a reality show or real news show image that you witnessed? Fiction is designed to be scary and news informative, yet you can be affected by either of them if they are on your scariest list. If you have too many scary images to choose the scariest one, it is time to read this chapter with eyes wide open and inject look-aways into programs with frightening images if you feel you just must watch. Think of finding your sweet spot between enough and too much suspense/crime/violence/scary stuff.

 The timely but short-lived yet ambitious drama *Rubicon* in 2010 gets a nod for timeliness in a show about the enormity of national security in a complex government. It was a sobering reflection on what was happening in the US.

Cops and Robbers have been plentiful ever since the comedy *Car 54 Where Are You* in the sixties. Things got more serious with *Hill Street* Blues in the eighties when this documentary-style groundbreaker came to your TV screen, winning eight Emmy awards. The use of slang and sexual situations was bold and sometimes met with resistance but has influenced TV ever since. This show was controversial at the time, but today's cop shows would make this one seem tame. Then *NYPD Blue* contained more violence while *The Wire*, a show about gang violence, corruption, cops, and criminals was a complex picture of Baltimore's troubles. Again, consciously notice that the degree and amount of violence is increasing with time. *Blue Bloods* has a more family-oriented sophistication.

Longmire entered in 2012, a show with a theme reminiscent of *Walker Texas Ranger* or even *Kung Fu*, in which the hero righted wrongs. And who doesn't like to see the good guys win? But *Copper* was about an Irish cowboy in the 1864 post-civil war era who does the right things for the wrong reasons. Again, *a caution for kids,* so watch but without the wee ones around. And *Copper* fits into the category of a multifaceted show like these next ones.

Western series became popular in the forties and fifties when they moved from radio to TV. In the sixties, they became multilayered; *The Wild Wild*

According to a study from Purdue University, supported by their department of communication, evidence suggests that crime shows have inspired people to pursue careers in forensic science and law enforcement.

West was a winner that ran from 1965 to 1969, combining a Western with a James Bond-like espionage thriller. When *Dr. Quinn Medicine Woman*, starring Jane Seymour, came to TV in the nineties, winning Emmy awards, a cowgirl had emerged with added interest of cowboys, Indians, and medicine, again layering genres, so it's more interesting. *Justified* in 2010 had a theme of a US marshal as an old western hero, again adding dimension to the everyday ordinary cowboy which is appealing to a new level of viewer sophistication. James Spader in *Blacklist* is his own kind of cowboy issuing renegade and violent justice.

Crime/legal shows abound. The reason has something to do with a universal fascination with death that has been on the agenda of most cultures since the beginning of time. "How did he die, who did it, and why" are all questions the mind presents. If the victims' circumstances resemble yours,

British-born David Schmid at State University of NY at Buffalo is the author of *Natural Born Celebrities: Serial Killers in American Culture*. Schmid speaks of crime writing and feels that while researching a subject you have to be simultaneously involved with it, and, at the same time, you have to keep it at a distance. Good advice for viewing crime shows, too!

you may begin to wonder if it could happen to you. Keep in mind that unless you are a very important spy/have a lot of money/walk alone at night/rip off your boss/date crazy people, or resemble Daniel Craig, you are probably safer than you think. Shows with victims include the ever popular *CSI, CSI Miami, NCIS, Law and Order, Law and Order: Special Victims Unit, Castle, Damages, Rizzoli and Isles, Hawaii 5-0,* and *24* to name a few of the most watched. Others of interest to viewers were *Cold Case, Criminal Minds, Rookie Blue,* and *Burn Notice*. Sometimes, as in *CSI* or *Rizzoli and Isles*, forensic science is critical to solving the crime. This is when your scientific mind gets engaged because scientific inquiry is one of the most potent motivations to stay interested. Just tune out if you are squeamish about autopsies. And any show that tells you there is a crime scene in the title like *CSI—Crime Scene Investigation* or *CSI: Miami* is a dead giveaway that there will be a corpse as the lead-in actor. *Hit & Miss*, about a British transgender assassin (you are now a conscious person, so you heard the word "assassin"), promises corpses.

Other shows of special interest included *Perception,* a series in which an extraordinarily gifted professor with schizophrenia solved crimes. While most schizophrenics aren't this well put together, it makes for an exciting twist; just don't imagine that *all* schizophrenics are as smart as Eric McCormick's depiction. *Touch* also fell into the special category about an extraordinarily gifted mute child who led people globally to the truths that set them free. His nemesis was the government, who tried to kidnap him for research purposes. These special people are so likable since they are more interesting than your neighbors, Bess and Fred; hence, the wide viewing audience.

Fantasy/high-tech dramas such as *Homeland, Blacklist,* or *Person of Interest* use sophisticated technology to prevent crimes, solve murders before they occur, and combine personal skills with technology. But the idea of a high-tech drama isn't novel. Movies such as *Time Machine, The Matrix, Total Recall,* and *Avatar* inspired you to transcend human capacities and limitations. Even comedies such as *Back to the Future* and Woody Allen's *Sleeper* used technology to accomplish the impossible. And if you recall Woody's orgasmatron, you might wish that it wasn't so impossible. Overcoming limitation with science or magic is a human fantasy, from the time you have dreams of flying until the time you develop a fantasy of recapturing your youth. Don't tell me you haven't imagined a problem magically disappearing! Even if you can't magically make warts disappear or transport yourself back to a simpler time in your personal life, you can have a great time watching a machine that keeps the flower shop manager/corrupt banker/

British-born David Schmid at State University of NY at Buffalo is the author of *Natural Born Celebrities: Serial Killers in American Culture.* Schmid speaks of crime writing and feels that while researching a subject you have to be simultaneously involved with it, and, at the same time, you have to keep it at a distance. Good advice for viewing crime shows, too!

hotel owner/favorite spy from being assassinated by his brother-in-law/
girlfriend/dog-sitter.

What's Drama Got to Do With You?

You have a lot to do with what is acceptable and desirable on TV. You have
reshaped what was once acceptable on TV with the goal of creating a more
humane environment. You can see the effects if you note the early black
and white *Tarzan* show in which Olympic swimmer Johnny Weissmuller
starred. He wrestled a rhino, a tiger, and an alligator—overpowering
them on camera with brute strength and fancy film work. You can't get
away with that today. HBO's *Luck,* a former drama about horse racing,
was canceled after the death of three of the horses and pressure from the
People for the Ethical Treatment of Animals. Your complaints show that
you won't stand for the abuse of animals. This is what I am talking about;
your voice *does* make a difference.

And there's more in the "what's that got to do with you" category.
Reasons you like certain shows can be very revealing. An old series called
the *Rogues* enjoyed popularity because the protagonists stole from the rich
and kept the goods for themselves in a hedonistic way. Getting away with
something for personal gain/fun/excitement/selfishness and little regard for
rules are at play here. As you watch, you vicariously get to be the bad guy,
have fun, get revenge, or kill the guy who stole your garden hose. It reveals
a darker side of the personality called the shadow, or side that you prefer
not to see and, even more, don't want anyone else to see. Your shadow gets
to come out and play vicariously during a drama. So put on your Sherlock
Holmes coat, and you may discover exactly why *you* like crime and drama
shows so much!

Crime Doesn't Pay Quiz

What was the worst crime you ever committed? Come on, nobody will ever know. As a therapist, I have heard it all, so you can't shock or surprise me as much as the dry cleaner who lived down the street, who once confessed he had torched his mother-in-law's business for the insurance. Hey, I once accidentally robbed a minister of a postcard. Yes, it was an accident, and if you don't ask, I won't tell. And if you are honest with yourself, that's all that matters. Did you:

____ Smoke marijuana (without inhaling, of course)

____ Buy/sell marijuana

____ Steal money from a cookie jar/drawer/purse

____ Sneak cigarettes from your parents/friends/music teacher/karate instructor

____ Drink beer/wine/Kahlua/Jack Daniels when underage

____ Shoplift that pair of Nikes/earrings/jeans you just had to have

____ Vandalize or paint graffiti on your school/bully's house/a bridge/rocks

____ Park in a handicapped spot

____ Sneak extra people into the drive-in movie to see *Star Wars/ Planet of the Apes/Hard Day's Night/Godzilla Meets the Blob/* other movie

____ Cheat on your taxes

____ Destroy your sister's Lego house/your science project/evidence

Crime Doesn't Pay Quiz
(continued)

Now, ask yourself, what was your motivation? More than one can apply.

____ Fun

____ Getting away with something/rebellion

____ Making a statement

____ Revenge

____ Acquiring or saving money/goods

____ Selfishness/little regard for rules

____ Covering your tracks

____ Impulsivity or passion

____ Not knowing any better

____ Attention

____ Juvenile insanity

____ Stupidity

____ Dark intentions

____ Excitement

____ Personal gain

____ Other

What did you decide? Keep your spy coat on while you check out the SpyTV for this chapter to see why your motivations matter.

SpyTV

Detect the *pattern of motivations* that you see in your life and on TV. It's time to choose which shows and actions you want to take in your own life. *Detect* which motivations of your own match those of the criminals you see on TV. The thief/murderer/sexual harassing boss/jilted lover/obsessive fan/career criminal has similar motivations, and so you sometimes actually identify with the criminal! Then *detect* how it makes you feel to act out of selfishness, revenge, fun, or impulsivity, if the patterns still exist. *Accept or reject* your motivations and actions as ones that will bring you a real conscious life. If you *accept* your motivations, then you can *respect* them. If you *reject* them, then you can *release* them with the trance breaker for this chapter, *aversion*.

To use *aversion* to break a trance of revenge, selfishness, or other motivation in yourself or an addiction to shows in which the criminals do the same, decide what motivation you would like to adopt as a *substitution* instead. If you had to view *American Horror Story* out of *selfishness* at the expense of everyone else in the family, picture the negative responses you got from them. If you found yourself ruthlessly viewing the *Copper* (rated CV) marathon due to a *need for excitement*, then you may decide that there are less intense ways to find excitement. Remember to *substitute* safer routes to excitement. You could catch a few reruns of a simpler time when *The Little House on the Prairie* was the Western of choice, or just change the channel all together and go to comedy or reality (not reality TV, your own).

Rene Balcer, *Law and Order*'s executive producer, believes that crime dramas have been popular in every culture around the world. He reminds us that the first story ever told was Adam and Eve, a love story. The second story was Cain and Abel.

Then it is time to continue with *aversion*. Think, for example, of times when you acted out of selfishness and how you felt afterward. If you parked in the handicapped spot, snuck cigarettes, or had to see the *NCIS* marathon, think of the guilt that followed. Think of how you felt, which thoughts were running through your head, any feelings in your stomach, heart, or chest. Now add to that, times when TV criminals or dramatic characters acted out of selfish motives, and think of how that makes you feel. Did you respond with the same distaste as with your own meager criminal past? Add your displeasure at the screen to the strong sense of displeasure that you felt for yourself. Are you having an adverse reaction to too many violent memories? This is *aversion*, and it is designed to cause you to turn away from any levels of suspense/violence that cause the adverse reaction. It's much like picturing a pound of fat/health problems/shortened lifespan all at once when trying to lose weight.

Then you can *substitute* a behavior of finding a win/win outcome, acting selflessly, or finding another more empowering strategy instead of selfishness. It can help you to break any viewing or life habit that you want to change. "Get sick of the old by overwhelming yourself with unpleasant images then substitute something new" is a formula for success.

Again I assure you that all of this knowledge does not ruin suspense for you. It makes you a conscious viewer who now understands why you like a certain show and what needs it may meet for you. It keeps you in a state of active attention rather than mindless entrancement. You will begin to notice not just who may have committed the crime but why it appeals to you and the techniques used by the producer to entice, hold, and amuse you. When you watch the TV awards, you could begin to develop an interest in seeing not only the stars but also David E. Kelley. Look that up in your Funk and Wagnall, or if you were born after 1980, then Google.

Making a Case to Rule Out Heavy Violence: Monkey Mind

If you remember from chapter 1, Gerard Echterhoff of Jacobs University in Germany wrote about mirror neurons in the brain. These neurons may cause you to feel empathy for the good guy and make you care about the outcome of the show, keeping you engaged in viewing. In his work at the University of Toronto at Scarborough, he explains how emotionally charged brutal, violent images trigger mirror neurons. As a result, they are more likely to become a part of the memory. They can result in nightmares and stored images of violent scenes, resulting in greater fear of the outside world. That fear may keep you at home watching and storing more violent images. Since the saving grace of the show's message is usually that there is justice in the end, some of the fear may be allayed, but the unrealistic estimate of how much crime exists in society remains.

There is another caution about watching violence on TV. In Echterhoff's work at Jacobs University, he also explains the phenomenon of false recall. Because people see someone performing an action on video, their brain simulates the action as if they were doing it themselves—falsely recalling actually doing it. As a result, they experience the empathetic mirror neuron effect. This could make violence viewing a precarious pastime. If you think you have done things that you witnessed on TV in the past, are you desensitized to performing the crime?

The Mirror Neuron System (MNS) Explains Monkey Behavior, Nut Attraction, and the Power of Sound (MNS)

The *Spirituality and Health* article, "Neurons of Compassion," explained that the mirror neuron system (MNS), possibly one of the most important discoveries of modern science, was discovered in 1995 because of an ice-cream cone and peanuts. It all happened at the University of Parma, Italy. Monkeys' brains were studied with small wires that could detect if the outer layers of cells were giving off electrical signals. While the monkeys indulged in the peanuts, the cells would fire, showing sequentially the activity of the mouth, hands, and fingers.

One afternoon, the research technician left the monkey hooked up to the electrode recorders and headed to lunch, taking a gelato back to the lab. He noticed that the monkeys had watched him eating his ice-cream cone, so he decided to check to see what their brain activity was during viewing. Even though the monkey had only watched him eat the ice cream, the brain neurons responded as if the monkey was actually eating the ice cream! The monkey's brain was "mirroring" what the experimenter was doing.

Why would the brain of a monkey or possibly a human for that matter simulate an experience simply by observation? Let's revisit the monkeys for a lesson in *anchoring,* a technique you learned in the politics chapter and *observational learning,* a technique from the beginning of *Get Reel.* Both anchoring and observational learning are solid foundations for understanding, and yet some researchers deny mirror neurons.

Technicians performing the experiment had the monkeys watch as they ate a peanut. The results were the same whether the monkeys were eating the peanut or watching it eaten by someone else. And there was another twist; if the monkeys simply heard the sound of a peanut being cracked open, even when it was out of their sight, their brains showed the same firing pattern as if they were cracking open and eating the peanut themselves. The sound had become anchored to eating. The same occurs to you when you hear someone crunching chips while you are viewing TV.

Think of the sounds of "freshness" in the ads for the super-sized, fried veggie wrap that comes to mind. You can merely hear the sound of the commercial or TV show in the background, and the brain makes a quantum leap into being there. You may recall the smell of a super-sized taco burger and dive into one.

For food ads, there is a short distance from having such a strong connection to hearing a sound and eating the food. But with the scary stuff, you experience the fear response generated by the scary music while the response becomes stronger each time you hear the eerie sounds of the ghost in the bathtub/ woods/armoire/briefcase. Certain music becomes an anchor for the shark about to jump out of the water and eat someone's arm/head/lunch. It all makes viewing far more experiential, and while the music from the movie *Out of Africa* may generate sweet nostalgia, the sounds from movies cause auditory anchors that keep you highly engaged whether you want to be or not. They contribute to the sense of suspense, the crime about to be committed, and the murderer coming up from behind the next victim or the twist in the plot about to emerge. You can even tell when two lovers will come onto the screen because you will begin to hear "their song."

I Feel Your Pain

In the grand scheme of research, the question remained, of what use were the neurons to human life? What purpose could mirror

Humans are the most imitative of living creatures according to the ancient Greek philosopher Aristotle, reports a *Spirituality and Health* magazine article on the MNS.

neurons have? Researchers began to look at baby primates.

Both young monkeys and human babies imitate parents' facial movements. Babies smile when they see their parents' faces. They move their mouths to eat and then to talk. They learned to imitate with their hands as they watched elders throw spears and start fires. Watching caused their brains to start mirroring as if they were actually completing the actions themselves. *The brain mirrored the behaviors so they could more easily learn to perform the actions.*

The implication is overwhelming for the viewing of violence. Does viewing of violence cause a memory for having completed the act? At least, the mirror neurons hold the memory. I can tell you that people have memories of some movies viewed on TV that they would love to remove. Scenes from *Blue Velvet, Cape Fear,* and *Interview with a Vampire* have haunted many since the viewing experience. It's because you're focusing on a face, asking what is the intention behind the beady/sharp/enigmatic/narrow eyes. You look, and you look harder. You ask yourself, "Are you the thief/murderer/swindler/safe cracker?" The more intently you view, the more the brain continues to attend, and the more the images become embedded in your mind. And you blink less, compromising your vision. At this point, you are not far from feeling a reaction of *aversion*, and may want to think of a new strategy to replace watching distasteful or haunting programs. *Substitution* would work here. You don't usually experience nightmares after viewing Comedy Central live or a documentary on aquatic life, such as swans/penguins/whales/dolphins.

And it raises the issue again of the positive potential of TV to teach. Is there a logical conclusion that viewing martial arts makes you a kung fu master? To a degree, yes, but you actually have to mimic the movements and practice to get the full effect. Having the neurons brings you to a place where accomplishing spear throwing or self-defense becomes easier. You have a sample of the behavior in your memory, and the mind thinks that the behavior has been completed. Try visualizing a perfect judo hold, golf swing, or even seeing your body healthy, and you may get powerful results.

Furthermore, studies from University of California Los Angeles (UCLA) show that humans experience psychological pain when they feel empathy with a victim. The pain forms the foundation for compassion. The studies show the same result for physical or emotional pain. Watching on the screen triggers emotions that result in empathetic reactions in your own brain. The more

> The MNS helps you better understand why children who watch large amounts of violence on television may begin to demonstrate aggressive behavior and reduced impulse control. Because the brain is wired to keep you connected to the outside world and what is happening there, that connection repeats within you as if it were your own experience.

you identify with a character, find them to resemble you, or have the same experiences as you, the greater the level of compassion. Because compassion is highly activated during the viewing of TV programs, you may have cried to see the islanders die on *Lost*, to witness Henry's helicopter crash on *M.A.S.H.* as he was killed on the way home from the war, or while watching the Huntsman get his heart ripped out by the evil queen on *Once Upon a Time*. Once you feel compassion, you care and you view again. Although recent studies question mirror neuron theories in humans, the effects of heavy violence viewing remain.

And when you see love on screen, you feel happy for the lovers, and, in a secondary way, you have an experience of that love. The Lifetime Channel is a good place to go for this experience. The life lesson here is that when you notice which characters you identify with in TV shows and in your real life and begin to really notice the impact that it has on you, you'll make the best possible choices in viewing and life. Perhaps this is one reason why research has shown that happy people who have happy friends are happier people.

Clearing Your Slate

If you can learn how to use a fork by viewing your mom do so, then you can learn to improve your golf game/ tennis game/leadership/dance skills/ relationships/health by imitation, too. Whether you watch these things

His Holiness the Dalai Lama tells us that if we want others to be happy, that we should practice compassion.

on video or TV or in real life, viewing is a prerequisite for much of what you learn. And there is so much more to learn and achieve. Vilayanur Ramachandran, an MNS researcher, believes however that while a monkey could reach for a peanut, only humans, because of their adequately developed mirror neuron systems, can accomplish great things.

It's fairly imperative, when accomplishing great things, to focus your mind and/or take action, which can be a challenge if you have too many conflicting messages, images, and memories in the brain. You may have visual memories of traumas, bad break-ups, and mismatched golf apparel that you want to erase. When you think of them, a sort of video plays in your mind, complete with sound and visceral feelings. If the mental replay of a break-up is running, replay it and look for cues that were there long before the final curtain. There were probably signs of trouble that you missed, and so the mental DVR replay can help you learn from experience, giving you a greater feeling of completion. You can note the red flags of a troubled relationship and be more aware if they pop up in the future. You can use this exercise for any life pattern that seems to repeat itself. Then it is time to heal. Unpleasant memories can have the heavy emotional charge that is attached to them lifted, and the memories can even be shifted so that there are more empowering ones to store in your memory. After all, why settle for memories of deep disappointment when you can transform them into hope? If you have an anchor or memory that remains troublesome, there are therapeutic cures. You may consult a therapist or try the suggestion below to get started now, if the memory is not intense.

To begin with one simple remedy, start to notice the continual stream of thoughts that go through your mind during the day. Observe them from a distance. Watch as you would watch TV with awareness, as a conscious observer, but this time don't participate, just observe. See what pops up. Notice if you obsess about who will win on *The Bachelor* or how the finale of *The Closer* affected the spin-off. Now because you have started to pay attention and because you are merely observing without involvement, the activity of the mind will shift. Negative thoughts may change slightly because it is less threatening to let thoughts come up. You are less involved, so you may be able to allow thoughts to surface without feeling threatened/bored/judged by the content. Now try "mind washing." Each time a thought emerges, take a breath and release the thought during the exhalation, as if sending it off with the breath. This is a good exercise to do after viewing and before bed to clear your mind of TV images, have a higher quality sleep state, and experience more pertinent dreams without the daily clutter that builds up in the mind. It's preventative for stress relief, at no cost to the observer, and beats high health-care costs. The following guidelines can assist with knowing when to dump the image of the shooting/robbery/car crash/ghoul/prisoner/vampire on steroids.

Take a Look in the Mirror: Ten Times to Shut Down the MNS

While viewing violence on TV, you can determine if the image is upsetting or disturbing to you. The visual images that occur during these times are powerful enough to stay with you. The key is to notice whether you experience any or all of the following thoughts or physical responses:

1. You feel disgust, fear, or extreme judgment while watching. (Not at yourself, at the criminal.)
2. You have a sick feeling in your gut. (You're such a conscious viewer.)
3. You have seen a show before, and you had images you could not shake. (Nightmares of JR Ewing III, making one of his many vile faces, perhaps.)
4. You begin to have symptoms of a stress response such as sweaty palms, rapid heart rate, or holding your breath. (Step away from the violence.)
5. A character sickens you viscerally. (Another conscious viewer trait.)
6. The show is using gratuitous violence and/or derogatory sexual scenes. (Do you really need to see another bloody victim/gun shot/ street fight at close range?)

7. You have been up too late and the show has you trapped, unable to go off to sleep. (Use *aversion*—think of your morning alarm going off.)
8. You consciously know better than to view what you are viewing. (Use *substitution, aversion and/or choice* to change the channel.)
9. You have seen this series before, and you know that it upsets you. (Experience is such a great teacher.)
10. Ineffective behaviors to reduce anxiety kick up during viewing. (Are you mindlessly eating, nail biting, yelling at the criminal out loud, jumping around the room in a trench coat?)

To reduce these symptoms, "Take a look in the mirror."

Take a Look in the Mirror

By doing this exercise, you may begin to develop the ability to be more aware of TV-based images you are storing on a daily basis. The same applies to Internet images. Decide how many of your daily thoughts contain the following ideas or similar ones. Check each item that applies.

____ What will a next episode of your favorite new show bring to the series?

____ Faces of actors

____ Memories of scenes

____ Visions of movies or TV shows that you liked and would like to see again

____ Disturbing flashes of TV content, a flash of a corpse, a bloody victim of violence, the cat falling off the roof on *America's Funniest Videos*

____ Memories of shows that relate to your personal experiences (*Seinfeld* memories not included; they are closely related to life experiences) such as memories of someone stealing your wallet, calling you on the phone after a fight, or tripping and falling at an inopportune time

---

The last item shows you how you make comparisons between your experiences and the ones that you watch on TV. How did it work out for the actor who was robbed, relieved, or embarrassed? Are you comparing your experience to theirs? These real-life comparisons to reel life are ones to watch consciously. This is not a dress rehearsal or a fictional experience. It is *your* life, and you won't win when comparing your life to the life of the model/biggest loser/*American Idol* winner/unhappy husband/schizophrenic professor.

RxTV: Cleaning Out the Closet

This exercise is applicable for any real-life experience. Remember that images are designed to be unforgettable. Anyone who has ever seen Gloria Swanson's face during the final scene of the movie *Sunset Boulevard* knows this. So it's time to release thoughts you identified during the Take a Look in the Mirror exercise. Use these RxTV prescriptions for letting go of thoughts from a distracted or overly full mind, or when you are flooded with too many images.

√ Notice the thought and see it leave you with the breath as you exhale.

√ See the thought roll away on a wave in the ocean, towed away by the current. This is another use for "mind washing."

√ Use the trance-breaking technique from the reality chapter, *substitution*. Deliberately think of something else and move in a new direction. Refocus on an empowering image and see it push the old image away from you with a slingshot-like push.

√ If you recognize patterns of disturbing media-related or other images, consider changing your activities to avoid stacking more of these images on top of one another, strenghtening the likelihood that the images will recur in the memory. For example, if you continually envision the dead body that is revealed at the beginning of many crime shows, tape the show, fast-forward beyond that part, and get to solving the mystery. My friend Ann, who is a personal trainer, needs to fast-forward beyond the theme song of Perry Mason reruns because it hammers in her memory all day.

√ If as you observe, you notice that disturbing or violent images run through an entire show, it's time to consider whether it is worth it to view. You may have to detox your brain after viewing in the same way you do after consuming too much fatty/salty/sugary/chemical-filled food/beer during Octoberfest.

√ If after using the RxTV, the thoughts don't diminish, you will need more time, assistance, and perspective. Accept where you are and decide what you want to do about it. Ask for help if you feel that you need it.

√ Don't be lulled into a false sense of security, thinking that you can just overdose on drama and violence and then simply breathe it away. Remember that violence viewing has a cumulative effect of creating a fear of the world outside of TV Land.

About Children and TV Violence

Whether televised violence is harmful to children was one of the first motivations for TV research. You may recall that young children presented with a punching bag were more likely to hit it after watching aggressive shows on television. But there is more to the story. Children's cartoons with violence that don't show consequences interrupt a child's growth in the area of decision making about actions that are potentially damaging.

And bullying and put-downs (subtle bullying) in comedies rarely portray the negative effects of such behavior in real life. Insult humor and bullying are epidemic, causing real-life schools to mandate bully-prevention programs. And the stress levels that are raised while watching bullying have

A study cited in a Scandinavian pediatric medical journal, *Acta Paediatrica*, found that symptoms of sympathetic nervous system activity, indicative of a stress response, were higher for middle-school boys after viewing violent video games.

been documented. The C for this chapter can raise conscious viewing for your children, too. Watch with them and talk about the consequences experienced by people who would perform televised actions in the real world. Note if shows give messages that misbehaviors are acceptable if it works out okay in the end. Let your children know that it doesn't work that way.

C—Note consequences for the characters. What messages does the show give about outcomes of characters' actions? Does crime sometimes pay? Watch these messages consciously and especially when viewing with children.

For more up-to-date information on *Get Reel* for this chapter, go to:

http://drnancyonline.com/category/rc-media-and-rxtv/

http://drnancyonline.com/category/current-news/

CHAPTER 8

DO YOU BELIEVE IN MAGIC?

Sci-Fi History Rap

Superman was the first, and George Reeves stars in this first verse,

Lost in Space moved to another land then came *Star Trek's* Spock pointy-eared Vulcan,

The X-files still are viral and live, *Battlestar Galactica* came in 1965,

Who wouldn't love the *Six Million Dollar Man*, then *Babylon 5* stole *Star Trek* fans,

Matt Groening animated *Futurama* in '78, while *Battlestar Galactica* rose as one of the greats,

Recent hits were *Flash Forward* and *V,* but couldn't compete with reality TV,

Now *True Blood* and *Twilight* bring vampires glory while others watch *American Horror Story,*

Spacemen, monster, and ghouls are still the rage, on Facebook and Google, more than *Frankenstein's* page,

But black and white classics still draw fans, and *Svengoolie* has a silly vampire clan,

Who follow him on Saturday night, since you still crave your dose of fright!

This chapter is brought to you by the new sci-fi hero, Writer Woman. Writer Woman knows good sci-fi and things supernatural and spiritual. She knows all about things that go bump in the night. Whether the topic is simply a superfast superhero or a real trip to heaven in the sky, get ready to explore it all … with Writer Woman.

Since dramas include so many supernatural themes, you will be guided through a whole chapter on the subject, and I know there are many of you who are happy about that. The reason I know that sci-fi fans are out there dates back to 2006. I was walking through downtown Pittsburgh (referred to as "dahn tahn" if you are a local resident) and found myself weaving my way through people dressed in costumes with furry bodies topped with animal heads. Imagine! Thousands of people wearing furry costumes, and it wasn't even Halloween.

So as not to keep you in unnecessary suspense, I will tell you that there is a national convention that is held in our town called the Anthrocon, the world's largest *furry fan club* in the world, with a Guinness world record of most mascots in a parade. Apparently the fursuit parade brought out enough members willing to design and wear their favorite costumes of fictional nonhuman characters with human characteristics to gain this prestigious record. It was clear that the print and television media have had an eerie influence on otherwise normal people.

Are you asking yourself why anyone would do such a thing? You would most likely pose this question if you weren't such a fan of the supernatural. If you are, then you know that

 There are forty Anthrocons in the world, with the largest one in Pittsburgh. The focus is on furries, anthropomorphic animal characters. Recent attendance was 5,179 with 1,044 furry costumes in the furry parade

these supernatural beings have strength, magic, talent, superpowers, and histories that would dwarf the greatest athletes, futurists, and inventors of our world. They are superheroes that can make or break anyone or anything with their supernatural gifts, and you wish you had their skills. If you had a Superman or Wonder Woman suit for any Halloween of your life or were ever a Star Trekkie, you know what I mean.

When William Shatner told his Trekkies to get a life on *Saturday Night Live*, he was speaking to everyone who is too wrapped up in fiction to live in the real world. The last time I saw Shatner, he admitted that he was more like the arrogant Denny Crane of *Boston Legal* than anyone else he had ever played in a movie, TV, on stage, or in an advertising role. But he also was very careful to say that no one should idolize him or the characters in any of his roles or see him as any better than anyone else just because he was a celebrity. He sang the song "Real" just to prove it, where through his lyrics, he admitted that just because you've seen him on your TV, it doesn't mean he's any more enlightened than you.

Okay, so now that your feet are on the ground, courtesy of Shatner, and your furry suit is hung in the closet for another year, let's explore your secret, spectacular superhero favorites. You can learn from them and use them as a tool while keeping a safe grasp on reality. It's very common to want at least one superpower! Come on, you can admit it. It's safe here. Haven't you ever wanted an intergalactic being to write the best term paper (bearing your name) ever submitted to your university? Or maybe you wanted a blond good witch or warlock to create a dust broom to clean with a twitch of the nose or a simple incantation? Perhaps you wanted a futuristic pilot to travel through the air and deliver you to work in a lofty spaceship, immune to rush-hour traffic. If you have, then you probably enjoy great moments in sci-fi. Yet you may be the superhero that you have overlooked while gazing at the talented heroes outside of yourself. Perhaps your trance is one of heroes as those with magic.

Wish I May, Wish I Might

Supernatural powers are anything that a superhero can do that falls outside the realm of science as you know it. Human and inhuman heroes as well as human mutants can have telepathy, superhuman strength, fangs, superfast healing, wall-climbing skills, telekinesis (ability to move objects), and many more traits that the average person may wish they had. But, really, which heroes would you morph into if you had a chance to, with wish fulfillment? Wishing you had the ability to rapidly teleport from home to work is a way of imagining that life was easier, and you love to watch those who can.

The superpower you would most like to have can be very revealing. If you could have any superpower, what would you wish for? It tells a lot about you and about your viewing choices. Many sci-fi shows and movies are based on *Marvel* or *DC* comics, like *Gotham* and *Agent Carter*, especially those involving superheroes. If these heroes' superpowers are the ones you most would want to have, then you have probably had

> A superpower of social media is that it affects your consumption of media and media products. Social media apps, blogs, video-sharing sites, social networks, and message boards interact between televised media and the Internet, attaching various degrees of popularity or value to the weekly series/superhero doll/You-Tube video/latest superhero app.

these desires for a long time—at least since you released your first comic book from its secure plastic wrapper and smelled the colored ink. You may prefer heroes who could annihilate the bully on the playground with one swift blow, dash away from him faster than a speeding bullet, halt the villain permanently with a polar blast, or just transport him or her to another planet. It's natural to want to have and be more in a supernatural way, with superpowers, but maybe the real hero is you. After you imagine that you are magical and come back to earth, you may be all that you need.

Why fantasize about eliminating stressful people with magic powers? In less-than-perfect families (are there any other kind?), children wish for the perfect protector, the perfect mentor, and the perfect love. And so do adults. But for kids, there is more fantasy involved that imprints itself in their brains, much like Hans Solo of *Star Wars* in carbon freeze. The perfect person is usually a morph of some media character, family member, teacher, or babysitter who can take care of anything that you can't. And those people become integrated into your psyche in positive ways that last for a lifetime. Their patience with handling anything from a spoiled child or a broken heart to a broken drainpipe becomes a part of your trance. Hurrah! You fantasize about real heroes rather than the heroes on the screen and build beliefs around positive role models. They are the Oprah for your life, the Donald and Suzy for your investments, and the Flash dancers for your dreams. And they become a part of you and what you believe about yourself. They form your belief and trance about the world and your place in it.

You as Superhero: Strength Finder

What are your *best strengths*?

_____ the *persistence* of Jean Valjean in *Les Misérables*

_____ the *integrity* of Nicolas Cage in *It Could Happen to You*

_____ the *vulnerability* of Meryl Streep in *Hope Springs*

What do you *do best*?

_____ Are you a great *friend* like Joey in *Friends*?

_____ Have *techie skills* like the guys in *The Big Bang Theory*?

_____ Have the ability to *help others* like *Frasier*?

What *challenges* persist in your pursuit of personal mastery?

_____ *relationships* like Hannah in *Girls*

_____ *protecting* people/animals/ideas from bad guys and bullies a la Mr. Reese in *Person of Interest*

_____ *work pursuits* such as *Two Broke Girls*

While you accept your challenges, hold on to the hero traits and begin to form a new trance, one that includes you, while you explore the ones outside of you that may lend themselves as role models. Make a list of your strengths; use them in positive statements about yourself. Repeat daily.

Now, it's time to explore ideas and fantasies of a perfect parent/ partner/ coworker/therapist/mentor/ dog trainer, so crank up your creative handle and go for a ride through the non-reality show genre.

The inventor of *Wonder Woman*, William Moulton Marston, scripted *Wonder Woman* in 1941 to fight for the US at Pearl Harbor in comic books. But creativity has many uses; Marston also created the systolic blood pressure test that formed the basis for the polygraph machine, later used in law enforcement for lie detector tests.

You are fully permitted to cringe at the following simplification of the supernatural genre, especially since some non-reality/sci-fi shows are so complex as to defy simplification. But for the sake of understanding, let me break a typical non-reality plot down for you. And here's a surprise that will take you back further than a ride with Cat Woman. *The stories are as varied as the powers but are usually predictable, and they usually come with a trance.* You need some sort of alien/monster/mutant ghost and a reason/plot for them to carry out, such as the end of the world/nuclear bomb/epidemic virus/ supernatural insemination/high school stranger danger/planetary takeover. The hero will need skills to accomplish an impossible mission, and so they may need to breathe fire/fly/understand all foreign languages (omni-lingual even for alien species)/move objects or have a memory eraser. Obviously you will need antiheroes, sometimes referred to as villains, to give the superheroes something to do and to remind you of things that are fearful. After all, fear is a natural part of you that, once triggered, can become a part of a larger destructive trance. It becomes a part of a belief that you are not enough and that magic/a laser sword/someone/something/X-ray vision is what you need. Superheroes are so much fun to watch, and they are perfect just as they are, Achilles heels and all. But to break the trance, remember that you are, too. Get real.

The stories, superheroes, villains, and superpowers are all interchangeable when writing or producing great sci-fi, with unlimited possibilities occurring through mixing and matching them. But why should I tell you myself when I can wave my Writer Woman pen, summoning a superhero to do it for me? I have invited the crème de la crème of superheroes to walk you through this guide. Superman will be your host today as you travel through *an example of story, superheroes, villains, and superpowers*. Please, no arguments from Batman, Spider-Man, and the Avengers who came in second.

The Anatomy of Sci-Fi: A Dialogue with Superman

Writer Woman: So, Superman, thanks for coming today to be our tour guide.

Superman: Hold on, I have to get out of a phone booth. Okay, so here's the deal. Imagine a team of mutant superheroes. Now plug in a team of mutant antiheroes. There, you have your *heroes and villains.*

Writer Woman: Yes, but there could also be children with superpowers who might be good or bad and …

Superman: (*slipping his arm through the sleeve of a tight red suit*) Stick to the basics. Those details just make the whole thing a fascinating blockbuster. The point is that the superheroes mutants are trying to *save the world* from the mutant villains in ways that you never could (*he's signaling to an invisible man to bring his business suit to the cleaners/back to the office/men's room for a quick slip on*). And there you have your *plot*.

Writer Woman: Superman, I hate to disagree with you, but maybe I could save them, and there were superpowers that made the whole thing, well, it made the whole thing … super.

Superman: Okay, but it helps if you have the superhuman mutant heroes with a *superpower* of a healing factor. It means that you can heal yourself after a battle with a mutant villain. Guess I could have used an X-man after exposure to kryptonite. I really have to go save Metropolis now. Just take the Anatomy of Sci-Fi Quiz for yourself.

> Marshall McLuhan predicted a generation ago that a new global village would occur through telecommunications. Facebook, Twitter, YouTube, Google+, Pinterest, and others are already influencing health, politics, education, science, and friendship.

Writer Woman: Aha! You *were* talking about the X-Men! (*Superman flying off tops of tall buildings*).

Superman (*later in the day*): It's all in a day's work (*while sipping a glass of wine with Lois*).

You: Feeling disillusioned by Superman's swift departure, you go to Facebook, Twitter, and your blog and trash the trailer for a Superman comeback movie, sharing a video preview that you and all of your friends harshly critique. You make a mock video of the scene starring your friends that goes viral. It gets the number-one spot on YouTube this week. The movie tanks at the box office. You have gotten millions of Americans to shut down their message boards for the televised version of the series, now in reruns. You have changed viewing behavior. After they said it couldn't be done ... but now you are feeling remorseful, even antihero-like. You wonder if there is any value in watching superheroes anymore. You decide to avoid more unrealistic or disempowering trances, and you get that it's time to turn off the Mutant Monster marathon. You can cheer up by playing the Anatomy of Sci-fi game.

Anatomy of Sci-Fi

Games help you to demystify superheroes, superpowers, and plots and take a look at the workings of sci-fi. Connect each plot in the column on the left with the corresponding superhero in the second column, then with the hero's powers in the third column by drawing a line between each one that is related. See how many you know. For example, you would match Captain America with powers of peak human potential and a plot of fighting for the country.

Plots	Superhero	Powers
Fighting crime	Superman	Magic lasso, omni-lingual
Fighting crime	Wonder Woman	High-tech weapons/gadgets
Saving the world	Batman	Invulnerability
Fighting antiheroes	Supergirl	Speed, strength, X-ray vision
Fighting vampires	Spider-Man	Magic, strength
Fighting global crime	Buffy	Leaping, climbing, jumping, making webs

Check your answers on page 163 after reading the viewer's guide below. The guide will help to jog your memory for the quiz if you miss any of the questions.

Viewer's Guide to Stories, Superpowers, and Semi-Human Heroes, Mutants, or Gifted Individuals

The Viewer's Guide to Stories, Superpowers, and Semi-Human Heroes, brought to you by Writer Woman, will challenge you to recall what you know about the supernatural lifestyle.

Possible stories/plots: save the world, save a dog, save a girl, save a city, save money, overcome a wolf, girl/villain/alternate universe, or dead person, stop a war between two warring groups of monsters, stop a war between humans and aliens/monsters/ zombies/ blobs/other

Semi-Human heroes: Superman, Spider-Man, Hulk, X-men, Avengers, Luke Skywalker, Wonder Woman, Supergirl, Green Lantern, Men in Black, Flash, *Star Trek* Crew, or *Buffy the Vampire Slayer*, a character and show with a complexity of traits of post-feminism and femininity, selected as one of the 100 Best Shows of All Time

Villains: Freddy Kruger, Frankenstein, Wolf Man, King Kong (really a nice ape who got type-casted), ghosts (can also be heroes), aliens, assorted monsters, mutants, dead people, vampires, extra-strong beings from earth/ alternative universe/other planet/other galaxy

Superpowers: These include body-based powers and object-based powers: omni-lingual comprehension (ability to comprehend Swahili or any other language), wall climbing (gets you there on time), flying (ditto), heat vision (helpful if you are crime fighting during the winter months), reality warping (makes you feel like you're losing your mind), lasso of truth (I think my parents used to borrow this superpower), bullet-deflecting bracelets, an invisible airplane (not on my must-own list but very helpful during attacks from villains), super-immunity, super-strength (increases your

> Avoid driving like Batman or James Bond. After using mature, high-risk video games, users demonstrated more risky driving habits and willingness to drink and drive. Since video games involve more participation than on TV, the impact is even stronger. The results were determined by increases of sensation seeking and rebelliousness.

popularity), telekinesis (go, Luke Skywalker), energy sourcing, which means giving energy to objects or people (wouldn't you like your pen to write books by itself?), ability to imbue or awaken powers (I could use this to emanate peace, burn calories, and bi-locate between London and Pittsburgh), ability to sprout wings or read minds (would "cut to the chase" in relationships), magic suits (no, thanks, sounds high-maintenance), invulnerability/super-immunity (helpful when faced with a car accident, gossip, or bully intimidation), and magic objects—high-tech super-gadgets, high-tech car

Villain powers: neck biting, tearing your head apart with super strength, changing faces to fool the unsuspecting, time travel, magic sword stuff, and the crème de la crème … reality warping and similar powers to the heroes but used for harm instead of good

Trances: These are based on whether you recognize the superpowers in you or see them only outside of yourself. They are inverses of each other: I am lovable / not as lovable; I am the hero / they are the heroes; life is scary, and I need super forces to succeed / I can master my own fear, and I have or can become all that I need to succeed; I need bulging muscles to be a superhero / I am okay as I am; the X-men are cool because they're different / I'm different but don't need to be cool.

Anatomy of Sci-Fi Answers: Buffy—fighting vampires with magic and strength; Spider-Man—fighting global crime with leaping, climbing, jumping, making webs; Superman—fighting crime with speed, strength, X-ray vision; Wonder Woman—saving the world with the magic lasso and omni-lingual ability; Batman—fighting antiheroes with high-tech weapons and gadgets; Supergirl—fighting crime with invulnerability.

Don't Try This at Home

Notice the heroes in the Anatomy of Sci-Fi. Their physical anatomies are perfect in the same way that movie and TV stars are. Wonder Woman and Superman look like they spend a good deal of time at the gym/running/

lifting weights/having facials and plastic surgery decade after decade, never aging naturally. But that is the magical way of legends. Not of viewers.

As you will learn in the gender chapter, there is a common and consistent stereotype of good guys/gals as beautiful, physically perfect specimens that only Michelangelo could reproduce. A study by individuals at Rutgers and Villanova Universities in 2012 found some interesting things about people who use plastic surgery to look as good as TV role models. Both men and women in the study reported that they felt cosmetic surgery was a positive thing to do to enhance appearance after viewing a reality show demonstrating cosmetic surgery. The study indicated that participants of both genders responded positively to the media message that it's a good idea to pursue serious measures to conform to cultural ideals of beauty. Other comments indicated that participants thought the idea was vain and pointless, but the majority bought the idea completely. And those decisions support the weight loss and beauty industries. TV hypnosis, anyone?

Real-Life Superheroes

There are many things that you can integrate from superheroes once you get past their fictional perfection. Take a deep breath, delete any idea that you have to look like a superhero, and move on because superheroes are still one of the most influential groups on TV and in print. The reason is because they are do-gooders, and do-gooders are always

Studies prove that black women show less internalization of media ideals of body image. In a Vassar and University of Michigan study, they showed less "wishful identification" with a favorite media persona.

a good influence on the nervous system—even in the case of real-life superheroes.

Take, for example, Mother Teresa. When people viewed her charitable behaviors in Calcutta, they felt warm and compassionate. When you *view others behaving altruistically*, you not only *feel real emotions* you also may feel *physical sensations of warmth*. If you feel like going out and imitating positive behaviors, then you have been influenced, resulting in a positive outcome. Following viewing of heroic, positive, and/or admirable role models, you feel positive emotions and physical confirmation that the feelings were, in fact, good ones. A common result is that you go out and do good things for others, proving that you integrated the experience through viewing. You, too, have become a real-life superhero by integrating or awakening the altruist within.

The *Stand Up to Cancer* special on September 7, 2012 is an example of viewing what feels good and then acting altruistically while shaping worldviews. If the *Jerry Lewis Labor Day Telethon* started the fire of televised charitable pledge drives, *Stand Up to Cancer* fanned the flame. Charitable work has long been seen as a source of meaning in life, bringing transcendence over daily reality as a form of spiritual practice. For Mother Teresa and large numbers of nuns and monks, spiritual practice is heavily charity based. Both belief and practice are parts of spirituality, with the idea that you can't have one without the other. Often fictional characters display similar positive traits. Didn't you cheer when Spider-Man showed mercy for his attackers? Weren't you inspired when Luke Skywalker overrode his familial connection to follow the light path of the force?

> While the brain mimics the blissful state of compassion, the same effect is negative with frightening images. Desensitization occurs when you wall off your feelings and reactions. You train them to be less sensitive so you can watch a ghoul/four-headed snake/zombies of the afterworld/sci-fi murder mystery marathon. This can occur in doctors who are less emotionally responsive to watching people get pricked by needles.

Actions often follow such inspired viewing experiences. After a viewing dose of do-gooding, you may

- become motivated to be like Luke Skywalker and take the high road;
- act with the same level of strength of character as Luke;
- develop an attitude of following a path of positive living that becomes embedded through repetition;

- master or recover from obstacles more easily, considering the power of the force; and
- take action to act out your inspired behavior, now or later.

Now or later is important because you may not immediately have the chance to save the world. In the review in chapter 1 about social behavior and modeling, I noted Bandura's research regarding how you learn from observation. So if you are watching Martha Stewart demonstrate how to mince as opposed to chop or slice, you may remember it later when you have an onion in your hand. If you do it over and over for special occasions until you are an expert mincer, enjoying the process of party planning and feeling generosity toward your guests, then you have just stacked a positive anchor. Mincing onions now is a source of positive memories and feelings of generosity that you absorbed from your TV. TV becomes your superhero for the day. You may even begin to feel great merely taking out your mincing knife as you begin the pattern of mincing. When you attach positive behavior to doing something over and over that you value, the anchor stacking is most effective!

> March 2008 proceedings of the National Academy of Sciences reported a study from Harvard and the San Diego University of CA. It provided evidence that cooperative behavior is contagious. People who benefit from kindness tend to pay it forward.

How does this make a TV watcher a better person? If you see a sci-fi hero whom you admire every week on TV and feel positively about making the world a better place, you may store those feelings and ideas for future use. Although you are not leaping from tall buildings, you may donate time to a food bank or to your sister who is moving to a new house. The feeling of wanting to make the world a better place generalizes to your life. When you start to act upon your positive feelings, making efforts toward others in need, you then know through experience how these observed behaviors work and how they make you feel. You repeat them because they feel good, stacking one memory on top of another until you have a built-in positive reaction to invitations or models for behaving altruistically. Anchor successfully stacked. You may or may not maintain the change permanently, but the more that you repeat it, the more likely you will be to maintain your new strengths.

And if you view a hero who is bound by green light-infused chains holding to the idea of final rescue from a mutant travel agent/wolf man/ bed-and-breakfast owner with protruding, sharp teeth, then you may absorb a model for holding on while having faith. See how this works? If you view someone who overcomes great adversity or public discouragement to follow a dream, then you may become more true to yourself through observational learning. You may become more capable of acting with greater faith in the moment and cope better when things look bleak. So you feel admiration, follow the same path, experience positive emotions while using the skills, and become a happier person. If you now feel like going out to rent the entire DVD series of *The Greatest American Hero* for inspiration or connecting with Writer Woman, feel free.

The Dark and Light Sides of the Force

Early sci-fi was scary. Favorite supernatural shows of all time include the early black and white *Twilight Zone* and *Outer Limits*. They often set out to convince you that you might have no choice when evil overcomes you. Ouch! Who wants to pull the covers over your head after viewing a car/ little boy/cattle farmer from whom you could not escape? But later popular sci–fi shows, including *Star Trek, Battlestar Galactica*, BBC's *Dr. Who, The X-files*, and *Lost*, did not try to influence you into powerlessness. The newer shows leaned more toward good vs. evil themes, with good winning out overall. And you must love them because you watch them. Why?

There is a universal theme in literature, movies, TV, and your real life of the good vs. evil theme. Darkness vs. light, God/angel vs. devil/evil spirit, right vs. wrong, generosity vs. self-interest, humanity as a whole vs. selfish ego, and you vs. the other guy/girl themes appear with regularity too common to miss. They are universal themes, a concept introduced in the love chapter. *And they are there because within everyone there is a balance of wanting to do the right thing vs. wanting to do whatever feels good or meets your needs at the time.* You may notice this inner conflict when choosing between eating the chocolate-cherry-pecan ice cream or saving it for your spouse/Santa Claus/tooth fairy/Writer Woman, lighting the way to understanding this conflict. And often this conflict is scary, even terrifying, leaving you in worse shape than before viewing.

If you view too many frightening images, desensitization automatically occurs as you wall off your feelings and reactions. Why is this instinctual? You cannot possibly absorb all of the alien blood and guts/slimy beings/ frightening monsters without feeling terrorized by your TV. While you hang on in the reel world to see how many corpses the villain/flying mummy/evil mechanical warlord will devour, you could be damaging your sensitivity and numbing yourself. And when you are numb, you are not viewing or living consciously. So weigh whether you want to watch a sci-fi murder mystery marathon or Shirley Temple reruns before you lose all sensitivity. Otherwise, you may experience a hypnotic state complete with blank staring, remote control twitch (I caught you rewinding to watch that really scary stuff), and inability to terminate viewing of even the scariest troll/metal robot/spirit from the past about to take over the earth/the neighborhood/your pantry.

Let's take Luke Skywalker's light and Darth Vader's darkness from reelity into reality. To personally understand some inner conflicts between the *dark and light sides of the self,* notice whether you have certain Darth tendencies. No, I am not asking if you breathe through a mechanical device or dress all in black. I mean do you recognize the side of yourself that you keep behind a metaphorical dark mask? There are so many things about you that you may know and hide or push away from your awareness, so much that you don't even recognize them when someone points them out. My neighbor's adult kids were visiting from Cleveland and lovingly asked their mom if she could see any resemblance in herself to meddling mother Marie Barone of *Everyone Loves Raymond.* They burst into belly laughter as she denied any similarity. See what I mean?

Everyone has parts of the self that are difficult to acknowledge because they don't show your best side. So you continue to present a positive face to your girl or boyfriend/partner. You may mistrust a partner who might love you and yet could steal your peanut butter sandwich. But your love life is a topic for another time. I'll get back to you on that. For now, come with Writer Woman as you shine a flashlight into the dark recesses behind Darth's/antiheroes'/aliens' masks and notice that you see the shadow side of the self projected on the screen. It is quite a successful maneuver by producers because you personally know people like Darth. Your boss/uncle/cleaning person may try to use his/her inner Darth to exert control over you. And it is always easier to see others' flaws than your own.

Think of the darker self projected as monsters of all kinds on the screen. Now think of the symbolism that was in the TV series *V* in which the aliens were perfect humans on the outside but when they unzipped their skin became repulsive and frightening. Or **in** the ABC comedy *The Neighbors*, the aliens' human skin disappears to reveal a slimy, green entity when people applaud too loudly. This is kind of how the shadow works. It's easier to see the negativity on the screen with the light overcoming the darkness than it is to take away the pretense and face the inner dark side of personal insecurities/inner green, slimy things/not doing the dishes/lying to your sister about dating the guy she used to date. But no applause; you don't need to expose the inner green, slimy thing until you are ready. Since everyone has those sides, *accepting yourself is essential if you want to be happy.* And the conflict resolution makes for great TV, a positive viewing experience, and a sense of personal satisfaction. When you saw Merlin's good magic overpower Morgana's evil magic on *Merlin,* you may have felt personally vindicated. And all is probably well.

The *Star Wars* movies and *Merlin* on BBC are two examples of shows that have a good balance of light and dark with humor for comic relief from all of the seriousness of the plot. You feel balanced after viewing. *Pay attention to this feeling as it is related to the point of the whole chapter!*

But all is not well if a show has a much greater proportion of darkness in it than light. In contrast, if the hero is nearly drowned, chased by outer and inner demons, transported into outer space, and tickled by flying wolves before he/she is saved, then you have paid a high viewing price for the long-awaited outcome into the light. The heavy images will stay with you long after the show is over, with little memory of the bright spot at the end of the hero's journey. Not every show needs to be *Les Misérables*. And if it is, then you will end up with a *negatively stacked anchor—a series of negative memories and feelings that are attached to one thing.* In the case of *Les Misérables,* the negative outcomes are attached to stealing with lots of great music. But in the case of sci-fi, the heroes' negative outcomes are attached to villains that represent the dark side and *could leave you feeling disempowered or just bad in a way you can't quite define.*

Imagine two superheroes called Yina and Yangte. Yina is a female superhero who only works with positive power but can be moody and passive, with little motivation to fight crime. She might rather watch reruns of *The Hulk* and overly plan her next crime-fighting move. Yangte is an antihero who works with dark energy and can be too aggressive at times but gets the job done, sometimes using his anti-powers long into the night, resulting in stress, elevated cortisol levels, and depleted adrenal glands. He will be visiting his doctor sooner than Yina. Unless, of course, Yina's couch-potato behavior causes a myriad of health issues.

But one cannot succeed without the other. Yina has to activate her inner Yangte to get up off of the sofa and put away the corn chips while continually working from the light side of the force. When activated, her superpower can audit information as it enters the atmosphere, saving small children with a gentle whisper

When you watch superheroes and antiheroes, your Inner Yina and Yangte are engaged. You identify with both the heroes and antiheroes, who evidence some of the strengths and high levels of motivation of Yangte and the heroes who rely on their gut feelings and ability to sense their inner Yina. Yes, you, too, have a light and dark side. And by now you know that Yina and Yangte are fictional heroes that represent two parts of you, as do the heroes in sci-fi.

that blows the villain away. And she can keep secrets, sometimes too many. Yangte needs to chill out sometimes and consider a more balanced approach to reaching his goals. His superpowers include the strength of ten men and a horse, clever deception skills, and the willingness to run over a small town with a tractor if it results in killing his prey. But there are very few characters or humans who don't require a balance. Wonder Woman certainly has drive and motivation, a trait of Yangte energy, yet she can chill out as Diana Prince when she is not saving the world. And Yangte may be able to learn deep relaxation and retire early.

In a psychological school of thought developed by psychologist Carl Jung, the two opposite parts of the self are referred to as the yin and yang of the self. The yin self is the light (female self) while the yang (male self) is the dark, *but both have positive/negative characteristics, and one does not exist without the other!* If you have an imbalance of yin in your personality, you may have challenges with getting your laundry/hair/taxes done, whether you are male or female. If you are highly motivated and have trouble relaxing and leaving behind your golf game/work/tattoo project, you may have a heavy imbalance of yang, or masculine energy. Both of these make up the inner Yina and Yangte that you see reflected in sci-fi shows that, when combined, are likely to cause you to wake up motivated yet smelling the flowers.

If both your inner Yina and Yangte would like a specific supernatural show, then you may like it, too, feeling better about your own ability to overcome your fears of your dark side after viewing. And what fears and personal conflicts/challenges are projected onto the screen in great supernatural shows?

- things that can overcome you (*X-Men*/mutants with strange deformities/floods/space ships/people who are really vampires)
- unappealing parts of the self (*Once Upon a Time*/monsters/insect people with bulging eyes/witches)
- time travel (*Back to the Future*—who wants to be transported to another planet right in the middle of your day?)

- multiple universes (You thought this was all there is?)
- fantasy futures (Will everything come out as well as it does on planet Starshine?)
- ethical dilemmas (No, you can't make love with an alien and expect good results.)
- combinations of historical figures, alternate history, and space travel with a conflict of getting back to the present time (*Bill and Ted's Excellent Adventure*—most excellent dudes!)
- sibling rivalry (Austin Powers and Dr. Evil's conflict put a damper on the relationship. Jaina and Jacen Solo of *Star Wars: The Clone Wars* were divided by Jacen's turn toward the dark side.)

Twins Jaina and Jacen Solo of *Star Wars: The Clone Wars* look like an example of the inner conflict between the whole, divided into dark and light, skillfully portrayed by Lucasfilm Animation. In the *Dark Crystal*, Jim Henson inspired you when both darkness and light were brought together as the evil Skeksis merged with the noble Mystics through the courage of the last remaining Gelfling. Sounds like just another Sunday afternoon in sci-fi world, but it is a great way to think of Yina and Yangte style heroes coming together to make a whole being. While the characters cope with conflicts that are removed from your own by various degrees, the conflicts are never removed from the joys and sorrows of every human being. They are stories that will haunt you long after you put away your iPad.

Things that Go Bump in the Night and Other More Serious Matters

In one week on TV, there were shows about ghosts in houses, celebrity ghost stories, ghost hunters, pet ghosts, ghosts unlimited, and more. You could watch *American Horror Story* (if you have strong immunity to fright), *My Ghost Story, Ghost Stories, Haunted London,* and *Ghost Adventures*, a show about an Ohio bookstore owner who is clearing the shop so the ghosts don't scare away business. I can't wait to see if a show about the real housewife ghosts from Atlanta will emerge. And some will watch it because of a universal fascination with the unknown, even if that fascination has been oversaturated with otherworldly beings. You can get enough of a good thing.

Moving from the ridiculous to the sublime, ghosts such as Patrick Swayze from the movie *Ghost* may have their spirits embedded in a fictional Supernatural Wall of Fame or as a star in the Supernatural Sidewalk. Patrick prevented people from getting killed, stopped his thief/former best friend from embezzling funds, and removed a villain from the planet before passing to the other side. *Casper,* also a ghost, is much like Patrick Swayze; he is a "good ghost." And why are there such things as good ghosts? Because the afterlife is supposedly not such a bad place in the reel or real world, and not all media ghosts are here to haunt you.

The supernatural world of the afterlife may involve religion or simply a restless ghost trying to take over your life/body/girlfriend/website. TV series dealing with the reel afterlife have carried substantial messages with leading ladies championing the cause of the real afterlife. *They had a strong influence on what you believe about the afterlife.* Some of these include the following:

- The series *The Medium,* based on a story of Allison DuBois, featured a medium who experienced communications from those who have passed over into the afterlife. The lead character's talents led her to work with the Phoenix district attorney's office to help with solving murders. But help from deceased victims during dream states caused some tension in a

A University of Toronto at Scarborough study addressed areas in the brain where thoughts of God were examined through activity in the anterior cingular cortex, which regulates when things go right vs. wrong. The God thoughts provided comfort to believers and stress to nonbelievers. The study, reported in *Psychological Science,* suggested that, for believers, thinking of God lowers stress, but for atheists, brain activity conflicts with their beliefs and raises stress levels

household with a husband and three daughters. *You might take away a message that the line between life and death is a thin one that Allison has been able to cross.*

- *The Ghost Whisperer* Melinda Gordon, played by Jennifer Love Hewitt, experienced similar challenges. But her ghosts talked to her when she was awake. While not everyone was willing to hear or believe that the messages were from ghosts, it was worth the struggle, as recipients of these ghostly messages acquired peace, released guilt, and moved on with their lives on TV. *Consider whether those on the other side can contact the living through an intermediary, a tenet of modern spiritualism.*

- Angels are a topic common to many religions and to many people's personal experiences. In *Touched by an Angel,* the angel Monica, played by Roma Downey, brought messages from God to people experiencing crossroads in life, although some of Monica's charges were reluctant to believe she was really an angel. The struggle is often one between the love she brings to the living and their fear of the message. *The show reflects a very human condition: the struggle between love and fear. Think of the things you desire to have, do, and experience that are interrupted by fear of failure or even fear of success, with fear as the common factor.*

In all three of these shows, the afterlife is a given, and they are serious takes on death.

God, Television, and Miracles

Movies such as *The Green Mile* suggest the possibility of miracles, a possibility that many people hope for. The dominating physical strength of one imprisoned character coupled with his extremely gentle personality shows that miracles can come from a strong yet gentle source. I see, in this movie, the characterization of a God both strong and gentle, working miracles through an imprisoned innocent man. The idea that God can work through many forms is also apparent in this interpretation.

Many religious and spiritually based television programs suggest

 An early Xerox commercial tickled your funny bone with a monk named Brother Dominic amazed by the Xerox copy machine. "It's a miracle," he reported, when speaking of the copier.

the same. The portrayal of miracles is, at times, physical with no scientifically explainable reason for an event or healing of disease. Real-life cases of spontaneous remission, rapid unexplained recovery from life-threatening illness, are often called miracles because they transcend most scientific explanations. At other times, the miracles are defined as the tiny messages that you receive from each other, from nature, and from everyday events.

Life after Death

Movies that you have seen on TV also speak directly to the afterlife. *What Dreams May Come* with Robin Williams may raise the possibility that the *afterlife is what you make it, based on your perceptions.* It may appeal to the "spiritual but not religious" viewers. And while Matt Damon in the movie *Hereafter* can talk to those in the next life, he makes no conclusion about what is there. *It's a feast for viewers who also don't know and may speak to you as a conscious viewer who is watching for movie messages.*

Defending your Life, a movie with Albert Brooks as Daniel Miller, and Meryl Streep as his love interest, also includes a cameo by Shirley McClain, of course! The recently deceased initially arrive in Judgment City where they ride on busses to a hearing and get to plead their cases for a place in heaven. Part of the process involves a video review of your life choices in a high-tech judgment court, choices both fearless and fear based.

Daniel's case is presided over by two judges, one who argues that Daniel should move on to the next phase. But the opposing judge, "Dragon Lady," thinks otherwise. If you haven't seen it, you might expect that Meryl Streep gets to go directly to heaven, while Albert has a bit of a struggle. But did you expect to find Rip Torn cast as Daniel's defense attorney Bob Diamond?

In *Defending Your Life*, Rip Torn's character explains to Daniel that humans use only 3–5 percent or their brain, which is mostly fear (there's that universal fear again). "When you use more than 5 percent of your brain, you don't want to be on earth, believe me," quips Torn. If Daniel proves to the judgment court that his fears are conquered, he gets to move on and use more of his brain, gaining the opportunity to experience more of what the universe has to offer. *It reminds me of a take on the afterlife as one step higher than where you happen to be at the time of death, but only if you've earned it.* Otherwise you get to come back to earth and overcome your fears. This is similar to concepts of Hinduism and Buddhism, two of the oldest spiritual practices in the world.

What you believe about the soul comes from what you have studied, what you have experienced, and your faith as well as media influence. You may witness many elements of your inner self in dramedies such as those on your Inner Committee in *Defending Your Life.* They're those parts of you called Inner Committee Members (CMs) They work together and have certain beliefs about your life and afterlife. These CM aspects of you are viewing TV and making decisions about whether to continue viewing, whether there is an afterlife, and even what to eat, drink, and Google.

Whether or not you believe in an afterlife, a further examination of *Defending Your Life* by your Inner Committee is in order. The movie may gently show you how your CMs work. *And the ways that this or any movie/ TV show may influence you are revealed.* If you apply the Inner Committee to Daniel's plight, it might look something like this.

Initially when he arrives in Judgment City, he gets to eat anything he wants without weight gain. Does this sound like the *inner child*? Certainly many have had this magical fantasy where biology is overridden by magic. He also gets unlimited entertainment, such as bowling and admission to comedy clubs free of charge. Wouldn't you like to be Daniel? But then along comes *inner fear.* Fear, and how you have handled life, is the one thing that you will be judged on in order to quality for admission to a boost in brainpower in the next life. If the judgment court determines that Daniel has conquered his fears, he will be sent on to the next phase

Defending Your Life was not the first media event to use technology for a transition into the beyond. *Heaven Can Wait,* starring Warren Beatty, suggested that souls wait to board a plane to their ultimate destination. More recently on the irreverent *South Park*, the oft-killed Kenny enters the gates of heaven to help God fight Satan with a video game.

of existence. Hmmm ... fear ... Daniel is set up to fear/not fear how he has handled his fear thus far. In his case, his *inner fear* (CM) takes control of the wheel of his life and dominates most of his trial. His fears are revealed on videotape for him to watch in full color. Even his past-life fears are recorded and can be viewed at the Past Life Pavilion, with an appropriately cast video introduction by Shirley McClain.

Following the Inner Committee theory, you might identify with the CM that *believes in you,* represented by your defense attorney Diamond, who is opposed by your *inner critic,* played convincingly by Lee Grant, the Dragon Lady. She reminds Daniel of every mistake he has made in overcoming his fear while he feebly attempts to explain. Even in Judgment City the verdict is not always right, though, which taps right back into a fear that even if you are worthy, you may be denied your desires. But, alas, there is a happy ending. When Daniel is about to be sent back to Earth and his life is on the line, he decides that he doesn't want to go back. His *inner motivator* and *drive* (inspired by Yangte) are awakened. You already know that Meryl Streep is destined for a better afterlife, and she so inspires Daniel that he performs a final feat of courage in order to be with her. His attempt results in an overturned verdict as the two are united. Does "fear is conquered by motivation" sound like a familiar theme of a day in the life of your Inner Committee? And that explains why these plots are so appealing to you.

Death after Life

Messages about the afterlife in the media reflect what you already know: that you have to die to get there. Death is a universal concern. Fear of dying is the number-two fear that people admit they have. Public speaking is number one; yes, you would rather die than speak in front of a room full of people. So this explains fascination with shows that

Teens watch different types of programming, depending on whether a teenager is religious, according to a study published in the *Journal of Media and Religion*. Surveys collected from over a thousand teens for the National Study of Youth and Religion found that more religious teens prefer less mature TV entertainment. Spirituality explained up to 27 percent of the differences in happiness levels among children in another study. As a conscious observer, what do you notice about either of these findings?

can offer clues about the afterlife, which many people fear. If you could choose how your life would end, you might prefer to go in your sleep of natural causes than to be run over in an airport by one of those beeping carts on their way to a departure gate.

The suspense runs high with death because it is the ultimate journey into the unknown, the most intriguing, suspenseful destination, the prize at the end of the life's journey (or not, depending on your views), and you want to know what comes next! It is a riddle to solve with so many possible options that you may not feel resolved unless you have had a near-death experience (NDE) and come back to life to tell about it. Even then, science says that the NDE is induced by brain activity, so you may or may not gain information from people who have had NDEs. You could not convince those who have had an NDE of that; their subjective experience is that the afterlife is very real. But the fewer ties you have to organized religion with already constructed views, the more susceptible you are to media impressions of the afterlife and religion. If you are viewing consciously, then you may pick up many ideas.

Life before Life

Actor Blair Underwood has taken it upon himself to share testaments regarding what is known about the other side prior to life. You may recall his major role on the NBC legal drama *L.A. Law*, one he portrayed for seven years. But while he has received Golden Globe and NAACP awards and has accepted the title as one of *People* magazine's "50 Most Beautiful People," he has also gathered stories for a book. These reports are from children who experienced recollections of what had happened *Before I Got Here: The Wondrous Things We Hear When We Listen to the Souls of Our Children*. Interestingly, Underwood portrayed the role of Saint Mark in *The Truth & Life*, a twenty-two-hour celebrity-voiced audio version of the *New Testament Bible*. Contrarily, he has recently played the lead role of Stanley Kowalski in the Broadway revival of *A Streetcar Named Desire*. Stanley is the classic bad guy. Yina and Yangte would be proud of Underwood, portraying both dark and light sides of the self.

Life during Life

In an October 2012 *Newsweek* article and in his book *Proof of Heaven*, neurosurgeon Dr. Eben Alexander reported his experience with the afterlife while in a bacterial meningitis-related coma. While his brain cortex was shut down, the part of the brain that controls thoughts and feelings, his mind experienced "brain-free consciousness." He reported that his mind journeyed to another larger dimension of the universe, one often described by those who've had NDEs and other mystical states. He decided that you are much more than your physical body, that death is not the end of consciousness. He was the first known person to have this specific experience.

But there are as many writers, scientists, visionaries, theologians, scholars, TV and movie producers, and mystics as there are views on the presence or the lack of a God and the afterlife. A reality show pitting these experts together could be called *Holy Rivals!* And religion is a sensitive subject since it is a reflection of an individual's sense of and belief about the soul. There are recent trends in religion that are reflected in the media for entertainment and/or enlightenment. And you may find them interesting and/or humorous, or just plain offensive lies. If you enjoy them, they will make you smile, but if you think they are offensive, then you will have a trigger response, quick and painful. Decide for yourself what you think; you'll get a challenge from the quiz below.

Profound or Profane?

Variations and trends in beliefs about God and religion are reflected in the media. Decide whether you find each depiction profound (or at least acceptable) or profane to heighten your conscious awareness of your views in the spiritual media arena.

Profound or Profane

With or without celebrities, the viewing of church on TV as opposed to attending a local community gathering on the Sabbath suggests a trend. The option of individual worship vs. community worship was not possible before the advent of television. *How do you feel about this trend?*

A shift in American religious practice from following one faith to pursuing various religious practices, changing faiths over a person's lifetime, or selecting aspects of various religions that resonate with the person has occurred. Another trend is toward multiple perspectives and diversity. The choices were played for laughs in some programs during the nineties. In a *Seinfeld* episode, character George Costanza, played by Jason Alexander, converts to win the heart of a woman. *Seinfeld* character Elaine, played by Julia Louis Dreyfus, agreed to be a maid of honor in a Hindu wedding but made the sign of the cross during the ceremony. *Is this all in fun or not?*

Profound or Profane?
(continued)

<table>
<tr><th></th><th><u>Profound</u></th><th>or</th><th><u>Profane</u></th></tr>
</table>

One trend was toward religious and traditional productions. *Last Temptation of Christ* and *Compassion of the Christ, Seven Years in Tibet,* and *Little Buddha* were movies that typified these trends, and televangelism brings religious tradition to the screen. A spoof on traditional stereotypes was Dana Carvey's portrayal of the Church Lady, one that was widely accepted as a takeoff. While some Catholics found the character offensive, others were sporting Church Lady bumper stickers with her famous slogan, "Isn't that special?" *What do you think?*

Some members of a third group, agnostics and atheists, hold that religion is just an attempt to avoid the feeling that life is meaningless. You/they may enjoy classic movies with these themes such as *Inherit the Wind* or *Elmer Gantry,* or comedies like Woody Allen's *Crimes and Misdemeanors* and *Monty Python's Life of Brian.* TV shows include some of Seth McFarlane's characters in *Family Guy* (the dog Brian) and *American Dad* or depictions of the characters in *Glee* and *The Office.* Dr. Gregory *House* is all about science. *Where do you stand? Are these depictions?*

Profound or Profane?
(continued)

	Profound	or	Profane

Belief in a divine presence is close to
the hearts of a fourth group, but they
find religion to limit the understanding
of that presence. They believe in
transcendence—a term used to describe
this phenomenon inferring that there is
some form of reality and meaning beyond
objective reality. This group will enjoy
the movies *Contact* and the *Matrix* or
TV shows *Star Wars: The Clone Wars* and
Battlestar Galactica. This group would be
the Independents in a political election;
it's not a position of "no position" but
one of continually viewing the spiritual
and political arena with fresh eyes, minus
preconceptions. *Is this belief…?*

RxTV: A Magical Viewing Experience

√ Everyone is entitled to his/her opinion and his/her experience with magical, supernatural, and religious viewing. Be mindful when speaking to others whose takes on shows disagree with your own. Listen consciously and respond as a conscious listener and viewer.

√ Enjoy any show with supernatural elements while considering how the show embeds messages. Pay close attention to the heroes, their skills/ powers/magical paraphenalia/challenges and the outcomes of them. Decide what you want to take away and keep for yourself in your own life.

√ If spirituality is a big part of your life, then enjoy books, movies, and TV that reinforce, expand, or challenge your point of view. Research shows that they may make you happier. Experts say that viewing what makes you happier makes your self-esteem stronger.

√ If you are not a spiritual or religious person, you can still enjoy spiritual, supernatural, and magical programming consciously, taking away positive moral and ethical messages without subscribing to any particular belief system.

Drawing the Invisible Line

Sexuality, race, and mental health are topics that have intersections with TV and religion. While it has become common to portray gay, lesbian, and alternative lifestyles in shows such as *Modern Family, Glee,* and *The New Normal,*

> Creator Jack Kenny felt that he had produced a family drama with the *Book of Daniel* with humor that genuinely explored the lives of the Webster family. They were good people with flaws, people who loved each other no matter what … and there was plenty of "what."

when sexuality and mental health show up on the same screen as religion, viewers and sponsors may not be ready. When the series *The Book of Daniel* was broadcast on TV in January 2006, it aired only a few episodes before it was dropped because of difficulty getting sponsors and because several local network stations refused to air this controversial program. The pastor Reverend Daniel Webster, portrayed by Aiden Quinn, received spiritual counseling directly from a modern human incarnation of Jesus in these therapeutic interventions.

But Rev. Webster was also dependent on prescription drugs, his wife was alcohol-dependent, he had a gay son and a daughter who had been arrested for drug possession. There were racial issues, embezzlement of funds by Daniel's brother-in-law, a bisexual secretary, a bishop involved with Daniel's father, and more. After four shows, it was dropped by NBC. No new attempt to portray so many of such characters has been presented since, but the videos are still available. See? Your opinions matter.

In Conclusion

Before signing off, Writer Woman would like to present an independently sponsored message for conscious viewing of the sci-fi movie *Avatar*. Writer Woman's interpretation is that it seems to merge superheroes, moral dilemmas, special effects, and high-level knock-off-your-socks entertainment. You can get out your popcorn to keep you in your seat, your spyglass for detection of the point of the big finale, and your conscious viewing skills for a look at some messages that you may find, beyond those that I found, that may become *positive anchors* for you.

An interpretation of the highest-grossing film of all time up to 2009, *Avatar*, is that it depicts a conscious way to end this chapter on the supernatural and to prepare you for your RCL degree. I will hold you in suspense until after the next chapter to grant your degree in the final chapter because what you are about to read before moving on is important.

In spiritual studies, an avatar is sometimes presented as a deliberate descendent of a deity sent to earth. Keep this in mind as you consciously view *Avatar*. When the avatar of this film, a member of a group of humanoids, chooses to save a planet along with its aliens and convert to their culture rather than to mine it for needed resources and upset its natural balance, a moral judgment has been made. The stance of the avatar is that even though you may need something, taking it from someone else at his or her expense is not likely to result in a friendly response or a positive reaction or even be the right thing to do. Aggressive attempts to sway the avatar toward the completion of his original mission are unsuccessful, despite bribery and promises. Talk about a superhero.

The aliens rebelled, and a battle was fought between the humanoids and alien Zegarell beings, so different from the humanoids that they were deemed unimportant. The symbolic struggle in the reel world between taking advantage of another planet for personal gain and the self-defense from such an attack can be seen in the real world as well. When people see others as too separated by distance, too different to matter, or as evil because of their differences, it creates a disconnect that can wreak havoc. Think consciously. Identify at least three times when this has occurred in your neighborhood, country, or in history. World peace may depend upon it.

SpyTV

Detect the messages in a televised religious or spiritual show or one that you consciously recognize has embedded spiritual messages and decide if you will *accept or reject them.* Then as you decide to *release or respect them,* if you choose to accept them, begin to *stack some positive spiritual memories with them.* You might recall an inspired feeling after viewing that reminds you of a time when you felt a spiritual experience in nature or at a ceremony. To *reject the message,* again *stack some positive anchors* that *mismatch* the message of the show that you would prefer to reinforce. If the message you choose to reject, for example, is that of a TV doctor who rejects any belief that is not scientific, recall times when this was disproven, when you felt that prayers were answered, when the angel of a TV series brought peace to someone or a time when you were inspired by a poem, sermon, or other experience.

C—Check out how you feel if you choose to watch something that you know is not feeding what feels good for you. Change takes time, so notice how it feels to view. You have definitely earned the right to choose by reading *Get Reel.*

For more up-to-date information on *Get Reel* for this chapter, go to:

http://drnancyonline.com/category/rc-media-and-rxtv/

http://drnancyonline.com/category/current-news/

CHAPTER 9

THE NEW ADVENTURES OF THE OLD YOU

Welcome to the Rest of Your Amazing Life

I spent this month wondering if you would toss your TV and computer out the window and get a library card or shut your TV down and log off your computer and get a library card or maybe just get a library card. While I think that you probably did none of the above, I am wondering if you have made changes in your viewing habits. I would neither want you to throw your TV out the window nor would I insist that you get a library card. Just be conscious. And here's what that might look like.

You're at home, kicking back and relaxing, consciously watching your must-see show. You have stacked together three recordings on your DVR/ Tivo that make you feel good, satisfy your needs, and give you the messages about yourself that you *want* to have or that just entertain you harmlessly. You have, in the same recorded collection, a couple of things that you have decided aren't the best ones, but now you view them consciously if you choose, rejecting anything that embeds itself in your head and takes you off course. You are remembering that producers are clever and that you can't catch all of the messages. Would you like to change that? There is time for the media to unleash potential and discover what Philo T Farnsworth knew. They have been doing so much right for so long that media has earned the right to become real. Direct them with your words and thoughts about what you need to *Get Reel*.

And when you watch TV, you might decide to watch *The Simpsons, a* show with a life of its own. They celebrated twenty-five years on the air reflecting life as you knew it on the screen. Their spoofs and parodies presented issues, staying close to a real topic while mocking it all the while. They tackled phobias, recycling, Broadway musicals, memory loss, spy flicks, shopping, gay lifestyles, suspense movies, snow plowing, popularity, mob mentality, the United Nations, little girls' dolls, Internet sensations, and you name it. If it happened in pop culture or real culture, they spoofed it or exposed attitudes about it. How else could they stay current and successfully remain on the air for so long? They show you how to laugh at yourself and everything else. This helps you break the trance. Who knows? You might see *The Simpsons* turn off their TVs!

But you don't necessarily have to turn them off. You have interrupted patterns of viewing unconsciously. You are now using "Wow," as you recognize things in programming or ads designed to present messages of any kind. You are having a great time with your TV, and you know when to turn it off. You have a full life, complete with significant others, less significant others (otherwise known as acquaintances), hobbies from needlepoint to extreme sports, and work that makes you say "Wow!" or at least makes you curious enough to say "Hmmm." If there are stressors in your life, you deal with them by enjoying nature, relaxing, calling a friend or mentor, thinking through the solution to the problem, and watching some TV of your choice to unwind. Maybe you have rediscovered who you really are/were before too many commercials, what you really want, and are pursuing your goals and dreams.

At this point in the *Get Reel* process, many people tell me that they have become conscious, that they want to make some changes in their viewing habits. The challenges that they report now have to do with:

- breaking old habits by using the trance breakers;
- substituting new behaviors;

- reminding themselves why they need to view consciously—what's in it for the brain and body; and
- and transferring conscious viewing skills to conscious living skills because *your TV viewing habits are metaphors for how you live your life.*

Or maybe you always had well-regulated viewing habits but have worked out some of the limiting messages that unconsciously held you back or made you feel incomplete. In either case, congratulations! You just won the Conscious Viewer award! You can read this last chapter with a smidge of smug. You went from *Get Reel* to Got Real and you can indulge in knowing that you got it!

I think the media is getting it, too. TV opened the subject of cancer with Showtime's *The Big C.* The show stepped up and may have made you ask the question of what you are doing with your time. As Laura Linney's character struggled with cancer, ratings soared, and if you were watching consciously, you were faced with thinking about your own legacy. What are you doing or what have you done with your time that makes a difference? If you can answer the same way as Betty White, then just relax and coast through the chapter. If not, pay close attention.

RCL 101: Reinventing Free Time

You don't have to be Jonas Salk to be an inventor of your life. You don't have to be Michelangelo to design something of great value. You don't even have to be Norman Lear to understand the social importance of your TV time. And it isn't necessary to look like a fashion model, "as seen on TV." You just have to take the tools you *do* have and become the master of your own fate, the keeper of your castle, and the lead dog in your autobiography. Perhaps whoever figured out that white vinegar could clean almost anything tried barbecue sauce, ammonia, and Jell-O first! The patent office is full of new applications for old fabrics, more effective shavers, and shoe sole inserts. The creative ideas are there, and *you* are the artist. And so the trance breaker for this chapter is *flooding.* And it means to flood yourself with new constructive choices and thoughts, as well as ones that already work so that you can replace any idea or viewing/life habit that isn't allowing you to be all that you are.

You will need some space to *flood* your life—space that text messages, e-mails, voicemails, urgent deadlines, Twitter posts, and Facebook entries do not allow you to have. Yet, they can help you to find your way into your future *if* you are focused. That means no drifting on to a website, YouTube, or pop culture video about J. Lo's new hairstyle or the Frank Sinatra documentary. This is where you get to *produce your own life*! Your e-mail's full box, your Facebook posts, and the Twitters that twitter all about are not the masters of your own destiny. *You* are! And it is time to write your script, complete with images of your future in Technicolor and HD with 3-D glasses! Knowing yourself very well will help you with this mission.

To begin this task of self-knowledge, consider that Monday morning heart attacks have been found to be associated with an emotional state called "joyless striving." It means that whatever you are doing in your career brings you no joy and has little meaning. It also implies reluctantly dragging yourself from where you are to where you aren't and don't want to be on Monday morning.

I have a friend, Tara, who is in this position. Whenever I call her at work, she wants to keep me on the phone in order to do anything rather than her job. I can't say that I blame her, based on her circumstances. Where in your life, if anywhere, do you feel joyless striving? And do you use TV and the Internet to block out your feelings and provide a cushion of temporary pleasure to avoid the question? Maybe you don't even find that you have a lot of trance, but you just use TV to anesthetize against a boring or painful life. Fine for a while but not at the expense of your health and happiness. You wouldn't want a diagnosis of life paralysis before you make your mark.

Ask yourself: Do you spend too much time striving for anything, without any enjoyment or fulfillment? Is it something your TV told you that you should want? The money chapter told you what messages you receive about what you *should* want to buy and be. Are you still listening and damaging your feelings of self-worth? Striving by itself is not such a bad thing—if you enjoy or value the process. After all, life is mostly journey, not much completion. This book took months, even years, to write, but it was finished on only one day, the day I stopped and decided it was done. If I hadn't appreciated the journey, I wouldn't have made it to the destination of writing *Get Reel*.

Mastering your viewing habits and addictions to movies, pawn shows, and George Clooney are a great beginning. But don't get too comfortable. There is more to fulfill in a Real Conscious Life. Before you reach for the remote, I have another suggestion for you—and it's important. By now, you know that I would not mention it if it were not at least as important as catching *America's Got Talent* in HD. And (*serious drum roll now*) I mean Ringo Starr/Phil Collins

As long as there have been Greek philosophers, their students learned that what happens to you is not as important as what you *believe* happens. Living consciously means separating the story about your life from the reality. If you change your story, you can change your life.

drumming; I mean a piñata from Madrid full of goodies and confetti important; I mean a Louis Armstrong trumpet made of gold serious. Live consciously. That's it—two words, just two. Live consciously. But as Ringo would say, it ain't easy. He was singing of love, and so are you. Real love for your Real Conscious Life (RCL).

By now, you know that I will give you the information that you need to get there and will give you a map, too. Mapping starts with a small organ of the body known as the brain. You remember your brain. Remember how it reacted to the idea of change? It said things such as, "Oh no! Change? Too scary for me! I'll just stick to what I know. It isn't working, but try something different? Way too scary!"

RCL 202: You Too Can Understand Neuroscience

By now, your brain has had plenty of time to *flood* with new ideas, washing the ineffective ideas out, and you have begun to feel comfortable with them. After all, you won the Conscious Viewer award. And you will continue to expand the award; as your brain constantly evolves, so will you. Now you will earn your RCL degree. And it won't be honorary because I will tell you how to recognize when you have gotten there. And you will bestow it on yourself.

This is the same brain that goes into an alpha brain wave state thirty seconds into viewing, where messages float in like dandelion fuzzies through unfocused, overly receptive attention. Remember this stage? It is a stage of receptivity. Your brain is empty like an empty basket, and so the media messages are filling your basket as if with eggs. By now, you have weeded out the rotten eggs and have some space in your basket.

If you feel like your basket/brain still needs a little more room, you might want to reread a couple of your favorite chapters from *Get Reel* to complete the RCL 101 jumpstart toward conscious living. You don't ever finish things that you never start, so if you detect that you need more time, this is step one. I will wait for you. You can find me in the next paragraph when you return.

RCL 303: Neuroscience and Intention—Creating Your Life

Since the goal of moving toward an RCL requires *breaking old habits, substituting new behaviors,* and *setting intentions* for your new life, it is time to remind yourself what is in it for you, mind and body. A few activities to tuck into your life will help you as you read this chapter.

In 2000, Sara Lazar, a neuroscientist at Massachusetts Hospital, found that while using a Functional MRI, you can detect miniscule changes in the brain during critical functions. Herbert Benson, a Harvard professor noted for the development of the Relaxation Response, asked Lazar to study the brains of monks and others who had completed long periods of contemplation and meditation. Findings showed that during meditation the parts of the brain involved in attention, the frontal and parietal lobes, had a significant amount of activity. Why would you care? Because these parts of the brain perform the higher-level brain functions such as thinking in contrast to the parts of the brain that are responsible for arousal and react to stress with fear and a flight-or-flight response. So that this does not become lost in translation, it means that if your two-year-old breaks your grandmother's elephant vase or expresses himself with Crayolas on an important brief you need for a meeting, you do not lose control but instead show an appropriate level of concern for the situation.

What's in that for you? Simply that relaxation can sharpen your attention and deactivate the parts of the brain that react stressfully. The more you relax, the more your thinking and attention abilities increase as these lobes further develop—and the less freaked out you may be over small things, like losing your recording of *Good Wife* in your DVR. Now, at the risk of pushing you into a life better than you have ever known, I must point out that relaxation or meditation could create changes in your way of thinking. It may seem less significant to see *Good Wife* at viewing time, knowing that you can watch it later, taking time to put on your relaxed Zen hat first. Heightened attention abilities, allowing for a sharp eye for the details of TV or life, are a gift you can give yourself. And you might not even miss the shows you don't see.

In 2011, when I gathered experts for a book entitled *Top Ten Tips for Lasting Happiness*, we talked of how just meditating and exercising can activate the parts of the brain that cause feelings of happiness. Now you may begin to understand why all of this brain research matters to you. This is a simplification of a lot of research and study, but I think you get the point. No study ever said that those who watch the most TV or who phone, text, and communicate on the Internet are the happiest. Those studies may come; no one knows. But for now, it is known that the best recipe for life includes healthy TV-viewing habits to allow for exercise and a period of daily contemplation and stillness. It also includes healthy diet, creative activities that get you into a flow state and make you lose track of time, and having a strong supportive social network, including some happy friends. At least that's what the research and my book collaborators had to say.

Can you do all of these things and watch TV? Especially when it is easier to just watch TV? Yes, it's called a balanced life, and it is yours for the gifting. And to learn how to gift yourself, move toward the next part of the course.

RCL 404: Manifesting Intentions for Your Life

If you are not yet convinced to hide the remote for a portion of the day, let me tell you another fact that may make a crucial difference in your thinking. Regular relaxation/meditation was found to not only increase attention but to reduce the aging process in the brain and increase intuition. Want to have more brain longevity and a better gut-level sense of what is right for you when viewing TV and living? Sounds like you may have found an answer. Not only will you have a greater power of observation/attention but more intuitive input for decision making as well. It's a win-win for your life and your viewing.

If you are interested in these things, you can find an unlimited number of materials on just how to accomplish these states. As I said, when I do any form of deep relaxation training with clients in my practice, I can get positive results with children in six weeks that it can take adults as much as six months to achieve. Really. I would not kid you. Children are less protective, allowing new ideas into their lives and also don't have the high levels of stress in their nervous systems to overcome. So if you have children, stress management and relaxation is something to consider for them, too.

But what about the ANTs you ask, the Automatic Negative Thoughts coined by Daniel Amen, that come up and don't allow you to quiet your mind? Aha! You are noticing that the brain, in its usual fearful response, is resisting. You were really paying attention. The Zen hat is on. And resist it will. However, it's just fine and will not stop you from conscious living. Just notice it, perhaps ignore it, or set

Matt Groening tells us that when your cable television is having difficulties that we should not panic. But he also jokes that we should resist the temptation to read or talk to loved ones.

your resistance off to the side for now and move on. What does that look like during a period of quiet relaxation? Just take a deep breath, release a thought on the breath, and come back to focusing on quiet, calm breathing. You can also do this at any time during your day to refocus from feelings of stress that are limiting your day. You might even need several minutes to clear your mind. And there is another reason to relax. It takes at least twenty minutes of relaxation each day to undo the stress in the body that is caused by the stress of that one day.

How do you know when you need to stop and relax even if you just take a deep breath and regroup? When you are having that pesky little symptom in your body that tells you that something is getting to you and that your body is pumping adrenaline in order to respond. Maybe you are watching *Silence of the Lambs,* and you are *holding your breath* to see who Hannibal Lecter eats next, or you experienced *heart pounding* while waiting for *The Mentalist* to track down Red John. Maybe you are even having *sweaty palms* or *tightness in the chest* while watching Spider-Man bounce off tall buildings in pursuit of a thief.

If you don't want to wear out your adrenals and end up feeling like Kirk Douglas's dying character, Uncle Joe, in the movie *Greedy,* pay attention to this signal. While a charming Michael J. Fox isn't out to get your money by singing "Ink a Dink a Doo" with you at the piano, your own stress symptoms will prematurely turn you into Uncle Joe.

Check out this abbreviated list to help you identify your reactions to stress so that you will know when you need to intervene with a deep breath or activity change.

Quiz: What's Aging You?

Place a check on the line after each symptom that you experience.

Headaches_____ (after nine hours of the *Twilight Zone* marathon)

Buzzing or ringing in your ears_____ (turn down the football game)

Faintness or dizziness_____ (yes, he did marry the heiress instead of the waif)

Voice quivering or shaking_____ (after telling the hero off for letting the city get taken over by aliens)

Dry mouth_____ (viewer overkill, no food or water in the past twelve hours)

Tightness in jaw/clenching_____ (hand over the remote, it's not your turn)

Sore muscles_____ (get up out of the chair)

Tightness in chest_____ (you have been at the computer watching *Damages* reruns way too long)

Weakness in parts of the body_____ (when was the last time you took a walk?)

Smoking_____ (chain smoking during a basketball game, step away from the pack)

Itching/hives___ (advanced reaction to junk snack foods like chips and gum drops)

Sweaty palms_____ (getting hot and bothered over not finding out who did it)

Nancy Mramor Kajuth, Ph.D.

Quiz: What's Aging You?
(Continued)

Place a check on the line after each symptom that you experience.

Tense and anxious feelings_____ (can't wait until next week to see if J.R.'s son takes over the ranch)

Bad dreams_____ (now you *know* it's time to kill the crime shows)

Your mind going blank_____ (media overload, you may need to hand over your phone, remote, *and* mouse)

Difficulty making decisions_____ (does it really matter whether you watch *Oprah* and tape *Dr. Phil* or tape *Oprah* and watch Phil?)

Obsessive thoughts_____ (compulsively checking to see if the descriptions are in yet on your TV's channel guide for the next episode of *Grey's Anatomy*)

Irritability_____ (just because *Mad Men*'s Don Draper didn't marry her doesn't mean you have to pout)

Tearfulness_____(if only Rodney had chosen Melissa or Carrie or Medusa)

Overeating_____(when the TV gets good, the munch gets going)

Blushing_____ (the sex scenes are really hot)

Trouble concentrating_____(the only thing on your mind is getting to the sports bar in time to get the boxing match on before the baseball fans get there)

Twitches, tics, spasms_____(been watching too many *Bewitched* reruns)

Quiz: What's Aging You?
(Continued)

Place a check on the line after each symptom that you experience.

Grinding of teeth, neck pain___(you know you want to tell off that lazy kid on *Wife Swap*)

Lower back pain____(you need a new La-Z-Boy to enjoy *Dog Whisperer*)

Heart racing____ (this is accompanied by the theme from the *Lone Ranger*)

Tightness in stomach ____ (worried about getting a life instead of just sitting there)

Nausea/indigestion____ (yes, she makes me sick in that outfit, too)

Loss of interest____ (nothing matters but the time with the tube)

Insomnia____ (can't possibly sleep until you see the end of the *Home Improvement/Frasier/I Love Lucy* rerun)

Fatigue____ (I give up, I'll get a real life)

Scoring:

If you have more than six symptoms, definitely start a relaxation practice. You will find resources at www.realconsciousliving.com. But any one ongoing symptom can be cause for concern. For example, back pain, headaches, or any chronic symptoms are your body's way of telling you that you are under stress and have been for some time.

RxTV: Stress-Free Viewing

√ Don't view beyond the programs that you have planned to watch. When *Sleeping with the Enemy* is over, get some shut-eye" of your own.

√ Plan your snacks to avoid indulging in foods that stress the body with too much fat, salt, and sugar. These are the ones that feel good going down and don't give you a food hangover the next day.

√ Hydrate frequently with water; it keeps your brain alert to the messages in programming.

√ Get up every hour to stretch and change position, if necessary. Get back your body awareness. You may not notice that you are uncomfortable if you are too absorbed in viewing an autopsy/juggling act/deal in a pawn shop/vampire bite.

√ Take the call from your mother/brother/dishwasher repair man/bank with a high-interest offer on your checking account. That's why there are pause buttons. Don't let viewing interrupt life; rather let life interrupt viewing.

Over a period of time with regular relaxation, you will find that you can relax at a moment's notice, interrupting the damage done by stress just by initiating the relaxation training technique of your choice. When I was beginning relaxation, I would relax every day at the same time. This is a good idea, by the way, because it makes relaxation as much a habit as viewing nightly reruns of *The Beverly Hillbillies*. One evening, while intently focused on writing an article for a deadline, I began to feel very relaxed, calm, and tranquil. I checked my watch and noticed that it was the exact time that I regularly did my relaxation training. I had done the work to train my nervous system, and my nervous system paid me back with habitual relaxation. It still does, by the way, so if Scarlett Johansson is on *Jimmy Kimmel, Conan, The Tonight Show,* or *Letterman,* I may sink into relaxation and miss it. But I will not miss a trick the next day!

An example of relaxing almost instantaneously through regular training occurred when I was working with a group of charming third graders on stress management. Relaxing is not only important for their health but it is an alternative to TV, much as reading a book can become. So once each week for about six months, I went to their classroom to teach a twenty-minute relaxation technique. I began each session with the statement, "Let's all take a deep breath and reeeeeelax."

One day, KDKA-TV, a local CBS affiliate station in Pittsburgh, contacted me to come in and tape a class with these third graders. They had seen an article about the program in the *Pittsburgh Post-Gazette* newspaper and thought it sounded unique. So I scheduled a forty-five-minute session with the students the day before taping to go over what I wanted to do for the production. When I arrived at their classroom, there were books open on the desk, but there were no children to be found. Setting out to find them, I checked the library, cafeteria, recess areas, music and art rooms—with no success.

I began to have a stress response as time ticked away, leaving little of the scheduled session left to practice. I went back to their classroom to wait for them, realizing that they would return at some time, but my stress response continued to elevate. I could feel the ANTs, the automatic negative thoughts and feelings, rolled in with a passion, ranging from anger at the classroom teacher ("How could she forget?") to fear ("How will we get it all done with so little time left?").

Clearly my brainstem was activated, and I was in no position to lead a relaxation activity. When the kids came back into the room with only ten minutes of rehearsal time left, they had been at a pep rally! They were cheering, chanting, hitting one another with pom-poms, running around the room, looking out the window at the football team practicing in their red and white uniforms, and generally acting out of control.

With my mind in overdrive, I wanted to yell as loudly as I could, "Pay attention!" But I had a moment of insight as I looked out over this impossible situation: this was the stress management class. I said in the same way that I always do, "Let's all take a deep breath and reeeeeelax." In doing so, my very well-trained nervous system relaxed instantly, and so did the students. They were so used to hearing the relaxation suggestion that they breathed slowly with my instruction for about two minutes and went from an activity level of one hundred down to zero. You could have heard a pin drop as they looked at me with total rapt attention, listened to the plan for the next day's taping, and reviewed everything in eight minutes that I had planned for forty-five. Their teacher was even impressed with the way that they attended to instruction for the rest of the day. If you are reading consciously, then you know that "Let's all take a deep breath and reeeeeeelax" is an anchor for relaxation.

RCL 505: Where There's a Will, There's a Strategy

Still not convinced? Is it because you don't have time to just shut down and turn off the celebrity news for just twenty minutes? If you don't feel the motivation to relax, exercise, or do any other things in life that you have been prepared to do by reading *Get Reel*, you may be having an issue with willpower.

So let me give you a great big hint here. If you keep your nose to the grindstone all day, attending to tasks diligently even when you don't want to, get up early to exercise and then come home and expect to have a healthier dinner or viewing diet, you may have already used up today's supply of willpower. It may be difficult to resist the European meringue cookies or another CV drama that has been

 Napoleon Hill tells us to exercise patience, persistence, and perspiration, and believes that these three things line the path to success.

keeping you up too late. Whenever you use up your willpower on one task, you have less for the second, according to research by Roy F. Baumeister at Florida State University. He indicates that willpower is a limited resource that can be used up. So if you've decided to call your mother after work but have used up your supply of willpower, Mom will miss you while you catch the new fall lineup.

Can you beat your own mental system and expand your willpower? Yes, by understanding why your self-control wanes. One reason is because you are hungry. Eating food before exercising willpower increases willpower and the likelihood of success with habit control. Baumeister and Matthew Galliot, PhD, found that even a glass of lemonade increased self-control by improving glucose levels. But there are other ways, so don't order the large pizza with everything on it yet. Once you exercise acts of self-control, blood glucose levels are reduced, resulting in poor performance on the next task requiring it. Low glucose is actually a predictor of failure in attempts to exercise willpower, so food may help to counteract this effect when you have decided that one, two, or three dramas are enough for now.

Practicing willpower is another way to strengthen it, in the same way that exercising a muscle strengthens the body. It's a mental exercise that increases the likelihood that you will become better with practice. That way, you will have more willpower so you will become less depleted after short bursts of self-control. And if you have been getting real throughout the first chapters of the book, you

> Heavy viewers of body image-related television programs, such as shows about models, makeovers, and fashion, had more body image dissatisfaction than light viewers of body image-related television programs. This relationship held true for current viewing and viewing ten years prior.

already have this reservoir built up. Give yourself credit. You are not as far away from your goals as you think. You may not know what you are now capable of doing until you try. If you want to relax every day to improve your mind, you can.

There are so many ways to learn deep relaxation, but that was the work of my book *Spiritual Fitness*. However, your journey to consciousness is a process. And you have time. Don't try to do it all like the Enjoli perfume woman who was going to "bring home the bacon, fry it up in the pan, and never let you forget you're a man." Don't overload yourself with ambitious goals, become anxious when you fail to use an unprecedented amount of willpower to accomplish them, and sink into depression. Otherwise, you may be found at the end of your life staring at Carroll O'Connor singing "Those Were the Days."

You may have to change your story about your life to exercise even the limited amount of willpower that you have. If you believe that you can't find time to relax, swim, find a partner, build a shed, or make baklava, after you consciously view the news, then maybe your story needs to be refreshed. The idea of story attached to life is not a new one; it was discussed in chapter 2 on politics and the news. But your life *is* news, to you and the people who care about you, and the story that you tell about it drives your life. *TV has shaped perception, which drives your story. But you don't need to do anything to be who you truly are. Just hold your perception, your story, as a constructive one; then what you do will move you in a healthy direction and will be a good choice for you and the maybe for the world.*

RCL 606: Everything You Always Wanted to Know about Creating Your Life but Were Afraid to Ask

Beliefs and prejudices can be deeply embedded in the cerebral cortex and influence what you think about what happens every day, but you can become conscious of them by looking at your reactions. For example, if someone cuts you off in traffic, and you decide that he is an illegal immigrant rebel on his way to take over the American banking system, you have a prejudice. Your mind unconsciously has gone to places that have taken root through past experiences, much as TV hypnosis may have. You have a hard time stopping those thoughts because they have been reinforced over time. The power of the attachment/anchor is increased when it is used over and over.

Your brain is in charge of your experience, not the other way around. In the same way that Neilson ratings decide what is on your TV, you decide what the Neilson ratings show about your viewing choices. The newly conscious you is viewing with discretion and driving the media industry toward what you like, will accept, want, and have to have. It's an outside-in process, but so is your DNA. What? Heresy, you say? If you are thinking, *My mom and sisters all experienced the heartbreak of psoriasis after age forty, and so will I,* or, *My dad and uncles all lost their hair, so the baldness gene is chasing me,* stop the ANTs. Where's your Zen hat? Your conscious viewing habits are about to become your conscious thinking and living habits.

Come with me on a ride through the brain. Imagine that you, Tony Randall, and Burt Reynolds are actors, playing out a scene that might occur in the brain. If this script bears a resemblance to a scene from a Woody Allen movie, it's intentional. Look over this script to see how it all works:

Tony Randall/Stimulus for Happiness: Mission control, incoming happiness arriving, proceeding toward the brain. Can I get a cue for the delivery to the cell?

(*Quietly, suspenseful music begins to play. You barely notice it, but then … you wonder if the message for happiness will get to the brain.*)

You/Resistance: I'm scared. Once it arrives, there's no turning back. I have to accept it. Can I put the positive thought on standby?

Burt Reynolds/Observer: Trouble with mission control. I'm ready to deliver to the brain, and the happiness has been launched. There's no turning back.

Tony Randall/Stimulus for Happiness: Prepare for delivery.

You/Resistance: Who knows what might be possible if I accept happy delivery? I'm scared to let go of staying home to take care of my cat, Mensa.

Burt Reynolds/Observer: Thought power released.

(*Regrets about delivery float around the thoughts. The delivery continues.*)

Tony Randall/Stimulus for Happiness: We've reached the destination.

(*Harmonica music plays "There's No Place Like Home." You can hear the sound of a champagne cork popping.*)

Burt Reynolds/Observer: The synergy is in motion. Stand by for more happiness.

You/Acceptance: Wow! Double wow (if you're from Pittsburgh). Why did I wait so long?

(*"Sweet Mystery of Life At Last I've Found You" reverberates in your consciousness. You start a charity for happy cats, and Mensa is your poster child.*)

Bruce Lipton, PhD, describes this process in *The Biology of Belief.* As a cell biologist and researcher at Stanford University, he went from being an unhappy man to a happy one—by choice. He was prompted to examine how this worked. Through very complex examination of the human cell, he discovered the answer. Dr. Lipton focused on the mechanisms through which energy, in the form of our beliefs, can affect our biology, including our genetic code. He conducted a series of experiments that reveal that the cell membrane, the outer layer of a cell, is the organic equivalent of a computer chip, and the cell's equivalent of a brain. He declared that cells respond to very basic perceptions of what is going on in their world. They perceive whether there is calcium, oxygen, light, hormones, or other stimuli in their environment. So does it also make sense that the cell perceives your thought?

This is a very brief summary of neuroscience, but I have to keep moving quickly to enhance the effects of rapid visual eye movement and compete with your TV. Back to how this affects your health and happiness legacy. Not only does your health improve with belief but, according to Lipton, your DNA gets the message, too. It no longer signals to your cells that while you may be predisposed to an illness, that they must get a certain genetic disease or condition. And that improved condition is passed to your children! (*Stars fall out of the sky, special effects of cells navigating the central nervous system dance in delight as the Disney song "A Whole New World," from Aladdin, plays in the background*).

I feel like I am starting to sound like a Direct TV commercial. Their script "When your cable goes on the fritz, you get frustrated. When you get frustrated, your daughter imitates you. When your daughter imitates you, she gets thrown out of school. When she gets thrown out of school, she meets undesirables. When she meets undesirables, she ties the knot with an undesirable. When she ties the knot with an undesirable, you have a grandson with a dog collar. Don't have a grandson with a dog collar," leads to the call for action toward changing from cable toward the dish. They are making illogical connections for your amusement and to capture you as a customer. Their ads are unforgettable. But there is a real connection between your thoughts, the biology of your cells, and your DNA. The more your thoughts evolve consciously toward good health, the more your mind-body connections strengthen positively, and the more your children get to experience the new and improved condition.

Now you might be getting curious about the possibility that your thoughts affect your health. If you are not feeling like the Woody Allenesque voice in the dialogue with Tony Randall and Burt Reynolds, then you are no longer resisting the idea that you can control your destiny. So maybe you could explore the idea that your beliefs affect your life. What beliefs about yourself have you gotten from your viewing? And what TV viewing habits have evolved for you at this point? How is your viewing different? And how does that apply to your life?

If you have let go of the idea that you need to approximate some impractical level of attractiveness, that you have to have a bigger car, that the other guy's political views are just wrong, or that reality is as it appears on TV, you are on the road to changing. Everything. Now. By *flooding* your perception.

Breaking Free

Think of a few beliefs that you have beyond the world of TV. List a few of your own, or pick from these if they fit. Below are some versions of the glass half full vs. half empty beliefs. If you answer them honestly, you will be applying what you have learned about conscious viewing. View objectively from a distance and see which apply to you.

I have bad luck / good luck.

I am the most/least qualified person for the job.

Life is difficult/challenging.

Good things come to those who wait. / Waiting for anything allows the next guy to get it first.

The world is a beautiful place. / The world is a scary place.

I am a good writer/teacher/leader/counselor/editor/financial planner/ other vs. everyone else seems to know more about what I do than I do.

What other beliefs can you detect about your life? Give yourself a few minutes to think about it and write them down. They are the joists in the house of your life, the foundation that you will build on and around. They determine your future. So *flood* yourself in a happy way; it could become a habit!

> So let's say you decide that the world is a pretty wonderful place in which to live. You go outside, and you see nature's beauty. You see nature's beauty, and you feel connected to all of life. You feel connected to all of life, and you feel a connection to something greater than yourself. Since this is something that lots of people tell me makes them happy, you now feel happy. See how this works, both in and outside of Direct TV?

Or try this one. "I'm a lucky person." You get online and try to connect with people who can help you find a new job. You connect with those people, and they connect you with other people. Those other people invite you to join their networking group. Because you feel lucky, you ask those people if they have any openings. Because you ask, you get an interview. See the domino effect of a positive belief? You might switch to viewing *The Newsroom* or even *The Office* for some serious or not so serious tips on work protocol.

Now consider the opposite. I have bad luck. Because I have bad luck, I am stuck in a job that I hate. Because I hate my job but need the money, I don't have time to look for a new one. Because I don't have time to look for a new one, I am stuck here watching *Desperate Housewives* on video.

Which one is likely to get you where you want to go? As you make the decision to consciously watch your thoughts, you change your mind consciously. And each change toward a more conscious awareness of good things coming your way increases your awareness of opportunities. Watch out for the automatic negative thoughts (ANTs) that come up and say, "Oh no you can't." Just observe them and move on. *Flood* them out as needed. Each opportunity increases your chances of creating the life you want. And you can still keep your cable TV, if you like and accomplish your goals.

RCL 808: Get Reel Final Exam: Earn Your RCL Degree

It's time to graduate into your Real Conscious Life. Without further ado, your final exam awaits you.

The Story of Your Life

Pick one choice for each question.

My life right now is:
1. Great
2. Fairly Great
3. Okay
4. Needs a therapist

When I don't know what to do, I:
1. Get curious about what might work
2. Try different ideas to see what might work
3. Ask around to see how others handled the situation
4. Freeze, unable to move forward

I am:
1. Highly capable of creating the life I want
2. Capable of creating the life I want
3. Conscious that I want to create a life
4. In need of a new story

People think I:
1. Am funny, smart, and successful
2. Like what I do
3. Am doing okay
4. Should change my ways in life and viewing

When I feel down, I:
1. Exercise, go for a walk, read something inspiring
2. Remain mindful of my feelings, watch comedy, vote for my favorite *American Idol*
3. Talk to a friend but don't insist on sticking to "my story"
4. Don't get much done

If I could do anything, I would:
1. Become a catalyst for good—build a real life for myself and others
2. Have the life that I want
3. Balance my budget and the scale
4. Not sure

Scoring: Less is more. Give one point for each item answered with number one, two points for each one answered with number two, and so on in the same fashion with the items answered with three and four. Add up your points.

6–11: You are on a roll. Share it with others. Watch TV in balance.

12–15: You have a story about your life that works for you. Consider keeping some good viewing habits while adding a few new ones.

16–19: It's time to tweak your story. Step away from the computer/TV/phone and set goals.

20–24: Major editing and a full rewrite are in order. Reread *Get Reel*. Earn your RCL. Make a difference.

RCL 909: Secrets for Graduates

Are you feeling sufficiently *flooded* with empowering ideas? The ones you have just read in *Get Reel* are supported by research and practice as ancient as the earth. The ancient yogis and philosophers have always taught that the reality we perceive as being "out there" in a fixed state is in fact just your illusion based on perception and belief. Instead, what we are actually dealing with is a field of infinite energy, shaped into possibilities that are in a constant state of flux. Your experience is, therefore, a result of past perception and conditioning. How you view everything determines how you will react to it. Beliefs and perceptions shape what you perceive and create in your real life. And conscious ones go together to create your RCL. What you ingest in the world/TV is imperative to creating these perceptions and realities.

You can use your RCL to your advantage if you *get curious* about some new beliefs and perceptions, make some *choices* about which ones are authentically true for you, and *note the consequences* of them. *Cover all the bases* as you *consciously view* TV and your beliefs and see which ones you might want to *change,* and then *consider* what to *cut out.*

Notice how you remained *calm* when I used the word *change. Now chisel away at a global community* of likeminded individuals living *conscious* lives who want to live a continuously changing, open-minded life and join them in real life, on the Internet, TV, Facebook, and wherever you find them.

Eleanor Roosevelt believed that if a child could have a fairy godmother that his/her mother should ask the fairy godmother to gift the child with gift of curiosity—the most useful gift.

It's your turn to have an RCL. And with this degree that you now bestow on yourself, with all of the rights and privileges attached to it, you can see how the letters feel after your name. Try it out. It will look something like this: Betty Grable, RCL, or Matt Damon, RCL. You have earned it. It comes with a lifetime guarantee of awareness and the ability to adapt to your environment, to create positive outcomes, and to enjoy watching TV. You can officially accept where you are, where you want to be, and understand how to get there. As spy James Bond tells us, we only live twice—before your Real Conscious life (BRCL) and after (ARCL).

Now go. Think of your life view as your camera lens determining whatever you see and perceive. Think of how you are shaping your life as you create whatever you want and need to move toward. Become a "wonder man" or "wonder woman" who wonders every day what possibilities there are in your life. It is truly time to *produce your own life.* Write a script, read it daily, see results. There will be time to expand your real life into your relationships, family, and work. And I'll be back, as Alfred Hitchcock would say, but for now …

C—Chisel away at a global community, in a bottom-up fashion that tells the industry what you really want. Statistics show what people are watching. If you like to see people get thrown off the island, then you will see more shows like *American Idol* and *The Bachelor*. What's good for the consumer is your decision. It's part of the privilege of having an RCL.

For more up-to-date information on *Get Reel* for this chapter, go to:

http://drnancyonline.com/category/rc-media-and-rxtv/

http://drnancyonline.com/category/current-news/

REFERENCES

Alexander, E. *Proof of Heaven: A Neurosurgeon's Journey into the Afterlife* NY: Simon and Schuster, 2012)

Amen, D. *Change Your Brain, Change Your Life* (New York: Three River Press, 1999)

American Psychological Association (2004). *Report of the APA Task Force on Advertising and Children.* Retrieved from: http://www.apa.org/pi/families/resources/advertising-children.pdf.

Balcer, Rene (April 3, 2014). Interview for the Writer's Corner Retrieved from: UrbanTimes https://urbantimes.co/2014/04/head-writer-of-law-order-rene-balcer-on-the-power-of-cultural-producers/

Baumeister, R.F., Galliott M., DeWall C.N. and Oaten M., (December 2006). Self-regulation and personality: how interventions increase regulatory success, and how depletion moderates the effects of traits on behavior. *Journal of Personality*, 74-6

Bobkowski, P.S. (2009). Adolescent Religiosity and Selective Exposure to Television. *Journal of Media and Religion* 8, 55-70.

Brady. Matt, (January 2009). *Spider-Man Meets Obama in 'Amazing Spider-Man' Newsarama*, 583. Retrieved from: http://www.newsarama.com/1899-spider-man-meets-obama-in-amazing-spider-man-583.html

Centers for Disease Control and Prevention www.cdc.gov/obesity

Chaevsky, P. (1976). Script for the movie *Network*

Dalai Lama XIV, *The Art of Happiness* (Hachette Australia, 2003)

Erickson, M. H. Healing in Hypnosis: The Seminars, Workshops and Lectures of Milton H. Erickson, Volume 1 (Sacramento, CA: Irvington Publications, 1988)

Echterhoff, G. Lindner, I, Davidson, P.S.R., Brand, M.University of Duisburg-Eessen, False Memories of Self-Performance Result From

Watching Others' Actions, *Association for Applied Psychological Science*. Retrieved from: https://www.psychologicalscience.org/index.php/news/releases/ false-memories-of-self-performance-result-from-watching-others- actions.html

Edwards, B. *Drawing on the Right Side of the Brain* (Los Angeles: Tarcher, 2012) Gruzelier, J. (September, 2014). Hypnosis Really Changes Your Mind. Presented at the British Association for the Advancement of Science Retrieved from New Scientist: http://www.newscientist.com/article/dn6385-hypnosis-really-changes-yourmind.html#.VV0V70tFtch

Greenwood, D.N. and Dal Cin, S., (October 2012). Ethnicity and Body Consciousness: Black and White American Women's Negotiation of Media Ideals and Other's Approval. *Psychology of Popular Media Culture*, 1 (4)

Hamilton, Allan, (September 2009). Neurons of Compassion: Have We Found The Basis for Empathy and Altruism? *Spirituality and Health*

Heinrich, J. (September, 2010). The Weirdest People in the World? *Behavioral and Brain Sciences*, 1-75

Hitchcock, Alfred, *The Alfred Hitchcock Hour*. Retrieved *from*: www.quotationspage.com

Illsley Clark, Jean. *Growing Up Again, Parenting Ourselves, Parenting Our Children, Revised Edition* (Center City, MN: Hazelden Information and Educational Services Publisher, 1998)

Joyce, N. (December 2008). Wonder Woman: A Psychologists Creation. *American Psychological Association Monitor on Psychology* Rhoades, S. A Complete History of American Comic Books (New York, Peter Lang Publishing, 2008)

Kick, Russ, *You Are Still Being Lied To: The New Disinformation Guide To Media Distortion, Historical Whitewashes, and Cultural Myths 2ⁿᵈ Revised edition* (Newbury Port, MA: Disinformation Books/Red Wheel-Weiser, 2009)

Kubey, R. and Csikszentmihalyi, M. (February 23, 2002). Television Addiction is No Mere Metaphor. *Scientific American*

Levinson, B. (2009) *Poliwood: An in-depth look at the Democratic and Republican Conventions in 2008*. Retrieved from: IMBd:http://www.imdb.com/title/tt1204953/

Lipton, B., and *Biology of Belief: Unleashing The Power of Consciousness, Matter, and Miracles* (Carlsbad, CA, Hay House, 2007)

Lindblad, F. (2008, November). Violent Video Games Affect Biological Systems, *Acta Paediatrica*, 98 (5), 166-172.

Matthews, V.P. (November, 2013) Violent Video Games May Emotionally Arouse Players. *Indiana University IU News Room.* Retrieved from: Stockholm University Website: http://www.su.se/english/about/2.291/press-releases/violent-video-games-affect-biological-systems-1.94

McLuhan, Marshall. *The Medium is the Message* (Berkeley, CA: Gingko Press, 2001)

Mitgang, Lee D., *Big Bird and Beyond: The New Media and the Markle Foundation* (NYC: Fordham University Press, 1989)

Mramor, N. (1990). Stress Management for Children Through Educational Television (Saybrook Institute Doctoral Dissertation)

Orenstein, P. *Cinderella Ate My Daughter,* (NYC: Harper Collins, 2011)

Ozersky, J. (September 17, 2010). Got Raw? *Time Magazine*

Paloucek, K. J. Believe It! (2010). *Channel Guide Magazine*

Poniewozik, J. (February 26, 2009). Gold Diggers of 2009. *Time Magazine*

Pope, K. (October 28, 2008). Poll: Too Much Money Spent on Presidential Campaign. *USA Today*

Powers, Ron (1973). Walter Cronkite Interview. *Chicago Sun Times* for *Playboy* Retrieved from: https://www.goodreads.com/author/quotes/30807.Walter_Cronkite

Proceedings of the National Academy of Sciences. (March 2008). Acts of Kindness Spread Amazingly Easily: Just a Few People Can Make a Difference. *Science Daily.* Retrieved from: http://www.sciencedaily.com/releases/2010/03/100308151049.htm

Rothenberg, G. J. (November 18, 2011). Drinking the Kool-Aid: A Survivor Remembers Jim Jones. *Atlantic Magazine*

Schmid, D. Natural Born Celebrities: Serial Killers in American Culture (University of Chicago Press, 2005)

Schwartz, E.I. *The Last Lone Inventor: A Tale of Deceit, Genius, and the Birth of Television* (NYC: Harper Perennial, 2003)

Sparks, G. and Huelsing Sarapin, S. (October 28, 2009). Researchers Rest Their Case: TV Consumption Predicts Opinion about Criminal Justice System. *Purdue University News*

The Obesity Crises in America (July 16, 2003) Surgeon General Committee on Education and the Workforce. Retrieved from: http://www.surgeongeneral.gov/news/testimony/obesity07162003.html

Tompkins, P. (October 2004) 'Proof of Heaven' Author: Science Is Being Forced to Take the Afterlife Seriously. Retrieved From: http://time.com/3449990/proof-of-heaven-author-science-is-being-forced-to-take-the-afterlife-seriously/

Tucker, K. (2010) *Entertainment Weekly's Special Oscar Guide Supplement*

Von Drehle, D. (2009, September 17). Mad Man: Is Glenn Beck Bad for America? *TIME*

Weston, G. TV's Cosmetic and Plastic Surgery Shows, Robert Thomson quote, *Cosmetic surgery.com* Retrieved from: http://www.cosmeticsurgery.com/articles/archive/an-157/

Zinczenko.D. and Goulding, M. *Eat This, Not That! 2013: The No-Diet Weight Loss Solution* (Emmaus,PA: Rodale Press, 2012)

Printed in the United States
By Bookmasters